Social Studies Competencies and Skills

Social Studies Competencies and Skills:

Learning to Teach As an Intern

John Jarolimek
University of Washington, Seattle

Macmillan Publishing Co., Inc.
New York
Collier Macmillan Publishers
London

Macmillan Publishing Co., Inc.
866 Third Avenue, New York, New York 10022

Collier Macmillan Canada, Ltd.

ISBN 0-02-360380-1

Printing: 1 2 3 4 5 6 7 8   Year: 7 8 9 0 1 2 3

Preface

This book has been prepared to serve the needs of preservice teachers who are in field-oriented, performance- or competency-based teacher education programs. Typically, these programs provide a mix of concurrent on-campus and field experiences for the student. Methods classes in programs of this type are often conducted in a clinical setting as opposed to a conventional college class. Also, these courses and the accompanying field experiences concentrate on helping the teacher-in-training, usually called the intern, develop specified skills and competencies deemed to be important to successful teaching.

In field-oriented, performance-based programs, the intern develops competencies and skills by conceptualizing them in the clinic and then by actually performing them with children in a classroom. Because of the strong contribution of the field-experience component, the clinic experience does not need to be as detailed and as intensive as the conventional comprehensive methods course. Correspondingly, this text is not as comprehensive a treatment of elementary school social studies methodology as books written for the conventional methods courses.

Each chapter of this book begins with a short vignette based on actual experiences of interns. This narrative puts the subject matter of the chapter in a practical, personal, on-the-job perspective. The characters in the introductory vignettes to chapters are composites of actual people this writer has known through the years. Although the names are fictitious, they represent various types of individuals one sees in teacher education programs as interns, field associate teachers, school district representatives, and clinic instructors. Among the interns in this book are a typical four-year college student suddenly struck by the reality of becoming a teacher; another who had successful work experience prior to entering the teacher education program; a recent divorcee who has teenage children of her own; an arts and science history major now entering elementary education; a beginning teacher who, because of an oversupply of teachers, is doing substitute teaching; a group of interns concerned about the reading ability of the children they teach; and a young, successful teacher who is just beginning to see her professional identity emerge. Anyone who has worked in teacher education will surely recognize these types. Interns using the book can easily identify with these characters, who confront problems like their own.

The introductions conclude with a list of basic competencies to be developed by the intern as the contents of the chapter are studied. The section headings within the chapters are cast as questions and correspond exactly to the Basic Competencies found at the beginning of the chapter. Immediately following the Basic Competencies, the intern is given advice regarding performance expectations as a result of (1) studying the chapter, (2) doing the related work in the clinic, and (3) engaging in supportive experiences in the field. The items on this list of expectations also appear at the ends of chapters in the form of a checklist. These items are stated behaviorally, which should make it easy for the intern to evaluate his or her performance.

Interspersed in the text are activities to be performed by the intern. These are called Intern Tasks. In all cases these tasks require the intern to do something that represents an application of the competencies or skills developed in the text. Presumably, many of these activities will be conducted in the classroom or in the school to which the intern has been assigned.

End-of-chapter material includes a checklist of the Intern Tasks. The page number listed after each task refers to the page in the chapter on which the task is presented. It is recommended that tasks be checked off as they are completed. This will ensure that the intern has firsthand experience with a variety of activities and procedures deemed to be important in teaching elementary school social studies.

It is not expected that all of the Intern Tasks will be completed by the intern in a single quarter or semester. Many teaching skills require time to develop; therefore, the intern should be allowed to complete these tasks at some time during the year or more of internship. The expectation is that *at the end of the intern experience* the student will have demonstrated the ability to perform those competencies and tasks defined at the beginning and conclusion of each of the chapters.

The success of field-oriented, performance-based teacher education programs depends heavily on the close cooperation of the clinic instructor, the field associate teacher, and the intern. To assist in involving the field associate teacher (known as the supervising teacher or the critic teacher in conventional programs) more completely in the methods training, the book periodically includes advisories to that individual. These suggestions should be taken seriously, because the field associate teacher has to be relied on to provide for the needed experiences if essential competencies and skills are to be learned by the intern teacher. Other school personnel should assist in counseling and advising the intern too: the field coordinator (who may also be the college supervisor), the building principal, central office social studies supervisors or specialists, librarians, instructional resource specialists, and/or others involved in the local teacher education program.

At the end of the text is a Certificate of Completion. If it is completed accurately, it will serve as a permanent record of the intern's training experience in social studies.

Although this book is designed primarily for students in field-based teacher education programs, it provides a ready-made program of study for *any* teacher to use in building professional competence in teaching social studies. It could be used to good advantage in workshop-type in-service courses conducted during the school year. In-service teachers taking such a course could complete the suggested intern tasks in their own classrooms. Such an arrangement would provide a good opportunity for the practical application of concepts and skills developed in the text and in the workshop and would be consistent with the idea of combining theory and practice.

John Jarolimek

Contents

Chapter 1

Orientation to the social studies

The reality of becoming a teacher had come as a sudden jolt to Pam Saunders. The excitement of college life and summer employment had made the time pass quickly since her parents had brought her to the campus that first fall quarter three years ago. And here she was into her teacher education program. She could hardly believe it. Besides, she had always thought of herself as a <u>student</u>. Now she was beginning to realize that as a teacher-in-training she would have to think of herself in a new role. She was challenged by the idea, yet the thought of the responsibilities it entailed made her uneasy.

There seemed to be so much she had to know and so little time to learn it all. The teaching of reading, language arts, math, science, social studies—social studies? All she could remember about elementary school social studies was a pageant her class put on when she was in the fifth grade in which she played the part of Sacajawea!

Pam has been assigned to a public school as a teacher-in-training. She will spend part of each day in the classroom of Mrs. Fitzgerald, who is known as a field associate teacher. She will also spend part of each day in the Teacher Education Clinic on campus, where she will be introduced to various methods of teaching. In this way her teacher education program is designed to combine theory and practice.

Pam is now in the Teacher Education Clinic and her musing is interrupted by the clinic instructor, who has just distributed something called Basic Competencies, the handout shown here.

SOCIAL STUDIES COMPETENCIES AND SKILLS

Basic Competencies—Social Studies

The intern teacher knows

1. The major purposes of social studies in the elementary school.
2. The differences between less desirable and more desirable practices in teaching social studies.
3. The themes and topics included in the various grades.
4. How various aspects of a social studies program are coordinated.
5. How social studies is scheduled in the daily program of an elementary school.
6. Some of the newer developments and trends in the subject matter of the social studies curriculum.

Perhaps you find yourself in a situation not too different from that of Miss Saunders. If so, this chapter will provide an orientation to social studies education. It is designed to help you develop those competencies identified by the clinic instructor.

INTERN ADVISORY

After completing this chapter, together with related work in the clinic and appropriate classroom experiences in the field, you should be able to do the following:

1. State a rationale for including social studies in the elementary school curriculum.
2. Provide at least two examples of each of the three major categories of goals for social studies.
3. List the themes or emphases most commonly found in the social studies curriculum of each of the grades K–6.
4. Provide examples of unit titles taught in the grade of your choice.
5. List six desirable practices in elementary school social studies and contrast them with less desirable practices.

6. Indicate the time of day and the amount of time you would spend on social studies in a grade of your choice.
7. Identify four topics representing contemporary concerns of and challenges for social studies.
8. Carry on an informal conversation with your field associate teacher about the purposes, trends, and developments in elementary school social studies.

WHAT IS SOCIAL STUDIES EDUCATION SUPPOSED TO ACHIEVE?

Every society inducts its young members into its way of life through the process of socialization. The social group is thereby perpetuated beyond the life span of individuals who comprise it at any one time. Modern societies the world over have established educational institutions to help families and communities with the socialization of young children. Thus, everywhere in the world the early school years include refining the use of the native language, learning the folkways and mores of the society, becoming familiar with the legal and political systems, developing character and morality built on the value system of the society, and developing loyalty and fidelity to the society. The United States is no exception to this general pattern, even though this country has state educational systems rather than a national system of education.

The scope and complexity of what a person needs to know in a modern nation such as the United States is enormous. In order to make it manageable from a teaching and learning point of view, schools find it convenient to divide the curriculum into various components: the language arts and reading; mathematics; science; health; music; arts; physical education; and social studies. Each component is assigned certain specific learnings with which it is centrally concerned; however, perceived in combination, these learnings are intended to provide socialization training and education that maximize the child's opportunities for self-fulfillment within the necessary constraints of group life.

Naturally, there is considerable overlap among the various school subjects. Children read social studies, science, and mathematics. They also use writing and speaking as they study these subjects. Mathematics often has elements of social studies and science in it. The reverse is also true. We are reminded, therefore, that it is not always possible, nor even sensible, to maintain rigid boundaries between the components of the school curriculum. They can and should support and enrich each other. Because social studies relates so closely to all of the other subjects of the elementary school curriculum, some teachers like to make social studies the integrating center of their instructional program.

INTERN ADVISORY

Goal statements indicate the general direction and intent of a program. Objectives, on the other hand, are more specific statements that tell what pupils are expected to learn. At the conclusion of this section, you will be asked to recall some things you learned when you were an elementary school pupil that can be placed in each of the goal categories.

There are numerous goal statements for social studies education. The National Council for the Social Studies (NCSS), a professional association, has issued statements dealing with the role of the social studies, as have many school districts and state departments of education. Nearly all of the fifty states specify the teaching of certain elements of social studies in their education codes. The following are typical examples of what is expected of social studies education:

1. Knowledge and information goals.
   Learning about
   a. The world, its people, and their cultures.
   b. The settlement, growth, history, and development of the United States.
   c. The neighborhood, community, and the home state; how people live and work there; how they meet their basic needs of life; and how they interact and depend on each other.
   d. The legal and political systems of the local community, the state, and the nation.
   e. The world of work and an orientation to various careers.
   f. Basic human institutions, such as the family.
   g. How people use and misuse the earth.
   h. The problems and challenges that confront people today in the realm of social living and human relations in the local, state, national, and international arenas.

    i. The basic social functions that characterize all societies, such as producing, transporting, distributing, and consuming goods and services; providing for education, recreation, and government; protecting and conserving human and natural resources; expressing esthetic and religious drives; and communicating with others.

2. Attitude and value goals.

    a. Knowing the common values of this society as defined in the historical documents of the republic, by the laws of the land, by court decisions, and by the religious heritages of this country.

    b. Being able to make decisions that involve choices between competing values.

    c. Knowing the basic human rights guaranteed to all citizens.

    d. Developing a reasoned loyalty to this country.

    e. Developing respect for the ideals, the heritages, and the institutions of this nation.

    f. Developing a feeling of brotherhood toward fellow human beings everywhere.

3. Skills goals.

    a. Social skills.

        (1) Living and working together, taking turns, respecting the rights of others, and being socially sensitive.

        (2) Learning self-control and self-direction.

        (3) Sharing ideas and experiences with others.

    b. Study skills and work habits.

        (1) Locating and gathering information from books and from a variety of other sources and special references.

        (2) Making reports, speaking before a group, listening when others are reporting, and listening to and following directions.

        (3) Reading social studies materials for a variety of purposes: to get the main idea; to locate a particular fact; to predict outcomes; to detect author bias; and/or to compare and contrast.

        (4) Using maps, globes, charts, graphs, pictures, and other visual materials.

        (5) Organizing information into usable structures such as outlining; making charts; making a time line; classifying pictures or data; arranging ideas, events, or facts in a sequence; taking notes; keeping records; and preparing summaries.

      (6) Conducting an inquiry on a problem of interest.
- c. Group-work skills.
  - (1) Working together on committees and assuming various roles in small groups such as serving as chairperson, secretary, or group member.
  - (2) Participating in a group discussion; leading a discussion.
  - (3) Participating in group decision making.
- d. Intellectual skills.
  - (1) Defining and identifying problems; relating prior experiences to a present inquiry.
  - (2) Forming and testing hypotheses; drawing conclusions based on information.
  - (3) Analyzing and synthesizing data.
  - (4) Distinguishing between fact and opinion; learning to separate relevant from irrelevant information and to recognize bias in persuasive materials such as advertising, political statements, and propaganda.
  - (5) Sensing cause-and-effect relationships.
  - (6) Comparing and contrasting differing points of view.
  - (7) Recognizing the value components in decision making.

Many believe that social studies education should and does have something to do with the development of civic and citizenship knowledge, attitudes, values, and skills. It is for this reason that most states require social studies to be taught in the public schools. These requirements are translated into specific course content (information, attitudes, values, and skills) that presumably helps children to become informed, rational, humane, and socially sensitive decision makers. The goals and purposes of the social studies closely parallel, and often overlap, those of the entire school program in the effort to help children become responsible thinking-feeling-acting human beings.

INTERN TASK 1-1

a. Try to recall two or three specific things you learned as an elementary school pupil that would fit in each of the three sets of goals presented in this section. Are these things still worth learning by pupils who are in school today? Why or why not?

b. Using the list of goals in this section, write a one-sentence explanation of the purposes of elementary school social studies.

Discuss your responses to these questions with your clinic instructor and/or your field associate teacher.

WHAT ARE SOME CHARACTERISTICS OF GOOD SOCIAL STUDIES PROGRAMS?

It is apparent from the foregoing examples that some goals are achieved through encounters with subject matter, whereas others are achieved through the *process* of the study itself. For example, to learn about the history of their country or the geography of the home state, or of life in another culture, pupils must obviously deal with the subject matter appropriate to those topics. On the other hand, to learn the skill of using the encyclopedia, the pupil must be involved in the process of using that reference. Similarly, to learn to inquire, the pupil must engage in investigative searches. To learn group-work skills, pupils must be involved in group-work processes. Soundly based social studies programs build content and process learnings simultaneously.

Although there is good teaching and poor teaching of social studies today, just as there always has been, programs of the past often overemphasized content outcomes and did less with process learnings. Recently, attempts have been made to achieve a better balance between these two types of outcomes. Other contrasts between less desirable and more desirable programs are summarized in Chart 1-1. Study the chart and then complete Intern Task 1-2.

Field Associate Teacher Advisory

It is recommended that Chart 1-1 be discussed with the intern. The contrasts shown in the chart may need some interpretation if their implications are to be understood by the intern. Point out that not all new programs today meet the "more desirable" criteria and not all programs of the past would be judged "less desirable."

Make arrangements for the intern to become familiar with the local social studies curriculum guide.

Discuss with the intern local regulations as to the amount of time required for social studies, how you schedule social studies in your daily program, and local policy regarding text-book adoption and use.

This would be a good time for the intern to get acquainted with the district social studies supervisor or consultant, if there is one. Perhaps the social studies supervisor would be willing to share in the responsibility of orienting the intern to the local social studies curriculum. The supervisor could also assist with Intern Task 1-2.

CHART 1-1.   *Characteristics of Less Desirable and More Desirable Social Studies Programs*

Less Desirable	More Desirable
1. Heavy reliance on history and geography.	1. Subject matter drawn from a broad range of social sciences; the humanities; and the experiences of pupils.
2. Emphasis on Western culture, ignoring large parts of the world.	2. A world view with attention to non-Western, non-Christian cultures as well as those of the West.
3. Rigid and formal programs; recitation procedures common.	3. Greater informality; more discussion; more pupil participation.
4. Much textbook teaching; fact-oriented.	4. Use of multiple resources with an emphasis on concept development.
5. Tendency to cover large areas and topics as in a survey.	5. More use of in-depth studies as cases and examples; learnings generalized and transferred to other situations.
6. Little relationship between in-school program and out-of-school behavior.	6. Application of learnings to out-of-school settings through social action.
7. Little emphasis on thinking as a major outcome of social studies.	7. Thinking emphasized as a major concern of social studies; inquiry strategies encouraged to develop reflective processes.
8. Emphasis on melting-pot idea.	8. Emphasis on pluralism and the contributions of many cultures.

CHART 1-1 *(Continued)*

Less Desirable	More Desirable
9. Values taught through exhortative procedures and by indoctrination.	9. Value clarification and a rational approach to value education.
10. Distorted pictures of social reality; failure to recognize the impact of science and technology; a largely rural focus; emphasis on the past.	10. Truthful pictures of social reality; greater urban focus; more attention to changes due to science and technology; speculation on the future.
11. Finding the *right* answers; memorization of answers.	11. Use of open-ended approaches to problem resolution; thoughtful responses to questions.
12. Little if any attention to racial and sex-role stereotyping.	12. Concern with racism, sexism, and racial and sex-role stereotyping.
13. Few options available to the teacher in terms of program design, teaching materials, and teaching strategies.	13. Many options available to the teacher in terms of various programs, texts, materials, and teaching strategies.
14. Reward of pupil behavior that is obedient, unquestioning; few pupil decisions required or expected.	14. Reward of pupil behavior that is inquiring; expects and requires pupil to make choices and decisions; requires reasoned obedience; helps pupil learn how to learn.

INTERN TASK 1-2

Contrast less desirable and more desirable social studies programs in terms of each of the following. Discuss your responses with your clinic instructor and/or your field associate teacher.

Less Desirable Program	More Desirable Program
1. Role of the teacher.	1. Role of the teacher.
2. Role of the learner.	2. Role of the learner.
3. Use of instructional material.	3. Use of instructional material.
4. Subject matter.	4. Subject matter.
5. Teaching procedures.	5. Teaching procedures.

WHAT GOES WHERE?

Children learn a great deal about social studies in their life experiences outside of school. This applies not only to informational aspects of social studies but to other dimensions as well. Children have many opportunities to learn about the world and its people through travel, television, and contact with adults. Outside of school they learn values and skills from their families and from contact with other persons in their social worlds. Consequently, hardly anything encountered in the social studies program will be totally new to all children, perhaps not even to *any* children in some classrooms.

The social studies program should be built on what the child already knows. This means that in introducing topics or units for study the teacher will need to explore with the children the extent of their prior experiences with the subject. Social studies programs are designed to build learnings sequentially year by year, but this cannot be achieved unless each teacher assumes some responsibility for maintaining continuity in children's learning.

Each year there will be study units and topics that are consistent with the emphasis suggested by the district curriculum for that year. Ordinarily, topics that are physically close to the child such as the school, family, neighborhood, and community are found in the primary grades. Topics that are more remote in space and time, such as the home state, the nation, and foreign cultures, appear in the middle and upper grades. It should be noted, however, that newer programs expand the world of the child early and very rapidly. For example, even in the primary grades it is not unusual to find children studying family living as it takes place in many parts of the world. Studies may begin with aspects of a topic that are familiar to the children, such as their own homes, schools, and families, but that lead to the study of these same institutions in other cultures. The movement from things that are close to those that are far away and back again is common in social studies programs today.

There is both similarity and variation in the subject matter of social studies programs from one location to another. For example, almost everywhere children study their home state. This is often placed in grade 4, although some districts place it at grade 6 or 7. Almost everywhere the study of the United States and its development comes in grade 5. Some districts also include the study of Canada and Latin America in that grade. Studies of other cultures often appear in grades 4 and 6, although some programs are inserting units on foreign lands in earlier grades. The primary grade programs often follow a sequence of school and family life in kindergarten and grade 1, the neighborhood and local area in grade 2, and the larger community in grade 3. Almost everywhere elementary school social studies programs have strong ties with the local area. This is as it should be because children are then able to draw examples of the concepts under study from their immediate environment. Teachers need to consult curriculum documents at the local level in order to find out precisely what emphases, topics, or units are suggested or required at each level.

Perhaps more important than the units and topics themselves are the basic concepts and main ideas that spiral through the program. Such basic concepts as interdependence, justice, cooperation, responsibility, culture, power, conflict, change, and stability are often selected to provide the organizing framework for social studies programs. These concepts are introduced in their simple variants in the primary grades through units on the school, home, neighborhood, and community and are expanded in meaning as children proceed through school and encounter units dealing with the state, nation, and the world. Those key ideas may be expressed in the curriculum documents as concepts, such as those just cited, or as generalizations such as these:

1. Events of the past influence those of the present.   (History)
2. Regions develop economic ties that make them dependent on one another.   (Geography)
3. The greater the diversity among culture groups in an area, the greater is the potential for conflict among these groups. (Sociology)
4. When people of different cultures come in contact with each other, selective borrowing occurs.   (Anthropology)
5. Every society or group develops laws or rules to govern the conduct of its members and to provide protection for them. (Political Science)
6. The interdependence of peoples of the world makes exchange and trade necessary.   (Economics)

SOCIAL STUDIES COMPETENCIES AND SKILLS

INTERN TASK 1–3

a. Visit your local curriculum library to find out what themes, topics, units, or emphases are required or suggested for the local district in which you are an intern teacher.

b Compare your local social studies curriculum with the characteristics of social studies programs shown in Chart 1–1.

HOW DOES IT ALL FIT TOGETHER?

Although most schools include the social science disciplines in their elementary school social studies program, they do not ordinarily conduct special courses in geography, history, economics, political science, or the other disciplines. The usual organizational format is one that combines components from more than a single discipline to form an interdisciplinary study around some topic of interest. For example, a sixth-grade class might study the topic "Crossroads of Three Continents—The Middle East." In such a study geography would be essential, as would be history, economics, and government. Doubtless, too, religious concepts would be included because this area of the world was the birthplace of three of the world's major religions.

Let us look at an example from the primary grades. Here there may be no concern about having the children identify the contributing disciplines, but the teacher knows that when children are studying the local landscape, they are dealing in a simple way with geographic concepts. When they learn about the need for rules and laws, they are beginning to understand ideas from political science, and when they study about life in early times, they are having their first brush with history. Most schools are introducing basic concepts from the social sciences and related disciplines in the early years of the elementary school, although they may not always be labeled as such.

Some units of study relate more closely to certain disciplines than to others. As an example, a second-grade class studying transportation in the local area is likely to deal with the natural environment, and thus pupils will learn something about local geography. It would be difficult for them not to include economic concepts in such a study because transportation systems relate so directly to the distribution of goods. This naturally takes the study into such concepts as interdependence, producer, consumer, goods, and services. Similarly, a fifth-grade study of the United States is usually historical in its emphasis, but it can and should involve concepts from other disciplines as well.

It is not the purpose of the elementary school to teach the social science disciplines apart from their relevance to social reality. They should be taught in ways that will help children build an understanding of the social and physical world in which they live. Unless children are able to understand the connection between what they are studying as history, geography, and so on, and something in their real world, the subject matter cannot make much sense to them. Constant awareness of the potential explanatory power of the subject matter of the social studies will do much to intercept an undue emphasis on capes and bays, places and products, battles and generals.

The subject matter of social studies is important in itself and should be carefully selected and well taught. It should not be perceived only as a vehicle through which process learnings are taught, although it obviously serves that important purpose too. That is, it is around some framework of subject matter that skills and values are taught and learned. The teacher needs to coordinate the social studies program in order to ensure balanced attention to skills, values, and content outcomes, carefully relating them to each other. It is not generally thought to be good practice to separate skills, values, and content outcomes into separate compartments as if they were unrelated.

The page from a teacher's guide for a fourth-grade text reproduced as Figure 1–1 provides a good illustration of how several outcomes can be achieved in a single lesson. The major thrust of this lesson has to do with expanding the meaning of the concept *division of labor,* but in the process at least six additional learnings are incorporated in this teaching strategy. These are identified in bold print in the left-hand column. Notice, too, that these learnings do not deal exclusively with the printed content of the book but involve pupils in getting meaning from pictures, working cooperatively, and engaging in a creative activity. Although attitudes and values are not directly stated as outcomes, they are implicit in the types of activities suggested for this lesson, such as appreciation of the contributions of each worker in the production process, willingness to do one's share on the small-group assignment, appreciation of the contributions that factory production makes to the nation's standard of living, and appreciation of the efficiency of the assembly line as a method of production.

Much of social studies teaching is directed toward the achievement of multiple outcomes, just as is done in the example cited. Informational learnings, skills, values, and attitudes are an inherent part of most social studies experiences. Thoughtful planning by the teacher will ensure that a balance of emphasis is maintained among the various outcomes that are a necessary part of social studies education for elementary school children. This example illustrates that such planning aids as teacher's guides and curriculum documents prepared by publishing companies and/or local school districts can be enormously helpful to the teacher in planning and teaching the social studies.

LESSON 10[1]

Learning outcome: The pupil relates changes in power to a second kind of division of labor.

Material used:

√ *Web of the World*, pages 25–27; pages 156, 158

Teaching strategy:

1. *Broadening the concept of* division of labor

The pupil gets the literal meaning of pictures.

- Direct attention to the pictures on pages 156 and 158. Question to be sure that pupils get the literal meaning of the pictures—each worker doing a small part of the making of an automobile.

- Invite speculation on how this kind of division of labor came about. Pupils should see that it can only happen when production goes on in a factory.

. . . develops hypotheses and understands their tentative nature.

- Invite speculation on the reasons factories were developed. "For thousands of years people made goods in their homes, or in small shops. Why did they, somewhere along the line, move the making of goods out of their homes and shops?" A second look at the assembly line pictures may help pupils see that the kind of machines that are now used to make things could not be in homes, because of their size and the need for power to run them.

2. *Reading to confirm ideas developed through discussion*

. . . uses evidence to test a hypothesis, to support an idea, to form a generalization.

- Have pupils read the section "Another kind of division of labor"

  ○ to check their ideas about the reason for the beginning of factories.

  ○ to connect the new kind of division of labor with the concept of dependence.

  ○ to identify another result of the new kind of division of labor.

3. *Acting out division of labor*

- Pupils can suggest five or six products that they are reasonably certain are made in steps in a factory—anything from toys to radios to automobiles.

The pupil works cooperatively with others.

. . . communicates information or ideas through creative activity.

- Meeting in small groups, pupils should discuss the steps that would probably be taken by several workers in assembling the item. After a few minutes of this discussion, children within each group may choose to be workers on the assembly line. As each group reports, each member should explain the particular operation that he performs as a worker manufacturing his group's item. If a group is willing to perform a bit, each can act out his job.

. . . sees cause-and-effect and other relationships.

- This would provide opportunity to emphasize the reasons why this kind of division of labor increases production.

Figure 1–1. This sample page from a teacher's guide accompanying a social studies textbook illustrates how multiple objectives can be included in a lesson.

---

[1]Phillip Viereck, Bertha Davis, and Joseph Decaroli, *Teacher's Guide for Web of the World and Its Related Media* (New York: Macmillan Publishing Co., Inc., 1973), pp. 12–13.

The tendency to overstress one aspect of the program at the expense of another is a frequent threat to a balanced offering. This happens because of an individual teacher's particular skill or interest in some aspect of social studies, or because of what the teacher thinks is important. For instance, one teacher may view the subject matter as being of greatest importance and, as a result, do little to include learning experiences that build skills and values. Another may be interested in and skillful in artistic work and, as a result, social studies becomes an art class with little done to develop social studies content and skills. Although these programs may have much about them that is commendable, each is limited in not attending to the important components of a well-rounded program.

INTERN TASK 1-4

Select *two* grade levels in which you have a special interest. Then provide a brief explanation (two or three sentences) of how the units listed below for those grades could be used to achieve multiple objectives concurrently. Check your responses with the clinic instructor and/or your field associate teacher.

1. All About Me (kindergarten).
2. Families Near and Far (first grade).
3. People Need People (second grade, emphasis on interdependence).
4. Getting It from Here to There (third grade, transportation).
5. Boom-Town Economics (fourth grade, early history of home state).
6. What Right Do You Have to . . . (fifth grade, rights and responsibilities).
7. Your Culture Is Showing (sixth grade, effect of culture on the individual).

WHEN SHOULD SOCIAL STUDIES BE TAUGHT AND FOR HOW LONG A TIME?

There is little, if any, reason to claim that any part of the day is best for teaching social studies. Where it is placed in the daily program is mainly a matter of teacher preference. Most often in the primary grades teachers will schedule reading instruction early in the day because they feel that children are best able to concentrate for a longer period of time when they are well rested. This principle applies to the scheduling of other language arts skills and mathematics as well. Because the social studies program is often activity oriented, it may be placed later in the day, thus providing a change of pace at a time when it is most needed. Just before or just after the lunch break are popular times for social studies in the primary grades. Depending on the nature of the program, primary-grade teachers might provide anywhere from twenty minutes to an hour for social studies. Most school districts have either guidelines or specific requirements as to the number of minutes to be spent on each school subject during the week.

In the middle and upper grades, a variety of patterns of scheduling is followed. Usually fifty minutes to an hour or more are provided for social studies, depending on the extent to which the teacher incorporates other learnings such as language arts, music, art, or reading into the social studies. Many middle- and upper-grade teachers select the first part of the day for social studies. Others use most of the afternoon, particularly if the program is heavily activity oriented. In departmentalized or cooperative teaching arrangements, still other scheduling formats may be used. In any case, for both primary and upper grades, social studies should be scheduled in one large block of time rather than fragmented into twenty- or thirty-minute periods two or three times during the day.

It hardly seems necessary to remind teachers that social studies deserves a high priority in the school program and needs to be taught in a systematic way on a regular basis. The fact is, however, that teachers are often neglectful of social studies. For instance, it may be taught in such a way that it becomes little more than arts and crafts. Or it may be combined with science instruction and thereby become another science class. Or it may be irregularly included in the day's program and become a "once-in-awhile" subject. Such haphazard approaches cannot possibly result in social studies education that has any significant impact on the social and civic behavior of pupils. One can only speculate on what the status of reading or mathematics achievement would be if those subjects were taught in this way.

INTERN TASK 1–5

a. The education codes of most states stipulate the amount of time (in clock hours) that is to be spent on social studies each week. These

minimum time requirements are usually different for primary, intermediate, and upper grades. Check local sources to find out if there are such requirements, and if so, what they are.
b. Decide when in the day's schedule you would prefer to teach social studies and provide a rationale for your choice.

WHAT ARE SOME OF THE NEWER CONCERNS OF SOCIAL STUDIES EDUCATION?

History, geography, and government are disciplines that continue to be important to the elementary school social studies program. However, as has already been noted, in recent years the content of social studies has been expanded to include other social science disciplines and the humanities as well. In addition there are a variety of subjects, topics, or emphases that figure prominently in present-day social studies programs but that do not fit neatly into any of the conventional disciplines. Some of these come from the experiences of children, as, for example, conflict resolution. Others stem from pervasive societal problems such as environmental contamination. The following topics represent concerns of this type and are likely to be a part of social studies education in the elementary school for several years to come.

Law-Related Education

There is a growing concern for the improved teaching of our legal system at all levels. Doubtless, much of this comes from the frightening increase in crime in recent years. But the major purpose of this emphasis is not to produce a "law-and-order" society in the repressive sense, even though law, order, and justice are obviously essential requirements for any society, particularly one based on democratic principles. Rather, there is increased awareness of the extent to which individuals are affected by the legal system, and that it is imperative for citizens to understand their relationship to the law. Indeed, it would be hard to think of any activity in a modern society from which some aspect of the law is wholly absent. The legal system protects the rights of individual citizens and also provides a mechanism for maintaining social order. These two values—individual freedom and social order—are both embraced by our society. Needless to say, the two often conflict, and it is the purpose of the legal system to ensure that one does not fall victim to the other.

Advocates of law-related education stress that these studies should take place within the structure of existing social studies programs. That is, as children study units on the home, family, community, state, nation, and so on, the legal dimension of each of these should not be overlooked. Moreover, law-related studies should be a part of the program of all grades from kindergarten upward in order to ensure the cumulative development of important understandings, attitudes, values, and skills that pertain to the legal system.

It is important to emphasize that law-related studies should include the broad spectrum of legal matters and not be confined to criminal aspects of the law. For several years many schools have conducted cooperative programs with local police agencies such as "Officer Friendly" or "The Policeman Is Our Friend." Such efforts have merit, of course, if properly implemented, but there is an even greater need for studies in the areas of civil law, consumer law, the judicial system, and other aspects of the law that also affect citizens daily.

Law-related studies usually are designed around a limited number of basic concepts such as justice, responsibility, freedom, citizen participation, authority, and fairness. These ideas are adapted to suit the level of maturity of the children and the subject matter of the program in various grades. In this way these ideas spiral toward increasing degrees of complexity as the pupils move through school.

Career Education

The approach to career education as a part of social studies is, in many ways, similar to that of law-related education. It, too, should be part of the regular curriculum at all levels rather than a separate, new program. Career education components can easily be incorporated in many of the existing social studies units and topics. Just as law-related education does not seek to train children to be lawyers, career education does not prepare pupils to make career choices while in the elementary school. The main purpose of a career emphasis is to help pupils develop an awareness of the world of work and to provide them with some knowledge of the vast number of career options that are available. There is an overwhelming amount of evidence that important decisions regarding career choices are often made on the basis of very limited information. Many, if not most, persons are not aware of the range of career choices available to them.

It is a mistake to view career education as a scheme to make "good little worker elves" out of pupils who will later find a productive niche in the work world, support themselves, stay off welfare rolls, pay their taxes, and do all this without grumbling. Sooner or later, however, all persons must make basic decisions about their lives, how they want to invest their time, what they perceive as worth striving for, and how they can achieve self-fulfillment. Many of these decisions relate to what one will do to earn a living. Career education aims to provide pupils with knowledge, attitudes, values, and skills that will enable them eventually to make those decisions intelligently. In this sense career education is a broad concept and should not be limited to providing occupational information.

Environmental Education

The contamination of the environment and the accelerated consumption of resources have posed serious threats to the quality of our life, perhaps even to human survival. Efforts to stem this trend toward disaster have taken the form of legislation, building citizen awareness, and education. Social studies provides a natural vehicle for the study of the social consequences of environmental misuse. As is true of other topics discussed in this section, environmental education needs to be a part of the program from the earliest grades. It, too, can and should be incorporated in many of the existing social studies units and topics.

As discussed here, environmental education is meant to be broadly interpreted to include everything that affects the quality of all life (plant, animal, and human) from the standpoint of the natural surroundings. It has to do with the web of life and the interdependent relationships that prevail among living things. In this sense environmental education seeks to engender a responsible concern in children. Continuing curricular attention to this important topic is required. Occasional units of study dealing with the environment are not in themselves adequate, nor is a once-a-year visit to the school camp.

There are several separate areas that are subsumed under the environmental education rubric. One is population education, another is outdoor education, another is ecology, and still another is conservation. All of these represent commendable efforts to sensitize young people to the importance of the environment to the survival needs of human beings. No one of them, however, is an adequate response to the broader goals of environmental education.

Human Relations Education

This is a broad area of concern that has to do with combating the evils of racism, with conflict resolution, with racial and sex-role stereotyping, and with the facilitation of harmonious person-to-person relationships. Additionally, human relations education includes multiethnic and bicultural studies in order to acquaint pupils with the pluralistic character of the culture of this society. With the recent emphasis on cultural plurality, there is the possibility of fragmentation of the society through separatist movements. Consequently, educational programs must aim toward the development of common core understandings and values that bind the society together in peaceful ways.

In a larger framework, human relations education strives to give a global perspective to human relations concepts. These thrusts have been identified by such descriptors as worldmindedness, international understanding, war-peace studies, world order, and global education. Much of the newer social studies material for children provides a world view of people and cultures. Conditions of the modern world make it imperative that American school children learn as much as they can about the many peoples of the world with whom they share this planet. Present-day emphasis is away from the study of "strange" people from faraway places. Today there are no faraway places; a twenty-four hour flight will take us anywhere in the world. Thus, the idea is to help children develop a sense of humanity and a feeling of kinship for people everywhere.

INTERN TASK 1–6

a. Explain how the topics in this section relate to the goals for social studies education listed on pages 4–6.

b. The inclusion of environmental education, career education, law-related education, and ethnic heritage studies in the social studies curriculum is being challenged by a parent at a public meeting. If you were asked to respond to such a concern, what points would you make?

Discuss your responses to these questions with your clinic instructor and/or your field associate teacher.

CHECKING YOUR PERFORMANCE

Intern Task Checklist

Task 1-1. a. Recalling things learned in the elementary school. P. 6 _____

b. Writing the purpose of elementary social studies. P. 7 _____

Task 1-2. Contrasting more and less desirable practices. P. 9 _____

Task 1-3. a. Finding out local district themes, topics, and units. P. 12 _____

b. Comparing local practices with the chart. P. 12 _____

Task 1-4. Achieving multiple objectives. P. 15 _____

Task 1-5. a. Finding out minimum time requirements. P. 16 _____

b. Preparing a daily schedule. P. 17 _____

Task 1-6. a. Relating topics to goals. P. 20 _____

b. Responding to criticism of curriculum content. P. 21 _____

Performance Checklist

In the field or in the clinic, the intern has

1. Stated a rationale for including social studies in the curriculum. _____

2. Provided two examples of the three major categories of goals. _____

3. Listed themes or emphases most commonly found in the curriculum for grades K-6. _____

4. Provided examples of unit titles taught in the grade of his or her choice. _____

5. Listed six desirable practices in social studies and contrasted them with less desirable practices. _____

6. Indicated the time of day and amount of time preferred for social studies in a grade of choice. _____

SOCIAL STUDIES COMPETENCIES AND SKILLS

7. Identified four topics representing contemporary concerns of, and challenges for, social studies. _____

8. Demonstrated the ability to be conversant about purposes, trends, and newer developments in elementary school social studies. _____

Field Associate Teacher Advisory

Tasks and performances should be checked off or initialed and dated by the appropriate local official, or the intern teacher can use the checklists for his or her own record.

INTERN ADVISORY

1. Become familiar with the magazines *Social Education, Instructor,* and *Teacher.* Know what they have to offer the teacher in the social studies area.
2. Talk to your field associate teacher about local and state councils for social studies. Attend one of their meetings.

Chapter 2

The teacher, the classroom, and the social studies

Ron Wilson had been a book salesman for a major publishing company for three years before he decided to enter teaching. He had been in and out of scores of classrooms, had observed numerous teachers at work, and had even conducted workshops for teachers, based on the textbooks his company published. His field associate teacher, Mrs. Milenka, knew of Ron's background, but being a secure and competent person, she was not threatened by his presence as an intern teacher.

Ron had been in enough classrooms to know a competent teacher when he saw one. And Mrs. Milenka was such a teacher. It was immediately apparent to him that children were psychologically and emotionally comfortable in her classroom. He could see that the relationship between the pupils and the teacher was one of respect and affection. The classroom environment gave him a feeling of orderly flexibility.

Mrs. Milenka, and teachers like her, are astute observers of the behavior of children. As a result, they get to know a great deal about the children they teach. This information is seldom recorded but reflects itself in a hundred different ways in the classroom each day as the teacher matches individual pupils with tasks and with books, sets objectives for children, asks questions, and supervises their work.

As Ron observed his field associate teacher, he took from his notebook the list of Basic Competencies the clinic instructor had given to the interns earlier in the week. "Whoever wrote these must have taken a page out of Mrs. Milenka's plan book," he thought. He wondered whether these were learned skills he saw being demonstrated or if one is born with them. He remembered the old saw about "Teachers are born, not made" and wondered how much truth there was in it after all. "Is teaching an art and not a science?" he asked himself. Certainly what he saw this teacher doing had elements of an artistic performance. But people do learn to be artists as well as scientists. If teaching is an art he was grateful to be studying with an artist as accomplished as Mrs. Milenka. He glanced down at the Basic Competencies again.

Basic Competencies—Social Studies

The intern teacher is able to

1. Arrange a suitable environment for teaching and learning social studies.
2. Take into account pupil variables that affect the teaching of social studies.
3. Use appropriate activities and learning resources to make social studies interesting and motivating for pupils.
4. Use a variety of strategies and techniques for teaching social studies.

INTERN ADVISORY

After completing this chapter, together with related work in the clinic and appropriate classroom experiences in the field, you should be able to do the following:

1. Classroom environment.
   a. Develop a nonthreatening classroom climate conducive to teaching and learning in which pupils can interact freely with each other and with the teacher.
   b. Arrange a flexible classroom environment suitable to teaching the social studies.
2. Knowledge of learners.
   a. Assess individual pupil strengths and limitations.
   b. Make appropriate pupil assignments.
   c. Formulate appropriate objectives that are understood by the learners.

3. Activities and materials.
   a. Provide varied activities that lead to desired objectives.
   b. Select and use learning materials needed for teaching social studies.
   c. Make social studies interesting, motivating, and meaningful to pupils.
4. Techniques and strategies.
   a. Ask appropriate classroom questions.
   b. Use a variety of appropriate teaching strategies.

HOW DOES A TEACHER ARRANGE A SUITABLE ENVIRONMENT FOR TEACHING AND LEARNING SOCIAL STUDIES?

There are visible and invisible characteristics of a social studies learning environment. The visible qualities have to do with the physical arrangement of the room: how the pupil stations are arranged, how learning centers are organized and placed in the room, what books and other learning resources are available, what displays and exhibits are present, and so on. The invisible characteristics reflect the emotional and social tone of the environment: the presence or absence of hostility, stress, and aggression. The invisible dimensions of a classroom environment are often referred to as the *classroom climate* or *classroom atmosphere*.

The term *social studies* implies that the classroom environment should be such as to make both *social* learnings and *study* learnings possible. There are several acceptable ways this can be accomplished. We will discuss two approaches from which the intern can extract characteristics that suit his or her preferences.

In our first instance we see social studies teaching individualized as much as possible for pupils. The learning surroundings suggest flexibility in order to accommodate individual learning styles, capabilities, and motivation. Information searches are conducted on an individual or small-group basis. Many activities and projects are done by small groups of pupils. Interactions are informal. Whole-class teaching is not avoided entirely but is kept at a minimum. Individual study, however, confined only to individual learning packets with no opportunity to share ideas with others or to discuss ideas in groups, is avoided. Pupil self-direction and independence are highly valued.

Not all teachers, nor all pupils for that matter, are comfortable with the degree of informality suggested by the foregoing description. They do their best work when they are in situations that are more structured. They are more inclined to formalize assignments given to individuals and groups. There is a greater reliance on the textbook as the core of the study units. Interactions between pupils and between the teacher and pupils are more formal. Outwardly such a classroom gives the appearance of being more orderly and organized, and indeed, it often is.

We have described two different approaches to the arrangement of the classroom environment, and there is nothing wrong with such variations. The learning environment of a classroom will reflect the teacher's personality, philosophy, teaching style, and competence. Therefore, there can be no set prescription of what a classroom environment should be like in all cases. The most important consideration is that it be a place that fosters and enhances the development of young human beings, not only in terms of their academic achievement but as total persons. This usually is found in classrooms that meet the following requirements:

1. There is evidence of unity and cohesiveness; pupils willingly cooperate to achieve class goals.
2. Pupils are involved in making decisions concerning the work and life in the classroom.
3. There is evidence of good interpersonal relations among pupils and the teacher.
4. Pupils are interested in what they are doing.
5. Not all pupils are required to do the same assignments and tasks, in the same amount of time, all of the time.
6. The physical makeup of the classroom (desks, tables, chairs, and so forth) indicates flexible use.
7. A wealth of social studies learning resources is provided.
8. There is much evidence of pupils' creative work products associated with social studies—constructions, murals and other art work, and written work—all of which suggests their active involvement in social studies learning.

INTERN TASK 2-1

Use the foregoing eight points listed to study the social studies environment in the classroom to which you have been assigned. For each of the eight points provide a short narrative documenting the extent to which the requirement has been met. Discuss your responses with your field associate teacher and/or your clinic instructor.

> ### Field Associate Teacher Advisory
>
> The intern teacher may need some assistance from you in completing this assignment. As a beginner, the intern may not know what to look for in detecting evidence of cohesiveness, for example. The exercise would be most helpful to the intern if you could provide some orientation to it, have the intern complete it, and then do a critique of and discuss the responses together.

HOW DO PUPIL VARIABLES AFFECT THE TEACHING OF SOCIAL STUDIES?

A steady stream of young humanity passes through the classrooms of the nation's schools each year—each child unique, each different from every other one, each a product of a particular set of environmental and hereditary conditions, and each on the way to becoming an adult of the twenty-first century. By the time the school receives these children, they have already come under powerful shaping influences in their homes and neighborhoods. They spend little of their time in school, actually—no more than five to six hours a day for about 180 days each year. The remainder of their time they live in another world, one that might be called their real world. What things are like in that real world makes a great deal of difference in what the child can or will do in school. The impact of out-of-school learning on the social development and social education of children vitally affects their social studies education.

The elementary school social studies program has to serve as an equalizing mechanism in the social education of young children. That is, children come to school having had encounters with different segments of the social world, and the social studies program can and should broaden the extent of those encounters. For example, a child may come from an upper-middle-class family. Let us assume that this child has had the advantage of a loving and caring family, with parents who have offered protection from many of the harsh realities of life. They have also provided an environment of affluence. The child speaks well, is curious and interested in learning, and is looking forward to school. The chances that this child will succeed in school are very high, indeed. Yet, with all the advantages, this child's encounters with the full spectrum of the social world are limited. The social studies program will need to build an awareness and understanding of the social worlds beyond what this child experiences on the basis of ordinary daily living.

Contrast what has just been described with another child who spends his after-school hours and weekends hustling customers for his older sister who is a prostitute. This child's family has always lived in poverty, and the child has spent much of his time on the street from the time he was able to walk. His language is colorful, but crude and profane. His real world has made him surly and distrustful. This child, too, has encountered a narrow segment of the social world, and for him the social studies program will need to provide an awareness and understanding of yet another slice of social reality.

These examples are cited to show the great range of backgrounds and experiences of pupils. A more detailed analysis would show that pupils vary one from another in interest, motivation, intelligence, ambition, physical fitness, reading ability, language facility, and, indeed, on any variable for which we can secure data. It is not possible to build a single program in social studies education that will serve the educational needs of children who vary so much in their individual characteristics. Specifically, this means that social studies programs must be tailored to suit the characteristics of pupils in the local school, and that within classes, instruction must be individualized.

No one single piece of information is going to provide anything in the way of a complete picture of a child's needs in social studies. This can come about only after careful observation on a day-by-day basis for a period of time. But because socioeconomic status is a summarizing variable, the teacher can use it as a rough screening device to get insights into such factors as motivation, achievement, and intelligence. To build awareness of the real world of children, the intern will find questions such as those included in the following exercise to be of assistance.

INTERN TASK 2-2

Respond briefly, but specifically, to the following questions, basing your responses on your observations of the neighborhood and the school to which you have been assigned as an intern. Discuss your responses with your clinic instructor and/or your field associate teacher.

1. What is the general appearance of the pupils? (well dressed and well groomed; rested; adequately nourished; in good health; and so on)
2. What does the neighborhood look like? (run-down; new homes; dilapidated buildings; apartments; or a center of business activity)
3. What would you estimate the income of parents to be? (high; middle; low; low-low)
4. What are the occupations of the persons living in the area? (professional; managerial; skilled; unskilled; or unemployed)
5. Is the population of the neighborhood fairly stable or is it highly transient?
6. What is the ethnic composition of the neighborhood? (all one group; mixed; what groups are represented, and in what percentages)
7. How do the pupils spend their time outside of school?
8. Is there anything particularly unique about the educational needs of the pupils who attend this school?

Field Associate Teacher Advisory

Advise the intern as to the sources of data in responding to this exercise. This would be a good time for the intern to have an interview with the building principal, who could provide information on several of the items.

Teachers accommodate pupil differences in social studies through imaginative use of methods and materials. The following competencies are needed:

The teacher is able to

1. Establish a flexible classroom management system.
2. Use a variety of learning resources.

SOCIAL STUDIES COMPETENCIES AND SKILLS

3. Arrange individual performance tasks in accordance with pupils' interests and capabilities.
4. Get pupils to develop and use creative activities in achieving social studies objectives.

These competencies can be observed in the following narrative.

Narrative	Competencies
Mrs. Milenka provides a classroom environment that is rich with materials related to the social studies unit. This allows pupils to explore various aspects of the topic on their own. She encourages pupils to wonder, to imagine, to be curious about what they see, to touch, and to feel. Much of the work in social studies is done in small groups in activity areas and learning centers in the classroom. She supervises and directs the work of these groups and that of individual children in accordance with their need for assistance. She provides a minimum of supervision for those who are self-directed and capable of independent work. She is usually physically close to those who read poorly or who are unable to work productively on their own. She arranges the small work groups in ways that encourage the involvement of those pupils who may be less interested or less capable than others. This helps them learn and provides avenues for greater acceptance of these children by the rest of the class. She maintains a flexible time schedule and will usually bring the entire class together for a summary and an evaluation session at the close of each day's work.	Establishes a Flexible Classroom Management System room environment variable supervision grouping pupils flexible schedule
The visitor to this room is impressed with the abundance and variety of learning resources. Mrs. Milenka makes use of a basic text, but there are also a great number of other reading resources available. She has three learning centers for the current unit. One consists largely of books and other materials for pupils who are good readers and want to do individual study and research. Another	Uses a Variety of Learning Resources reading

center is where the audio and visual materials are used: filmstrips and audio tapes that can be operated by the pupils. The third center consists of learning packets and other self-study material. In addition the room has interest centers that contain displays, artifacts, maps, a globe, an encyclopedia, study prints, and an abundant supply of magazines. Because these learning resources are systematically arranged, they do not give the room a cluttered look.

learning kits and packets

interest centers

There is a considerable amount of teacher participation with pupils on a one-to-one basis. These contacts are not of lengthy duration, but they are frequent. In this way Mrs. Milenka is able to negotiate a pupil contract, make an adjustment in an assignment, or help a child find a needed book. She likes to think in terms of performance capabilities of individual pupils and assigns responsibilities accordingly. Even though pupils are working on several projects and assignments at the same time, she seems to know where each pupil is, what each is doing, and what level of performance can be expected from each.

Arranges Individual Performance Tasks

pupil contracts

individualized assignments

Looking about the room one sees much evidence of the children's creative work. Here is a small construction project underway. Over there we see a group of pupils preparing a mural. The bulletin boards have posted on them several pieces of pupils' writing and illustrations. It is apparent that these children are expressing their ideas and feelings through several channels of communication, and in the process their creative abilities are being tapped.

Develops and Uses Creative Activities

expressive activities

variety of methods and media for pupil communication

INTERN TASK 2-3

a. Compare your own efforts to individualize social studies teaching with those of Mrs. Milenka in the narrative.
b. Rate yourself on a scale of 1 to 10 on each of the four competencies discussed. Also, have your field associate teacher rate you on those

SOCIAL STUDIES COMPETENCIES AND SKILLS

competencies on a scale of 1 to 10. Compare your ratings. Indicate areas needing improvement. Discuss this activity with your clinic instructor.

Note: Defer this exercise until you are teaching regularly.

WHAT RESOURCES AND ACTIVITIES ARE USED IN TEACHING SOCIAL STUDIES?

In order to do the kind of teaching being described here, an abundance of learning resources is required. But, of course, not all learning resources are self-teaching devices; therefore, good teaching involves not only the availability of materials, but also the thoughtful selection and use of them. Most forward-moving school districts now encourage teachers to use multimedia approaches to social studies instruction for these reasons:

1. Not all pupils learn in the same way; different media are able to appeal to the learning styles of different learners.
2. The reading ranges among children who are randomly selected to form elementary classrooms are great, averaging three to five years in the lower grades and five to ten years in the middle and upper grades.
3. Each of the media has peculiar strengths and limitations in the way it conveys messages.
4. The impact of a message is likely to be stronger if more than one sensory system is involved in receiving it.
5. Material to be learned varies greatly in its abstractness and complexity.
6. The use of a variety of media has motivating and interest-generating qualities.
7. Inquiry-oriented teaching modes require wide-ranging information searches and sources.
8. Different sources may provide different insights on the same subject; there may be discrepancies or inaccuracies that go undetected if a single source is used.

The most widely used learning resource in social studies is the textbook. Almost all school districts provide a textbook for each child in the middle and upper grades, and ordinarily it is the same book for each child in the room. Textbook use is less common in the primary grades partly because of the reading level of pupils and partly because of a long tradition of informal social studies instruction based on direct experience. Because of their widespread use and misuse, the beginning teacher should become thoroughly familiar with textbooks and know what can and cannot be done with them.

There is no such thing as a good easy-to-read social studies textbook. Children almost always find them challenging, if not hard to read. This is because the ideas are complex and the specialized vocabulary is difficult. Social studies texts are designed more to be studied and thought about than read in the way a child reads a storybook. Reading in the social studies is discussed more extensively in Chapter 7.

If one looks for learning resources beyond the textbooks that are available for classroom use, one finds the full range from next to nothing to almost everything on the market. Some schools pride themselves in having the latest innovations in educational hardware. However, teachers often find the most helpful learning resources to be neither exotic nor unfamiliar. They are simply improved models of long-standing and reliable learning resources:

1. *Trade books*—that is, nontext, "library" books.
2. *Encyclopedias*—*World Book* and *The New Book of Knowledge* are the ones most commonly found in elementary school classrooms.
3. *Filmstrips*—including sound filmstrips that are synchronized with an audio recording.
4. *Films*—usually 16-mm with sound, also available in film loop cartridges that may be 8-mm.
5. *Pictures, charts,* and *study prints.*
6. *Maps, globes,* and *map-charts.*
7. *Overhead transparencies*—commercial and teacher-made.
8. *Audio recordings*—on tape and conventional disc records.
9. *Television.*
10. *Learning kits* and *packets*—for individual study, commercial and teacher-made.
11. *Simulation games.*
12. *Free and inexpensive material.*
13. *Community resources*—including resource persons, museums, libraries, exhibits, and field trips.
14. *Newspapers, magazines, classroom periodicals,* and *pamphlets.*
15. *Special references, The World Almanac,* and an *atlas.*

Ideally, a particular learning resource is selected and used because it can serve a specific purpose better than some other resource. This means that there must be objectives if an intelligent selection of learning resources is to be made. Once the objectives are identified, any learning resource that helps pupils achieve those objectives most efficiently and effectively is appropriate.

Much the same can be said for learning activities. Teachers are urged to use a variety of learning activities for many of the same reasons they are urged to use multimedia approaches. The activities traditionally associated with social studies are reading, responding to and/or discussing questions, and making reports. For many years the more exciting programs in elementary school social studies have involved the learner in a broad range of pupil activities. But even today social studies programs tend to be bookish and formal, with few activities beyond those that require well-developed linguistic abilities.

Learning activities are sometimes thought of as means to ends— that is, they are used to achieve objectives believed to be important. Teachers are cautioned not to have pupils engage in activities simply for the sake of doing activities. This is good advice, but it is not always easy to separate ends from means in social studies. For instance, while participating in an activity, children may be having valuable experiences that are in themselves important social studies outcomes. When they work together, plan, search for information, and test ideas, they are learning and applying process skills. What is important here is that these process outcomes be consciously identified as objectives by the teacher.

CHART 2-1. *Learning Activities for Social Studies*

Type of Learning Activity	Examples		Purposes Served
Research	Reading Writing Interviewing Note taking	Collecting Map work Reporting Using references	To Gather data Practice data-gathering skills Answer questions

CHART 2-1 *(continued)*

Type of Learning Activity	Examples		Purposes Served
Presentation	Telling Demonstrating Illustrating Dramatizing Exhibiting	Announcing Giving directions Pantomiming Relating events	To Share ideas with others Practice communication skills Clarify ideas Encourage initiative Apply information
Creative experiences	Writing Sketching Illustrating Sewing Soap carving Manipulating Comparing	Drawing Modeling Painting Constructing Singing Dramatizing Imagining	To Express ideas creatively Encourage creative abilities Stimulate interest Extend and/or enrich learning

Appreciation	Listening
	Viewing
		Describing
		Reading
			To
			Develop attitudes and
			  feelings
			Provide valuing experiences
			Extend and/or enrich
			  learning

Observation or listening	Observing Visiting places of interest Viewing pictures or films Listening to recordings		To Gather information Build observation and perceptual skills Compare and contrast
Group cooperation	Discussing Sharing Helping one another Doing committee work	Conversing Asking questions	To Develop group-work skills Use socialization skills Engage in larger projects
Experimentation	Measuring Demonstrating Conducting experiments	Collecting	To Clarify complex procedures Develop inquiry skills Gather information

CHART 2-1 (continued)

Type of Learning Activity	Examples		Purposes Served
Organization	Planning Outlining Holding meetings	Discussing Summarizing	To Clarify relationships Prepare a plan of action Organize ideas
Evaluation	Summarizing Criticizing Asking questions	Reviewing	To Clarify direction and purpose Assess progress toward goals Modify plans

INTERN TASK 2-4

a. Make an inventory of the resources available for teaching social studies in the school where you are an intern teacher. Solicit the help of the librarian in your building or the district specialist in instructional resources. Compare what you find with the list in this section.

b. Using the list of activities in Chart 2-1 as a guide, keep a log of the activities used in your classroom in social studies for a two-week period. Discuss this with your clinic instructor.

c. Add to the list of "purposes served" in Chart 2-1. Discuss these with your field associate teacher as they apply to the work in your classroom.

Field Associate Teacher Advisory

In the section that follows, the intern is advised to move into teaching social studies *gradually*, beginning with more formal procedures and then moving to more informal activity- and inquiry-oriented strategies. How this comes about, of course, depends almost entirely on the field associate teacher. It is strongly recommended that the microteaching experiences suggested at the end of the chapter be provided early in the term to help the intern get a feeling for teaching social studies. It is important that the intern's early teaching experiences be successful.

In conducting the critique of the microteaching, use the three questions provided. Try to get the intern to respond to them without your help, but provide cues that will lead to insight. It is important for the intern to begin early in learning to analyze and evaluate his or her own teaching.

WHAT TECHNIQUES AND STRATEGIES ARE USED IN TEACHING SOCIAL STUDIES?

How one goes about learning should have something to do with the nature of what is to be learned. For instance, it would be foolish to believe that young children learn how to work in small committees by listening to the teacher read an account of how people work in groups. Group work involves skills that require practice if they are to be learned. The pupil has to participate in the process of learning them on a firsthand basis. No amount of reading about group-work skills or hearing about them will make a person proficient in their use any more than reading about the techniques of playing second base will make an individual a good second baseman. If, however, a teacher wanted to provide children with information about early European settlements in this hemisphere, reading an account to them might very well be the best means available to achieve that objective. In this latter case the objective is to transmit information, not to have pupils develop proficiency in a skill.

How one goes about learning should also have something to do with the characteristics of the person doing the learning. A well-presented series of lengthy, technical lectures on the westward movement, for example, might be wholly appropriate to a college course in American history. But no matter how well they are presented, such lectures would be inappropriate for fifth graders studying the same topic. It is obvious that we can do some things with some groups that we cannot do with others.

The techniques and strategies to be used in teaching social studies, therefore, can best be understood by looking at the goals of the program and the objectives to be achieved. If we want children to gain information, this can be achieved through reading, viewing, discussing, and other procedures that involve the transmission of informational messages. These are referred to as *expository* teaching strategies. They have come under criticism in recent years because of the tendency to overuse them with young children. If we want children to develop critical habits of thought, to search for data independently, to be able to form hypotheses and test them, we use *inquiry* teaching strategies. If we want children to learn to work with each other, to plan together, or to apply what they are learning as they are learning it, we would use *activity* teaching strategies. *Demonstration* strategies can be a part of any of the others and would be used to improve the communication process through showing, doing, and telling. What is called discovery learning is a variation of inquiry. These modes of teaching—expository, inquiry, activity, and demonstration—are discussed in detail in other sources.[1]

Beginning teachers are usually most comfortable starting with an expository strategy. The teaching situation can be controlled sufficiently well to reduce management concerns to a minimum, the objectives can be made very specific, the pupils' study materials can be preselected by the teacher, and the process can be entirely teacher directed. First encounters with teaching social studies should be short—twenty- to thirty-minute episodes—and involve teaching a simple concept or skill. This initial teaching experience might be based on the textbook, with heavy reliance on the suggestions presented in the teacher's manual that accompanies the book. After a few experiences of this type, the novice will have gained some confidence in the teaching role, will know how to gauge pupil responses, and can begin to add variations, such as increased use of visual material, discussion questions, and pupil follow-up activities.

Having achieved a backlog of success experiences in the expository mode, the teacher might plan a demonstration. Some aspects of map or globe use would serve well for this purpose. Pupil follow-up work to the demonstration might be individualized, perhaps giving individual pupils some choice in what they will do. This can be succeeded by a class discussion of the individual follow-up activities.

While doing this type of rather formal, teacher-directed expository teaching, the questions asked by the teacher will be informational, requiring the pupils to do little more than recall what they have read or observed. The teacher is not concerned with much beyond the literal comprehension of what has been taught. With increased experience and confidence, the teacher should begin asking

[1] John Jarolimek and Clifford D. Foster, *Teaching and Learning in the Elementary School* (New York: Macmillan Publishing Co., Inc., 1976), pp. 89–112.

some questions that require other intellectual operations, such as interpretation, analysis, synthesis, or application. These reflective questions should not be ones that can be answered by recalling factual information but should require pupils to respond to such queries as "Why?" "How do you know?" "If that happened, how do you explain . . .?" "Can you summarize . . .?" "What conclusion can we come to?" "What other problems does that raise?"

These questions will gradually lead the teacher and the class away from exposition and in the direction of inquiry. In time, pupils will be raising questions and problems themselves and will speculate about their solutions. These hunches will be converted into hypotheses that result in pupil searches for data, which will necessitate the wide use of resources, individualized assignments, and a variety of interesting pupil activities. At this stage the intern is well on the way to developing professional maturity in the use of teaching techniques and strategies in social studies.

The intern often spends some time observing the field associate teacher prior to trying his or her hand at teaching. Teaching looks deceptively easy when one observes a master doing it! Everything seems to happen in an unhurried, yet deliberate, way. The transactions between teacher and pupils exude a feeling of confidence and assurance. Watching such a teacher, the observer might think, "Anyone could do that!" And, interestingly enough, the more skillful the teacher, the easier the process appears to be. It is only when the intern attempts to emulate the teaching behavior of the field associate teacher that the complexity of teaching becomes apparent.

The intern cannot possibly be expected to match the teaching performance of the master teacher. If this were possible there would be no need for a training program. Thus, the intern must not be discouraged if early efforts are not as polished as desired. Time is an important dimension in learning how to teach. What is important at this point is that initial efforts at social studies teaching be simple, brief, and teacher directed, to ensure a *successful* experience for the novice. Armed with the confidence of successful experiences, the intern can then move toward more imaginative teaching strategies.

INTERN TASK 2-5

Before taking on the responsibility of teaching an entire class, the intern will find it helpful to engage in a few microteaching sessions: a smaller group, a shorter period of instruction, and a reduction in the quantity of material to be taught. Microteaching should involve no more than a half-dozen pupils and should not last more than fifteen to twenty minutes. There should be a single specific objective.

Arrange with your field associate teacher for microteaching experiences as a preliminary to your whole-class teaching. The following sequence is suggested:

a. Plan a presentation to six pupils in which you explain a social studies concept or a process of your own choosing that would be appropriate for the grade level in which you are placed. This should be done in an expository mode of teaching. That is, decide what is to be learned and present it, rather than involve the pupils in a discussion. You may use any media you wish. Limit your presentation to fifteen minutes.

In preparing this presentation, begin by writing precisely what it is you want the pupils to learn. This should be done in a single sentence by completing the following stem: "As a result of this presentation, pupils will be able to . . . (write, list, identify, solve, compare, recall, construct, and so on.)"

Have this objective reviewed by your clinic instructor and your field associate teacher *before* the presentation is made.

Have your field associate teacher observe your presentation. Following the presentation, prepare a critique of it with your field associate teacher in terms of the following questions:
(1) Did you achieve the stated objective?
(2) What went especially well in the presentation?
(3) If you were to reteach the episode, what would you do differently?

b. Follow precisely the same procedure as in (a), but with a different group of six pupils and using a *discussion* format.
c. Follow precisely the same procedure as in (a) and (b), but with a different group of six pupils. This time use a *demonstration* mode in which you show them how to do something—that is, a skill.

CHECKING YOUR PERFORMANCE

Intern Task Checklist

Task 2-1.   Studying the classroom environment.   P. 26   _____

Task 2-2.   Observing the neighborhood.   P. 29   _____

Task 2-3.   a. Comparing your ability to individualize instruction with that of the teacher in the narrative.   P. 31   _____

b. Rating your ability to individualize instruction. P. 31   _____

Task 2-4.   a. Making an inventory of learning resources.   P. 36   _____

b. Keeping a log of classroom activities.   P. 36   _____

c. Extending list of purposes served.   P. 36   _____

Task 2-5.   a. Microteaching: teaching a concept or process.   P. 40   _____

b. Microteaching: conducting a discussion.   P. 40   _____

c. Microteaching: performing a demonstration.   P. 40   _____

Performance Checklist

In the field or in the clinic, the intern teacher has

1. Demonstrated the ability to develop a nonthreatening classroom climate conducive to teaching and learning, in which pupils can interact freely with each other and with the teacher.   _____

2. Arranged a flexible classroom environment suitable to teaching the social studies.   _____

3. Made assessments of pupils' ability to learn social studies.   _____

4. Made appropriate pupil assignments.   _____

5. Formulated appropriate objectives that have been understood by learners.   _____

6. Provided varied activities that lead to desired objectives.   _____

7. Selected and used learning materials needed for teaching social studies.   _____

8. Made social studies interesting, motivating, and meaningful to pupils.   _____

9. Asked appropriate classroom questions.   _____

10. Used a variety of appropriate teaching strategies.   _____

SOCIAL STUDIES COMPETENCIES AND SKILLS

> *Field Associate Teacher Advisory*
>
> Tasks and performances should be checked off or initialed and dated by the appropriate local official, or the intern teacher can use the checklists for his or her own record.

INTERN ADVISORY

At this point in your work you should arrange a conference with your field associate teacher and discuss how well you are making progress in the direction of achieving the Basic Competencies included thus far. It is not expected that you will be able to perform them all satisfactorily at this stage of your training, but you must be able to do so before the conclusion of your internship.

Prepare a brief summary of this conference and submit it to your clinic instructor and to your field coordinator.

> *Field Associate Teacher Advisory*
>
> It cannot be expected that the intern will be able to perform the Basic Competencies discussed in this chapter early in the term. Nonetheless, some progress should be made toward their achievement even at the early stages of the internship. At the conclusion of the training period, the intern must be able to perform these competencies at a level commensurate with that of a beginning teacher and should not be approved for certification until it has been demonstrated to your satisfaction that he or she is able to do so.

Chapter 3

Social studies subject matter, skills, and values, and how to teach them

Early in the term Kay Woodruff and her field associate teacher, Nancy Juarez, were talking informally about the subject matter of elementary school social studies. This was of more than ordinary interest to Kay because she had a Bachelor of Arts degree with a major in history. She had originally intended to be a high school history teacher but became interested in elementary school teaching as a result of something called a "302 experience" at her university. This involved volunteer work as a teacher aide as a preliminary to admission to the teacher education program. Kay found that she liked working with young children and was flattered by the way they responded to her. Kay was an honor student and liked history as a discipline, but she was not sure she really understood social studies as a school subject.

"When I took my undergraduate course in social studies methods several years ago," Mrs. Juarez said, "social studies was defined as 'those portions of the social sciences selected for instructional purposes.' For all practical purposes this meant history and geography that could be simplified for elementary school children. Since then the trend has been to broaden the base of social studies, not only to include other social science disciplines, but also to include the arts, humanities, current social problems, and the personal concerns of pupils."

"But don't children need to develop the mental discipline that comes from the systematic study of a single subject before they attempt to integrate knowledge from several disciplines?" Kay asked.

"Our purpose is not to make social scientists and historians out of these children. We want to provide them with a citizen's knowledge of social reality and of human societies," replied Mrs. Juarez. "We are basically concerned with developing good citizenship. There are many good citizens who have never studied the social sciences—may not even have heard of them. As for integrating knowledge from several sources, this is not a problem for children. They are less inclined to compartmentalize knowledge than are adults."

Conversations along this line continued between Kay and Mrs. Juarez throughout most of the year. Kay raised some difficult issues with Mrs. Juarez: Is it the purpose of social studies to conserve or to reform society? Does social studies take a position of advocacy on social issues? Isn't much of what passes for social studies education simply propagandizing for "the system"? What evidence is there that social studies makes any difference in the behavior of pupils? Wouldn't social science *be a better term than* social studies? *Then, in a lighter vein, Kay would ask slyly, "Do you say social studies is or social studies are?"*

Mrs. Juarez explained to Kay that the profession itself did not have good responses to some of these questions, nor was there consensus among specialists on these issues. Kay appreciated Nancy Juarez's candidness and intellectual honesty. She was also impressed with her professionalism and her commitment to the social studies concept. What Kay did not know then, but would learn several months later from one of her former history professors, was that Nancy Juarez had a master's degree in history.

The list of Basic Competencies related to subject matter and planning that the clinic instructor had provided the interns made little sense to Kay Woodruff at the time it was distributed. The list seemed to be so much educational theory that was remote from what she imagined social studies teaching to be. But between the work in the clinic and her experiences with Nancy Juarez and the children, Kay learned to organize her social studies program along the lines suggested by the Basic Competencies.

Basic Competencies—Social Studies

The intern teacher is able to

1. Identify, define, and explain key concepts and generalizations relevant to elementary school social studies education.
2. Use concepts and generalizations as organizing frameworks for planning and teaching social studies.
3. Convert subject matter into thought forms appropriate to elementary school pupils.
4. Select subject matter appropriate to the development of the main ideas and the development of related attitudes and values and skills objectives.
5. Use appropriate strategies for teaching various types of social studies learnings:
   a. Informational learning.
   b. Concepts and generalizations.
   c. Skills.
   d. Attitudes and values.

INTERN ADVISORY

After completing this chapter, together with related work in the clinic and appropriate class experiences in the field, you should be able to do the following:

1. Explain the difference between a concept and a generalization and provide several examples of each that are appropriate to social studies.
2. Show by an example how concepts and generalizations provide organizing frameworks for planning and teaching social studies.
3. Using the topic "People Change the Earth" illustrate by specific examples (by defining the concepts to be developed and the subject matter to be used) how it could be presented at a level of difficulty suitable to the grade level in which you are teaching.
4. Using what you have done in number 3, show by specific example how the attitudes, values, and skills learned are built around the core subject matter selected for study.
5. Teach a concept or a generalization to the class to which you are assigned, using one of the strategies discussed in this chapter.

6. Teach a social studies skill to the class to which you are assigned, using the strategy discussed in this chapter.
7. Conduct a simple values-clarification exercise with your class.
8. Identify a children's book or a story that would be particularly useful in highlighting a general value that is embraced by this society.

HOW DO CONCEPTS AND GENERALIZATIONS RELATE TO SOCIAL STUDIES?

If asked to tell what a village is, most adults would probably say something along this line, "A village consists of a group of persons living in a rural area in a cluster of homes smaller than a city or a town." For most purposes this is an adequate definition to make communication possible. But *village* had a much more elaborate meaning for the Indians of British Columbia, as explained in Margaret Craven's novel *I Heard the Owl Call My Name.* On the boat trip north, the young priest, Mark Brian, recalls what his bishop had told him about the village:

> The Indian knows his village and feels for his village as no white man for his country, his town, or even for his own bit of land. His village is not the strip of land four miles long and three miles wide that is his as long as the sun rises and the moon sets. The myths are the village and the winds and the rains. The river is the village, and the black and white killer whales that herd the fish to the end of the inlet the better to gobble them. The village is the salmon who comes up the river to spawn, the seal who follows the salmon and bites off his head, the bluejay whose name is like the sound he makes— "Kwiss-kwiss." The village is the talking bird, the owl, who calls the name of the man who is going to die, and the silver-tipped grizzly who ambles into the village, and the little white speck that is the mountain goat on Whoop-Szo.
>
> The fifty-foot totem by the church is the village, and the Cedar-man who stands at the bottom holding up the eagle, the wolf and the raven! And a voice said to the great cedar tree in Bond Sound, "Come forth, Tzakamayi and be a man," and he came forth to be the Cedar-man, the first man-god of the people and more powerful than all other.[1]

[1] From *I Heard the Owl Call My Name*. Copyright © 1973 by Margaret Craven. Reprinted by permission by Doubleday & Company, Inc., and George G. Harrap & Company.

This is a superb example of a concept because it illustrates so well the richness and depth of meaning that can inhere in a single word label: *village*. It also illustrates how vital experience is in developing such meanings. It is doubtful if anyone who did not actually grow up in the village culture of these North Coast Indians could understand and appreciate the full meaning of *village* as they conceptualize it. Yet the novelist does very well in conveying the meaning by skillfully building word images for us of things that are familiar because they come out of our own background of experience.

Concepts are sometimes described as abstract categories of meanings. They are abstract because they are removed from specific instances. For example, *island* is the word label for a geographic phenomenon consisting of land completely surrounded by water. Kauai is one specific example of such a set of conditions. There are thousands of other specific examples of the concept *island*. But to know that Kauai is an island (that is, a body of land completely surrounded by water) is not to know very much about that beautiful outcropping of land in the Pacific. To early Hawaiians, Kauai had a meaning closely akin to that of village to the North Coast Indians described earlier. Concept definitions, therefore, tell us only about those qualities or attributes that a class or group of examples *have in common*. They do not tell us about the unique features of particular examples.

Other concepts and some specific examples of each are these:

1. Mountains: Alps, Rockies, Cascades, Sierra Nevadas.
2. Forms of government: monarchy, democracy, dictatorship.
3. Consumer goods: shoes, cars, television sets, furniture.
4. Producer: farmer, factory worker, contractor.
5. Political party: Democratic, Republican, Independent.
6. River: Mississippi, Hudson, Missouri, Columbia.

It is relatively easy to provide examples of concepts such as these. But it is not so easy to provide one- or two-word examples of such concepts as

justice	*colonialism*	*culture*
equality of opportunity	*free enterprise*	*interdependence*
legal system	*role*	*franchise*

The meanings of these concepts can be developed by description or by definition, providing the descriptions and/or definitions are rooted in the experiences of the learner—that is, in something that is already known. This means that if we are to develop new concepts or extend the meanings of those partially understood, it is critical to link them to prior experience and knowledge.

Social studies material is literally loaded with concepts. The following paragraph was selected at random from a fourth-grade social studies textbook. The concepts have been italicized here to call attention to them:

> Long before Chicago became a *manufacturing city*, it was a *trade center*. Today it is the busiest *marketing center* of the *nation*. Every *year* there are *dozens* of *trade fairs* in Chicago. *Producers* and *buyers* of *goods* gather there to do *business* with each other. They also learn from one another about the latest *products*. *People* come to Chicago from all over the United States. The Furniture Fair and the Shoe Exhibit are two of the biggest such *fairs* held each *year*.[2]

If you try to simplify this paragraph by substituting simpler words for those that are italicized, you will find that you cannot do so and still have the paragraph convey the same meaning. It is clear from this example that concepts carry much of the meaning of social studies.

INTERN TASK 3-1

Before proceeding, make certain you are able to identify social studies concepts. Select a page at random from a child's social studies text, preferably one used in your classroom, and identify all the social studies concepts on that page. If you do not have a text available, use the article "Homestead Act" in the H volume of *World Book* encyclopedia. Check your accuracy in identifying concepts with your field associate teacher.

Let us return to the village concept cited earlier and ask the question: What can we say about the relationship between the village and the people who live there? Several things could be said, of course, but the following will serve our purpose:

[2]Phillip Viereck and Bertha Davis, *Web of the World: Interdependence of People and Places* (a fourth grade textbook) (New York: Macmillan Publishing Co., Inc., 1973), p. 257.

The village embraces the total culture of traditional North Coast Indians.

This statement expresses a relationship between the concepts *village* and *culture*. Such relationships are called generalizations and are expressed as declarative statements. Because generalizations are relationships between two or more concepts, they are summarizing statements that have wide applicability. They can be transferred to many situations. For example, the generalization cited does not apply only to one village but to *all* villages of traditional North Coast Indians. That is what makes it a generalization. The generalization "All human societies have a culture" has even broader applicability. It would apply to *any* human society, anywhere in the world.

In social studies we are usually concerned with four types of generalizations:

1. *Those that describe*: In any society there are more consumers than producers.
2. *Those that show cause and effect*: The closer one goes to the equator, the warmer will be the average annual temperature at sea level.
3. *Those that express a value principle*: Individuals are not allowed to do things that endanger the health, safety, or well-being of others.
4. *Those that express a law or theory*: The economic development of a country requires domestic savings that can provide enough capital to finance the investments needed to guarantee an adequate rate of growth.

INTERN TASK 3-2

At this point you should be able to identify, define, and explain social studies concepts and generalizations. Select three unit topics from the following list and provide examples of five concepts that might be included in such units. Then, using the concepts you have identified, write a generalization that expresses a valid relationship central to each of the topics. Have these checked for correctness by your clinic instructor.

People Change the Earth (K–8)
School Living (K)

Families and Their Needs (1)
The Shopping Center (2)
Life in the City (3)
Our Home State (4)
The Westward Movement (5)
Crossroads of the World: The Middle East (6–7)
Colonial America (8)

HOW ARE CONCEPTS AND GENERALIZATIONS USED AS ORGANIZING FRAMEWORKS FOR PLANNING AND TEACHING SOCIAL STUDIES?

Concepts and generalizations are used to organize the subject matter components of the social studies program. The relationship between concepts and generalizations and subject matter is twofold and reciprocal. On the one hand, subject matter provides the specific detail, the examples, the illustrative support, and the vicarious experience that give concepts and generalizations meaning. Concepts and generalizations cannot be developed without in some way being linked to subject matter and to one's experience. On the other hand, subject matter will be more effectively understood and, therefore, better remembered if it is focused on key ideas such as concepts and generalizations. We know that much of the subject matter studied is forgotten, but that the residual learning—that is, the key ideas—is long-lasting. This is not to say that all subject matter is forgotten or that it is unimportant.

Figure 3-1 shows how one textbook series incorporates concepts and generalizations from the social sciences to develop a conceptual framework for the program. This one is selected from grade 5. Although the subject matter of the text deals with the United States and other people of the Western Hemisphere, you will notice that the generalizations are not content-specific. They could be developed with and/or applied to other parts of the world. We say they have high *transfer value.*

In making plans for teaching, one teacher focused on key ideas as illustrated on page 53.

Conceptual Framework Established in this Level[3]

Level Five *This summary of generalizations indicates the multi-disciplinary approach embodied in the contents of Lands of Promise. The length of a column does not necessarily indicate the depth to which that dis-*

ECONOMICS	GEOGRAPHY	SOCIOLOGY
☐ The wants of people are unlimited; the resources needed to fulfill their wants are scarce.	☐ The way people use their natural environment reflects their values and technology—their culture.	☐ The family is a basic social unit which fulfills many of the needs of its members.
☐ When a good or goods are scarce, the price for them is high. As the supply of goods matches the demand, prices tend to fall.	☐ People shape and adapt the natural environment to meet their needs; they also change and adapt their culture to suit the environment.	☐ People's values and beliefs greatly influence how they will act in a given situation.
☐ As the price of goods rises, the supply offered in the market tends to increase.	☐ The physical features of an area influence settlement patterns in that area.	☐ Status and prestige are relative to the values sought by a social group.
☐ Standard of living is related to productivity.	☐ The accessibility of an area is an important factor in its growth and development.	☐ Every known society of any size contains a hierarchy of social classes.
☐ When people support themselves by hunting and food-gathering, an area can support only a small population.	☐ Cities tend to begin and grow as centers to serve the areas surrounding them.	☐ Groups of people cooperate and work together when faced with a common problem.
☐ Growth in population creates an increased demand for goods and services.	☐ The development of an urban center depends heavily upon availability of transportation and upon the productivity of its hinterland.	☐ People who differ from the majority culture, in readily apparent ways, run a greater risk of being treated unfairly than those who do not differ.
☐ The economy of a region is related to available natural resources, human knowledge and skills, and tradition.	☐ Most modern countries are dominated economically by core areas which are highly industrialized and urbanized.	☐ The greater the diversity among culture groups in an area, the greater is the potential for conflict among these groups.
☐ Transportation is an important factor in the location and development of economic activity.	☐ Regions of the earth can be defined on the basis of a single feature or on the basis of several features.	☐ Increased industrialization and urbanization is accompanied by changes in the social structure of a society.
☐ Regional specialization and interdependence tend to accompany economic and population growth.	☐ Water is the key to settlement and development in the drier areas of the world.	☐ Population growth is presenting people with some of the most challenging problems of modern times.
☐ The development of markets is tied to the development of transportation and communication systems.	☐ Regions develop economic ties that make them dependent on one another.	☐ The trend toward urbanization has created urgent problems of group living and urban management.
☐ The interdependence of peoples of the world makes exchange and trade necessary.	☐ The unwise use of natural resources can result in tremendous cost to future generations.	
☐ The economic development of a country is enhanced by increased trade and specialization.		
☐ Economies that are based on a single crop or product are less stable than those that are diversified.		
☐ Most modern societies perceive economic welfare as a desired goal for their people; universally, poverty is devalued as a human condition.		

Figure 3-1.

[3]Bertha Davis, *Teacher's Guide for Lands of Promise and Its Related Media* (New York: Macmillan Publishing Co., Inc., 1974), pp. vi–vii.

Social Studies/Focus on Active Learning

cipline is woven into the book. These generalizations are cited only once in the chart, although they may appear in the lists of generalizations for several different chapters.

POLITICAL SCIENCE	ANTHROPOLOGY	HISTORY	PHILOSOPHY
☐ Every society or group develops laws or rules to govern the conduct of its members and to provide protection for them. ☐ The decisions, policies, and laws made for a given society reflect and are based on the values, beliefs, and traditions of that society. ☐ Government must rest, to some extent or in some form, on the consent of the governed. ☐ Political and economic power is not evenly distributed, even in democratic societies. ☐ Political stability within a country is conducive to economic development. ☐ In modern societies, government plays an increasingly important role in the development and use of natural resources. ☐ Cooperation between nations is facilitated by a common heritage and similar social institutions. ☐ The rule of the majority is a major tenet of American democracy.	☐ Although they may contain cultural diversity, culture regions are often identified in terms of the dominant cultural group. ☐ People moving into a new environment tend to take their ways of life with them into the new situation. ☐ Maintaining a cultural identity is important to most culture groups. ☐ Culture is transmitted within a society through education by the elders, imitation and learning by the young. ☐ The increased and more frequent contact of persons from various cultures made possible by modern-day transportation and communication systems is resulting in extensive cultural diffusion, cultural borrowing, and cultural exchange. ☐ When people of different cultures come in contact with each other, selective borrowing occurs.	☐ The early history of a country or region has a definite bearing on the culture of its people. ☐ Events of the past influence those of the present. ☐ All regions in a country do not grow and develop at the same rate. ☐ Causes are rarely simple, often complex. ☐ Change in a culture may result from factors generated by the culture itself. ☐ Violence and war are not effective solutions to basic human problems.	☐ Each culture has certain significant values and beliefs that influence its development. ☐ All societies have holidays, feasts, and festivals that help to celebrate and perpetuate traditions, beliefs, and customs.

Our Environment

Organizing Idea

Environmental factors influence where and how people live and what they do; people adapt, shape, utilize, and exploit the environment to their own needs.

This generalization provides the focus for the study. Notice how similiar it is to those listed in Figure 3-1.

Main Ideas to Be Developed

1. Our environment includes everything around us.
2. We make use of the environment in order to live.
3. People can adapt to their environment and can also make the environment adapt to them.
4. The natural environment consists of things made by or placed here by nature.
5. The "man-made" environment consists of things made or placed here by human beings.
6. We can make proper or improper use of the environment.

These generalizations are specific to the topic studied. Teaching episodes will be planned around them.

Essential Concepts to Be Developed

Needs	Exploitation
Wants	Conservation
Natural resources	Pollution
Adaptation	Web of life
Population	Litter

These concepts are essential to the understanding of the subject as it is being planned and will be presented.

Field Associate Teacher Advisory

Make certain the intern teacher understands the conceptual framework of the social studies program in your school. Discuss the local social studies curriculum guide with the intern in terms of its rationale and conceptual framework. If a curriculum guide is not available, discuss the rationale and conceptual framework of the social studies textbook series you are using as these are explained in the accompanying teacher's guide.

HOW CAN SUBJECT MATTER BE CONVERTED INTO THOUGHT FORMS APPROPRIATE FOR ELEMENTARY SCHOOL CHILDREN?

Social studies concepts and topics can be studied at various levels of complexity. Kindergarteners and first graders often study the family and family life. Yet a graduate student working on a doctor's degree in sociology or anthropology might take an advanced seminar on the same subject. The United States Supreme Court struggles with the meaning of justice in a complex case, yet children in the elementary school learn about the meaning of "liberty and justice for all." How does a teacher go about setting the complexity of subject matter, concepts, and generalizations and present them in ways that make sense to children? The following are suggested:

1. Define concepts and key ideas in childlike terms. For example:

Concept	For a Young Child This Means
Justice	Being or playing fair
Laws	Rules
Equality of opportunity	Seeing that everyone gets a turn
Cooperation	Working with others
Responsibility	Doing your part or doing your duty

2. Select content samples (subject matter) with which pupils can identify. This does not mean that topics selected for study must in all cases be physically close to the children. The usual assumption is that things that are physically close to children will be more familiar than those far away. This is not always the case. Children can study about things far away that are psychologically close to them. On the other hand, things that are physically close may be psychologically remote. The lifestyles of families who live across town, for example, may be as unfamiliar to a child as those of people halfway around the world.

3. Develop ideas only to the point where children can apply them to reality. It takes time for children to learn concepts. They build the meanings of ideas cumulatively over several years. Do not expect children to learn complex concepts to completion in the early grades. The tendency is to try to teach children more than they want or need to know about a concept or a subject at a particular time.

4. Rely heavily on diagnostic approaches to teaching. Find out how much pupils already know. This can usually be accomplished through informal class discussions in which children respond to open-ended questions the teacher has prepared in advance. Observe how well they use new terms and concepts naturally and easily. Be aware of the level of interest in what is being studied. Draw on the experiences of pupils in planning and teaching social studies. Encourage children to talk about what is studied as it relates to their lives.

INTERN TASK 3-3

Interview four or five children from your class individually to determine their understanding of selected social studies concepts. Use a straightforward procedure and everyday concepts. For example, you might say, "What does the term *family* mean to you? What is a family, anyway?" (Or use *community, city, park,* and the like.) When the child responds, probe gently to get an elaboration of what the concept means to the youngster. You might vary the procedure by including abstract concepts such as *justice* and *freedom,* or quantitative concepts such as *several years later* or *long ago.* These experiences will provide you with firsthand knowledge of what it means to convert subject matter into thought forms appropriate for elementary school children.

HOW IS SUBJECT MATTER SELECTED IN ORDER TO ACHIEVE THE MULTIPLE OBJECTIVES OF SOCIAL STUDIES?

There is some variation in school district policies, but typically elementary school teachers do not have a great deal of choice about the subjects and topics to be included in the social studies curriculum. These are either designated by the district curriculum guide or the district has adopted a textbook series that pretty much determines the units and topics to be included. Teachers do, however, have a considerable amount of latitude in deciding how those topics will be developed and what ideas will be singled out for emphasis. It is those ideas that really determine the specific subject matter. An example will illustrate how this comes about.

Let us say that the fifth-grade curriculum guide calls for a unit on Canada. The guide also indicates what the emphasis is to be and the major generalizations that are to provide a focus for this unit:

Canada: Land Giant of the Western Hemisphere

This unit should provide pupils with a comprehensive view of Canada as it is today. This does not mean that historical information will be excluded, but simply that the stress is to be interdisciplinary with an emphasis on contemporary life. The unit should treat Canada as a whole rather than focus on a particular small sample of Canadian life and culture. Whereas the similarities between the United States and Canada should be studied, it is important to present Canada as a nation distinguished by its own nationality and culture. Some emphasis must be placed on how it is different from the United States. The long-standing tradition of cordial relations between the United States and Canada also should be stressed. The following generalizations should emerge as a result of the study of Canada:

1. The physical features of an area influence settlement patterns and transportation routes. (Geography)
2. Maintaining an ethnic identity is important to most members of a cultural group. (Anthropology)
3. The use of available resources depends on the nature of the economic system, the values of people, and their level of technology. (Economics)
4. The early history of a country has a definite bearing on the present culture of its people. (History)

How does the teacher go about selecting subject matter about Canada that will be in accord with the focus suggested by the curriculum guide?

One option available to the teacher, obviously, is simply to teach whatever is included in the children's textbook. If the textbook treatment is in harmony with the focus suggested and the teacher makes enlightened use of the books, this is not an altogether undesirable procedure. We would like to think, however, that the teacher will be able to develop a more imaginative approach and, in the process, make better use of the text and other learning resources that are available on this subject.

The basic question here is this: What is it that the pupils are expected to learn about Canada that is consistent with the suggested emphasis? Or, what are the main ideas about Canada that will receive attention in this unit?

In order to respond to this question, the teacher should do some self-study with the thought of selecting six to eight major ideas to be included in the unit. The public library, *The World Almanac*, encyclopedias, and the pupil materials in the classroom can be used for this purpose. Let us assume that the teacher has done this research and decides that the following main ideas will be developed in the unit:

1. Canada is a country with a unique, northern geographic location.
2. Canada is a large, regionally divided and diverse country.
3. Canada is a highly industrialized and technologically advanced country.
4. Canada is an urbanized country, rapidly becoming a nation of city-dwellers.
5. Canada is an exposed country, open to a multitude of external cultural, economic, and political influences.
6. Canada is a multi-ethnic country with two predominant linguistic groups.[4]

After the teacher has selected the main ideas, such as those listed here, it is possible to select the essential related concepts and the specific subject matter, as shown by Chart 3-1.

CHART 3-1. Essential Cognitive Elements of a Unit on Canada

Main Ideas	Essential Concepts	Subject Matter Synopsis
1. Canada is a country with a unique north-	Arctic Latitude	Location and size of Canada along with its dominant physi-

[4]CONTACT, Number 5, Canada Studies Foundation, 252 Bloor Street West, Toronto, Ontario M5S IV5, September 1974.

SOCIAL STUDIES COMPETENCIES AND SKILLS

CHART 3-1. (continued)

Main Ideas	Essential Concepts	Subject Matter Synopsis
ern geographic location.	Coastline Heartland Natural boundary Political boundary	cal features, unique natural regions, and climatic characteristics; population distribution; location in terms of other nations of the Northern Hemisphere.
2. Canada is a large, regionally divided and diverse country.	Regionalism Prairie Maritime Offshore Province	Brief history of Canadian development; political and natural regions; occupations of its people; regionalism as a social, economic, and political factor in Canadian life.
3. Canada is a highly industrialized and technologically advanced country.	Natural resources Minerals Raw materials Technological change	Development of Canadian resources for export and domestic use; rise of Canadian industry; transportation and communication systems in Canada.
4. Canada is an urbanized country, rapidly becoming a nation of city dwellers.	Metropolitan area Trading center Manufacturing center Urban environment	Move toward urbanism with cities gaining in their influence over the lives of all Canadians; problems associated with urban sprawl and urban renewal: Toronto, a case study.
5. Canada is an exposed country, open to a multitude of external cultural, economic, and political influences.	Foreign investment Nationalism Cultural influence	Influence of foreign investments in Canadian industry and agriculture; the American presence; cultural influences from the States; influence of immigration on Canadian development.
6. Canada is a multiethnic country with two predominant linguistic groups.	Ethnic group Bilingual Bicultural Heritage Minority Cultural mosaic	Historical background of Canadian bilingualism; effect of bicultural life on social, political, and economic decision making; status of native people in Canada.

Thus far we have discussed subject matter selection only in terms of informational outcomes—that is, cognitive objectives. But what about skills, attitudes, and values? How do they fit into the picture? Objectives that deal with skills, attitudes, and values are structured around the subject matter, too, and are developed concurrently with informational objectives. Unless the curriculum guide specifically indicates which skills, attitudes, and values are to receive attention—and usually it does not—the matter is left to the judgment of the teacher.

In the example of Canada it is reasonable that map and globe skills would be a necessary part of main ideas numbers 1 and 2. All of the main ideas will require information searches that will provide a way to teach and apply research and inquiry skills. The teacher will doubtless plan activities that require the children to use group-work skills. Attitudinal outcomes can hardly be ignored because the curriculum guide states explicitly, "The long-standing tradition of cordial relations between the United States and Canada also should be stressed." Values will come into the study as pupils begin to examine the trade-offs involved in Canada's becoming an urbanized country, exploiting its resources, assimilating its native people, and maintaining an official bicultural position.

These suggestions provide some possibilities for the coordination of information, skills, attitudes, and values objectives. The essential point is that it is around the basic subject matter that all of these objectives are achieved by children.

WHAT ARE APPROPRIATE TEACHING STRATEGIES FOR THE VARIOUS TYPES OF SOCIAL STUDIES LEARNINGS?

For purposes of analysis, those who write on the subject of education often discuss the attainment of concepts, attitudes, values, and skills separately in terms of *cognitive, affective,* and *psychomotor* objectives. In the classroom, however, these objectives are usually achieved concurrently. It is nearly impossible to separate concepts from skills and attitudes and values in a complex and highly interrelated field such as the social studies. This was illustrated in the sample lesson provided in Chapter 1. Nonetheless, some instruction is directed mainly to the attainment of concepts, some mainly to attitudes and values, and some mainly to skill development.

Informational Learning

Some of the things children are expected to learn in social studies are informational and do not fit neatly into any of the categories of concepts, skills, attitudes, or values. These learnings are largely cognitive and are, at least to some extent, factual. Such learnings might be regarded as important elements of the cultural heritage that are transmitted through instruction from one generation to the next. Information about the growth and development of the United States, folklore and legends, traditions, community and state history, and basic information about the geography of the world are examples of such learnings. They are usually transmitted to learners through the use of some form of expository teaching, such as reading, films, or narration.

Except in a general way, there is no agreement as to what should be included in informational learning. The usual assumption is that it is the information contained in the textbooks or that which is designated in the curriculum guide or course of study. In some cases what is to be taught may be specified in the education code of the state. The tendency through the years has been to place too great an emphasis on informational outcomes with a corresponding neglect of concept development, attitudes, values, and skills. Also, emphasis may be placed on elements of information that are trivial, not often used, or not even known by well-informed, educated adults. The judgment of the teacher is crucial in selecting the elements of information that pupils are expected to learn and remember on a long-term basis.

INTERN TASK 3-4

Identify six items of information relating to social studies that you believe should be learned by the pupils in the grade you are teaching. Why did you select the particular items that you did? Now interview individuals not associated directly with the education enterprise, such as a lawyer, a physician, a member of the clergy, a gasoline station owner or some other businessman, a police officer, a government official, and/or others, and have them respond to the question: What information, attitudes, values, or skills does a citizen need to know, hold, or practice? How do their responses differ from yours? Discuss your choices with your field associate teacher and/or your clinic instructor.

Teaching and Learning Concepts and Generalizations

As has already been explained, concepts and generalizations are not in all cases specific to particular topics and this has important implications for how they are taught and learned. The key guideline in the development of concepts and generalizations is the *breadth of experience* the pupils have with them. For example, if the teacher is developing the concept *desert* and shows the learners one picture of a desert depicting sand dunes and camels, that single mental image will constitute the extent of the learner's understanding of the concept *desert*. Years later the learner might be traveling through the desert in the southwestern part of the United States and be surprised to find irrigated cropland and no evidence of sand dunes or camels. In this case the learning was not abstracted from the specific example provided by the teacher. A better teaching procedure would have been to give several examples of what is and what is not a desert, followed by their descriptions and, finally, a definition.

Concepts are learned by citing examples, providing descriptions, and establishing definitions. There is some evidence to suggest that concept learning is enhanced when all three of these processes are used in developing the meaning of concepts.[5] Let us apply this procedure to an easily understood concept such as *island*:

Examples:	Long Island, Maui, Catalina, Ireland, Iceland, Greenland, Vancouver.
Nonexamples:	Lower California, Denmark, Italy, Florida (all peninsulas).
Description:	Islands are places that have water all around them. They may be wooded, consist of farmland, or be just an outcropping of rock. They may even consist entirely of a city, as in the case of Manhattan Island. But what is on the land has nothing to do with whether the place is an island.
Definition:	An island is a land mass surrounded by water.

This simple example provides good leads as to how the teaching of a concept might proceed. One could begin by exposing the learners to

[5] Jack D. Simpson, "The Effects of Critical Property Identification and Form of Instance Presentation on Children's Concept Attainment in the Social Studies" (Ph. D. dissertation, University of Washington, Seattle), 1975, pp. 42–43.

examples and nonexamples. From this a description could be made, and from the examples and description a definition could be generated. The procedure could also be reversed. One might begin with the definition, develop a description, and then have the learners search for examples and nonexamples. What is important here is that all three of these processes—examples, description, and definition—should be used, rather than one.

There are specific strategies that have been developed for concept attainment. The intern should try these in the classroom by following the directions provided here.

INTERN TASK 3-5

Strategy One: Listing, Grouping, and Labeling.

Directions:

Step 1. Provide pupils with an experience that affords them an opportunity to make a great number of specific observations, such as a trip to the supermarket in the primary grades, a walk through the community, items sold in a department store, products manufactured in the home state or city, means of transportation and so on.

Step 2. Following the experience in Step 1, have pupils list as many specific things as they can remember seeing. As children list items, write them on the chalkboard randomly, just as they are suggested.

Step 3. Ask pupils to study the list to see whether the items might be grouped in categories (that is, which items seem to belong together). Then group the items into the categories that seem to go together.

Step 4. Have pupils suggest labels for these groups. (These groups are concepts, bearing such labels as fruit, vegetables, transportation, communication, services, and so on.)

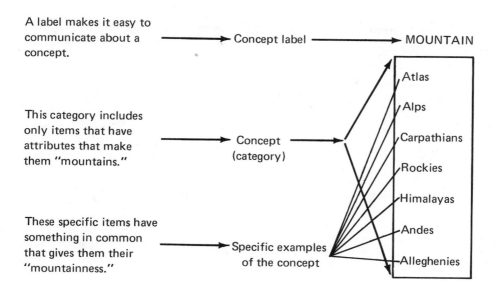

A label makes it easy to communicate about a concept. → Concept label → MOUNTAIN

This category includes only items that have attributes that make them "mountains." → Concept (category)

These specific items have something in common that gives them their "mountainness." → Specific examples of the concept

Atlas
Alps
Carpathians
Rockies
Himalayas
Andes
Alleghenies

INTERN TASK 3-6

Strategy Two: Experiencing, Hypothesizing, and Testing.

Directions:

Step 1. Provide pupils with extended firsthand exploratory experiences with the concept. Make sure pupils see the concept in many different settings. Encourage pupils to identify numerous examples of the concept. For example, if the concept to be studied is *culture change*, pupils could cite examples showing the effects of the introduction of technology, changing agricultural practices, changes in government, and so on. Clarify any subconcepts and terms related to the main concept and essential to its understanding.

Step 2. Encourage pupils to discuss the concept and to speculate on how the concept relates to other concepts already known to them and/or how it can be helpful in understanding relationships. These speculations should be stated as hypotheses that can be tested. For example, in the case of culture change, some hypotheses might be

When people are isolated from other people for long periods of time, culture changes come about more slowly than when there is frequent contact with outsiders.

Or:

New tools and new power sources hasten culture change.

Or:

Ways of working are more easily changed than are beliefs about God and the meaning of life.

These statements should not be assumed to be true or false but as hypotheses to be tested.

Step 3. Have pupils make a data search to test the hypotheses they have generated.

Step 4. On the basis of data collected, formulate tentative conclusions. From this, other hypotheses should be generated and the search continued.

Step 5. Continue the study with additional firsthand experiences, hypotheses formation and testing, and concluding, until the meaning of the concept has been extended and refined.

This strategy is especially useful in developing the meanings of concepts that are not easily defined, such as *culture, power, authority, freedom, democracy,* and *social change.*

INTERN TASK 3-7

Strategy Three: Recognizing Examples and Nonexamples.

Directions:

Step 1. Identify the label for the concept to be studied. (For example, *metropolitan region*.)

Step 2. Provide learners with the identifying features of the concept. These are known as its major attributes or critical properties. (For example, in order for a place to be a metropolitan region, what characteristics *must* it have?) These should be written on the chalkboard or otherwise displayed.

Step 3. Provide examples that illustrate the presence of the major attributes. Show that the attributes are present in each of the examples. These examples could be visuals or narrative accounts.

Step 4. Provide nonexamples of the concept. Show that the attributes are not present in each case.

Step 5. Present examples and nonexamples and have the pupils identify the attributes and tell why each is an example or nonexample in terms of the presence or absence of the attributes.

Step 6. Have the pupils find examples and nonexamples. These should be shared with the group, and pupils should explain why each is or is not an example of the concept.

Step 7. Test to see whether pupils can identify examples and non-examples of the concept.

This strategy is useful in teaching concepts whose critical attributes can be clearly identified and on which there is consensus among experts.

Teaching and Learning Skills

When we teach someone a skill, the object is to get the learner to be able to do something proficiently in repeated performances. This means that practice is an essential ingredient in teaching and learning a skill. Skills need to be understood by learners and should, therefore, be taught in meaningful ways. But nothing can take the place of practice that is conducted with the intent of improving performance. In cases where we find children with inadequately developed skills, we usually find that they have not practiced them sufficiently to develop proficiency.

Practice should not be confused with meaningless and routine drill. Practice exercises must be interesting to the learner and the

learner must be highly motivated or the practice may be done carelessly and inaccurately, thereby preventing improvement. Pupils can
practice doing skills incorrectly as well as correctly. It is not always
necessary to perform exercises when engaging in practice. Children
practice skills when they apply them in achieving other objectives.
Indeed, in social studies much of the practice of skills comes through
using them and applying them in functional settings. It is necessary
to make use of skills on a regular basis in order to maintain the desired level of proficiency.

Teaching and Learning Attitudes and Values

It is often claimed that attitudes and values are "caught, not
taught." That is another way of saying that attitudes and values do
not lend themselves well to the kind of direct instruction used to
teach information, concepts, generalizations, and skills. Often attitudes and values are the result of affectively toned experiences with
ideas, topics, things, or people. Typically, children will reflect the
attitudes and values of high-status adults with whom they associate
closely—primarily parents. In addition to parents, this group of significant others, whose behavior, attitudes, and values children emulate,
could include other close relatives, teachers, and religious leaders.
It is clear that the development of attitudes and values of the young
is a partial responsibility of the school, one it shares with the home
and other agencies and institutions.

From the standpoint of socializing children into the life of society, it is imperative that they develop a commitment to those
general attitudes and values embraced by society. These general
values serve as guidelines to behavior: once internalized, they monitor the conduct of individuals, thereby making orderly social life
possible. General values are derived from our legal and judicial systems, our great documents of freedom, our religious heritages, and
our cultural traditions. There is no single source to which the teacher
can refer to see these general values listed. Nonetheless, they are
apparent in a variety of forms that we see around us each day—in
the laws of Scouting, for instance; in slogans on public buildings; in
the slogans on our paper currency and coins; and in rules for sporting
events. General values such as these are the most evident:

Freedom	Honesty
Human dignity	Loyalty
Equality of treatment	Consideration for others
Equality of opportunity	Responsibility
Fair play	Courage
Trustworthiness	Truthfulness

With very young children these values are taught in more or less direct ways by the adults who surround them. One might even say that young children are indoctrinated with such values as honesty, truthfulness, consideration for others, fair play, and so on. Parents reward children when their behavior reflects these values and punish them when it does not. When this is done gently, with compassion, and consistently, children learn what is expected of them, they internalize these values, and in the process they develop a conscience. But these values have a rational basis in terms of group life, the general welfare, and social responsibility. Therefore, as children mature, more can be done with the meaning of these values in terms of their social consequences.

General values are taught naturally through the daily life in the classroom. It is in this way that children experience on a firsthand basis such general values as consideration for others, fair play, and honesty. It is expected that the child will see such behavior modeled by the teacher, and for some children the teacher may be the only adult in their lives whose behavior reflects such values. General values can also be conveyed to children through any or all of the following:

1. Studying the history and development of the United States, stressing the ideals that inspired it, and showing that as a nation we are committed to certain human values.
2. Studying the biographies of individuals whose lives reflect the general values of the nation.
3. Studying the legal and justice systems.
4. Celebrating holidays that reinforce values and the ideals associated with the holiday.
5. Analyzing the meaning of such statements as the Pledge of Allegiance, Preamble to the Constitution, and the Bill of Rights.
6. Building an awareness of situations that are not consistent with the professed values of society; learning that reality does not always reach the ideal.
7. Conducting cross-cultural studies to make comparative analyses of value systems.

SOCIAL STUDIES COMPETENCIES AND SKILLS

INTERN TASK 3-8

Arrange with your field associate teacher to select and teach social studies skills following the directions provided here. Notice that an example of how the steps are applied appears on the facing page.

Skills Teaching Strategy

Directions:

Step 1. Make sure pupils understand what is involved in performing the skill. Show them how it is used. Provide the children with a good model of the skill in operation.

Step 2. Break the skill into components and arrange them sequentially. Develop the teaching sequence step by step, having the children do each component as it is presented and explained. Supervise carefully to make sure children's responses are correct.

Step 3. Have the pupils perform a simple variation of the skill under your close supervision. This is to ensure that the pupils are performing the skill correctly.

Step 4. After it is established that the pupils are performing the skill correctly, provide for supervised practice, using simple variations that ensure pupil success.

Step 5. Gradually increase the complexity of the variation of the skill and begin having pupils apply the skill in situations in which it is useful. Continue this procedure until the desired level of proficiency is achieved.

Step 6. Continue to practice the skill at regular intervals, largely through functional application, in order to maintain and improve performance.

Field Associate Teacher Advisory

The intern teacher should become thoroughly familiar with the social studies skills listed in Chapter 1. It is essential that the intern teacher select skills and teach them to pupils following the directions provided here.

Example of Steps in Skills Teaching Strategy

Skill: Using the directory of a newspaper to find needed information.

Step 1. Secure a newspaper, preferably a Sunday edition, and show how difficult and time-consuming it is to find some bit of information if one has to leaf through the entire paper to find it. Have pupils try their hand at finding items without using the newspaper directory. Show how easily one can find information with the aid of the directory.

Step 2. a. Make sure pupils know how to use the dictionary and the encyclopedia prior to teaching this skill.

b. Acquaint pupils with various sections of the newspaper: general news, classified ads, sports, editorials, weather, and so on.

c. Teach pupils the specialized vocabulary associated with the newspaper: vital statistics, obituaries, market quotations, masthead, dateline, syndicated, and so on.

d. Teach pupils what items are included in the various categories listed in the directory, and how they are arranged. For example, what is included in the Arts and Entertainment section; how are the classifieds organized; and how does one find out what arrangement is used?

e. Provide a newspaper for each member of the class and have the pupils locate easy items using the directory such as the television schedule, sports, and the comics. Supervise to make sure everyone is performing the skill correctly.

Step 3. Follow Step 2 immediately with an exercise requiring pupils to locate items making use of the directory. Supervise and assist as needed. Check responses.

Step 4. Assign pupils to find information in the next day's newspaper. This should be done on their own without teacher supervision. Check responses.

Step 5. Bring to class copies of a different newspaper from the one used thus far in which a slightly different directory format appears. Assign pupils to find information in this paper without your assistance, to see if they can transfer and modify their skill from one situation to another. Check responses.

Step 6. From time to time have pupils make use of the directory to locate needed information. Observe the accuracy and extensiveness of use of the directory.

The individual interpretation of general values to decision making in one's daily life gets us into the area of personal values. The relationship and the distinction between general values and personal values can be clarified by the following example. The concept *beauty* is a value embraced by virtually everyone in this society. It would be unusual, indeed aberrant, for an individual to prefer to be surrounded by ugliness rather than beauty. We say, therefore, that beauty is a general value. But philosophers from time immemorial have told us that "Beauty lies in the eyes of the beholder." In other words, what seems beautiful to me may not seem so to you—or to anyone else, for that matter. Interpreted in this way, beauty becomes idiosyncratic, unique, peculiar. We say it is a personal value.

Naturally, personal values must be handled much more delicately in the teaching process than is required when dealing with general values. Schools have a responsibility to reflect and to promote general values that characterize this society. This does not apply to personal values. Individuals sort things out for themselves, and they behave accordingly. In the last analysis it is the individual who makes the choices that affect his or her life, and it is the individual who enjoys, or suffers the consequences of, those choices. Thus, although the school should not and does not tell pupils what their personal values should be, it can provide experiences that will help them develop a sensitivity to the value dimension of much personal decision making.

In order not to ignore the personal value dimension entirely, and yet not be in the untenable position of telling children what their personal values should be, schools in recent years have engaged children in *valuing* experiences. These are sometimes referred to as value-clarification experiences. The purpose of such experiences is simply to get the youngsters to examine the kinds of value choices that are being made and to understand more fully why they are being made. Valuing experiences and value clarification might explore such things as what the child sees as major forces that guide his or her life: What sorts of things symbolize success for the child? Who are the persons admired as heroes? What qualities do they have that make them heroes? What would you do if you had a free day and could do anything you wanted to do? What are ten (or any number) of things you really like to do? If you could do anything you wanted and would be a success at whatever you did, what would you choose to do? Professor Sidney B. Simon and his colleagues have assembled a great number of exercises of this type that are interesting and that can be useful in values clarification.[6] Role playing, which will be discussed in Chapter 9, can also be used to involve children in the valuing process.

In using value-clarification procedures, the teacher is cautioned not to pry too deeply into the personal lives of children. Teachers are not psychologists and value clarification is not psychotherapy. These exercises should be kept simple and participation by pupils should be optional. We cannot know what detrimental effects might result if the inner psychological space of a child is exposed to public view.

Value clarification can take place only in a risk-free environment where learners are secure in suggesting alternatives. The teacher presents a situation in which there is a conflict between two values, both of which are prized. One must not have children make a choice between something that is legal and something that is illegal, or something that is moral and something that is immoral, ethical or nonethical. The choice, rather, is between two or more "goods," and this is precisely why the choices are always difficult. After a situation is presented that is likely to elicit value responses, the situation is discussed from several points of view until several alternative solutions surface. The likely consequences that flow from each of these solutions should be considered. It should be made clear that there is no one solution that is right for everyone. (This should not be confused with other kinds of choices and responses where there is clearly a right answer.) Value-clarification exercises often present good settings for role playing as the following example will illustrate.

In this account, a situation is presented in which an individual is not doing anything illegal, but he is violating the norms of the neighborhood and is creating a public nuisance. The situation has to do with the conflict between the need for conforming behavior on the one hand and personal freedom on the other.

The householders in the story propose three courses of action: (1) talk to the individual, (2) call the police, and (3) do nothing. As pupils try to resolve the dilemma presented, they should consider

---

[6] Sidney B. Simon, Leland Howe, and Howard Kirschenbaum, *Values Clarification : A Handbook of Practical Strategies for Teachers and Students* (New York: Hart Publishing Company, 1972).

each of these alternatives and the consequences of each. They should also suggest other alternative solutions to the problem.

A Fly in the Oak Street Ointment

Directions: Most of us have been in situations where someone would not or could not do his or her part on some project that required everyone's cooperation. This is a story about such a situation. Listen to the story and then we will talk about what you think the neighbors should do about the problem they face.

You never saw any waste paper, empty beer cans, or other trash lying around Oak Street. No sir. The homeowners on Oak Street took a great deal of pride in the appearance of their neighborhood. No question about it. The houses were neatly painted. The lawns were so neatly clipped and weed-free that they could correctly be called manicured. Even the birds seemed to be a bit more tidy when they played in the trees and in the yards along Oak Street! Everyone there did his or her part to keep Oak Street the best looking neighborhood in the city.

Everyone, that is, except the old fellow who moved next to Stendler's last winter. His lawn had not been cut yet this year and here it was nearly the first of June!

"If he doesn't cut those weeds before they seed, the wind will blow them into everyone's yard in the whole neighborhood," said one irate resident of Oak Street to a couple neighbors one Saturday morning. "I think we ought to talk to him about it. Trouble is, you never see the guy."

"It sure is disgusting," said another. "It spoils everything that the rest of us are doing. Depreciates everybody's property. He shouldn't be allowed to get away with it. We should call the police."

"I agree that it looks bad," said the third neighbor, "but he really isn't doing anything illegal. In this city there is no law that says a man has to keep his property looking like his neighbors'. Some places have such a law but we don't here. Besides, maybe we are the ones with the hang-ups with all this neat neighborhood stuff. I say 'live and let live.' It really is his own business."

1. What do you think would be the effect of each of the three solutions proposed in the story?
2. Can you think of other ways of dealing with this problem?
3. Can you think of examples from your own life experiences in which your freedom is restricted because you live with, or close to, other people?

Have the pupils consider the situation from several perspectives:

1. The neighbor is a bachelor who just is not concerned about the appearance of his property.
2. After thirty-five years of marriage, his wife died six months ago, and he is so despondent over his loss that he has little interest in the property they bought just before her death.
3. His lawn mower is broken (or he doesn't have one); his wife is in the hospital and he is so strapped for money that he cannot afford to have the mower fixed or to pay someone to do the job for him.
4. He works long days, every day of the week, and never gets home during the daylight hours.
5. He has some debilitating physical condition that makes it impossible for him to mow the lawn.
6. He doesn't like grass lawns so he is planning to cover his front yard with green concrete but hasn't gotten around to it yet; meanwhile, he sees no point in wasting his time and energy mowing the lawn. He doesn't even own a lawn mower.

SOCIAL STUDIES COMPETENCIES AND SKILLS

CHECKING YOUR PERFORMANCE

Intern Task Checklist

Task 3–1. Identifying concepts. P. 48 _____

Task 3–2. Writing generalizations. P. 49 _____

Task 3–3. Interviewing children to gauge their understanding of concepts. P. 55 _____

Task 3–4. Identifying essential information. P. 60 _____

Task 3–5. Concept development: listing, grouping, and labeling. P. 62 _____

Task 3–6. Concept development: experiencing, hypothesizing, and testing. P. 63 _____

Task 3–7. Concept development: recognizing examples and nonexamples. P. 64 _____

Task 3–8. Teaching a skill. P. 68 _____

Performance Checklist

In the field or in the clinic, the intern teacher has

1. Explained the difference between a concept and a generalization and has provided social studies examples of each. _____

2. Demonstrated by an example how concepts and generalizations provide organizing frameworks for social studies. _____

3. Adapted the topic "People Change the Earth" for teaching at the level assigned and defined the concepts and subject matter to be used. _____

4. Illustrated by specific examples how learning attitudes, values, and skills is built into the unit "People Change the Earth." _____

5. Taught a concept or generalization using one of the strategies discussed in this chapter. _____

6. Taught a social studies skill, using the strategy discussed in this chapter. _____

7. Conducted a simple values-clarification exercise. _____

8. Identified a children's book that highlights a general value. _____

Field Associate Teacher Advisory

Tasks and performances should be checked off or initialed and dated by the appropriate local official, or the intern teacher can use the checklists for his or her own record.

Chapter 4

Approaches to social studies instruction

Carol Jacobs dropped out of college in her junior year twenty years ago when she and her former husband were married. She is now nearly forty years of age, a mother of three teenage children, divorced, and back in school, completing requirements for teacher certification. Other than some work with the PTA when her own children were in school, Carol has had no contact with elementary education in recent years.

Mrs. Jacobs had observed some social studies teaching as a part of her teacher education program but was confused about what she saw. Some teachers seemed to handle the subject much as she remembered her own teachers doing when she was in the elementary grades. These teachers relied heavily on the textbook and tended to present formal lessons that stressed factual material from history and geography. Other teachers operated at the opposite end of the continuum and conducted what Carol referred to as a "non-program." What the children were doing seemed to lack any planned focus. In between these extremes she observed a range of practices varying in their degree of informality and structure.

As she thought about social studies and her own personality makeup, Carol knew she could not possibly function in a situation that was totally unstructured. At the same time, she also knew she could not be comfortable with a program that was rigid and formal. She often thought of the experiences of her own children and what teachers and activities they found interesting and worthwhile. She remembered that they really liked social studies projects and activities, but they also liked to think they were learning something important.

Carol's clinic instructor emphasized that there are several sound approaches to social studies instruction. Because of personality differences, what will work well for one teacher may not work well for another. Similarly, groups of children differ in how they react to certain teaching procedures. "In any case," the instructor went on, "there are basic competencies that every teacher must be able to perform in order to teach social studies satisfactorily. These are on the list you have just been given."

Basic Competencies—Social Studies

In planning and teaching social studies, the intern teacher is able to

1. Select and use a suitable approach to planning and teaching social studies.
2. Use a variety of instructional resources in teaching.
3. Include a variety of learning activities for pupils.
4. Make long- and short-range plans for teaching social studies.
5. Use an appropriate format for preparing social studies teaching plans.

INTERN ADVISORY

After completing this chapter, together with related work in the clinic and appropriate classroom experiences in the field, you should be able to do the following:

1. Describe essential differences between a highly structured approach, a modately structured approach, and an informal approach to planning and teaching social studies and know which is best suited to your teaching style.
2. Identify three social studies textbook series by publisher and describe the distinguishing features of each. (You will need to examine these books at your school or in your campus curriculum library.)

3. Identify the titles of six trade books that would be appropriate for use in elementary school social studies units. (You will need to examine these books at your school library.)
4. Select a topic and identify the main ideas related to it.
5. Plan and teach a short sequence structured around the text adopted for use in your classroom.
6. Develop a short-range plan structured around a main idea using the format of Chart 4-1.
7. Develop and teach a lesson using a plan similar to the one in Figure 4-1.
8. Develop a unit using the format suggested on pp. 90–91.

WHAT APPROACHES TO PLANNING AND TEACHING SOCIAL STUDIES CAN A TEACHER USE?

In this section we will examine three approaches to social studies instruction. To some extent each one requires the teacher to perform the basic competencies identified at the beginning of this chapter. The purpose is not to persuade the reader that any one of these approaches is superior to the other two. Rather, each will be presented without prejudice, leaving the reader to analyze it and to evaluate it in terms of its suitability as a way of teaching social studies.

A Highly Structured Approach

A highly structured approach is one that is largely planned in advance by the teacher, who often relies on the textbook or other curriculum documents in determining the nature and content of the program. If pupils help in the planning, they do so minimally and usually in matters that do not alter the basic content and emphasis. That is, they might exercise some choice concerning individual activities to be performed but would not suggest alternative topics to be studied. Reliance on the textbook as the prime data source is complete. Variations in requirements to accommodate pupil differences would include varying the lengths of assignments or varying the amount of time needed to complete them. All pupils deal with the same basic subject matter.

If we follow a teacher through the steps in planning and teaching social studies in this way, we would observe the following:

The teacher

1. Surveys the text to find out which units are included and decides how to apportion the amount of time available to each one. The recommendations of the textbook authors may be used in making these decisions.
2. Studies the teacher's guide accompanying the text to find out how the program is organized and what major goals and objectives are stressed. These goals and objectives may be accepted as appropriate for the program.
3. Uses the teacher's guide for teaching plans and pupil activities.
4. Uses additional resources and activities for enrichment, extension of learning, and for individualizing learning. Some of these are suggested by the teacher's guide, including those provided by the publisher of the text series as satellite materials.
5. Evaluates learnings as suggested by the text and teacher's guide, focusing mainly on informational learnings, basic concepts, and related skills.
6. Uses formal teaching procedures consisting mainly of question and answer, some discussion, an occasional pupil report, and map making; there is infrequent use of drama, art, music, or construction activities.

A Moderately Structured Approach

A moderately structured approach has some of the same characteristics as the one just discussed, but the reliance on the text is not as complete, more of the teacher's personality is apparent, and it is not so thoroughly preplanned and teacher directed. Pupils are more involved in planning and there is greater use of a wide range of instructional materials and activities. The formality that characterizes the highly structured approach is missing. Pupils feel freer to voice their own opinions and views on issues. Interactions are more along the lines of true discussion as opposed to question-and-answer procedures. The teacher has a sensitivity to pupil individuality and provides for pupil variations in ability and motivation. Pupils may be thoroughly involved in expressive activities such as construction, art, music, role playing, and simulation games. This is not a completely pupil-centered approach, yet it is not one that is wholly teacher directed either.

If we follow a teacher through the steps in planning and teaching in this way, we would observe the following:

The teacher

1. Examines the curriculum guide and the textbook to find out what topics and units are expected to be included in the program.
2. Establishes broad goals and objectives for the year. Takes into consideration those suggested by the curriculum guide and textbook teacher's guide, but makes his or her own.
3. Tentatively selects topics to be studied; consults teacher's guide and curriculum guide in this process, selects some that are suggested, omits others, and adds some. These topics may be modified as the program develops and as pupil interests and capabilities are better known.
4. Decides on sequence of units selected, time allotment for each, taking into account holidays, seasons of the year, and so forth.
5. Uses some teaching suggestions from the teacher's guide and curriculum guide but develops many of his or her own ideas for activities and strategies.
6. Develops and uses learning packets, self-paced materials, learning centers, and pupil contracts; also, individualizes learning through use of small groups.
7. Plans for and uses many instructional resources in addition to the textbook. This includes pictures, packets, library books, films, filmstrips, recordings, and artifacts.
8. Uses a variety of informal evaluative techniques and devices such as discussion, observation, pupil conferences, teacher-made tests, checklists, and experience summaries.
9. Maintains an easy, relaxed instructional pace but stays close to teacher-pupil planned treatment of the unit topic.

An Informal, Pupil-Centered Approach

Teachers who are interested in open education find it to be an attractive approach to teaching social studies. Although it requires considerable preplanning by the teacher, the program itself is not structured in advance, as are the other two approaches that have been discussed. Study units and pupil experiences are planned jointly by the teacher and pupils in terms of the interests, backgrounds, and needs of the pupils. Thus, the unit emerges under the guidance of the teacher, who relies heavily on pupil initiative and interest. Children help decide what they will study. They raise questions about the information they are interested in getting and search out relevant sources. They plan ways of working, activities in which they will engage, and ways of sharing ideas with one another. Pupils are encouraged to become involved in assuming responsibility for what they are to learn and how they will go about learning it. The boundaries between the various disciplines contributing to social studies education are blurred; indeed, the social studies units often incorporate learnings from the total elementary school curriculum.

If we follow a teacher through the steps in planning and teaching in this way, we will observe the following:

The teacher

1. Formulates broad goals and objectives for the year in terms of anticipated social and intellectual growth of the pupils.
2. Studies pupil backgrounds; develops an awareness of the social milieu from which pupils come.
3. Prepares motivating (or facilitating) questions dealing with social issues and topics to arouse pupil interest.
4. Provides books, artifacts, displays, visuals, construction materials, and other items to motivate pupil interest and curiosity in engaging in inquiry.
5. Encourages pupils to suggest topics for study and to suggest possible questions and problems for exploration.
6. Guides pupils in exploratory information searches.
7. Assists pupils in developing an in-depth study of topics and problems selected; plans are refined and/or modified as the study progresses.
8. Individualizes the program in accordance with pupil interest and need using interest centers, individual study contracts, individual study materials, projects, and activities.

9. Closely relates social studies work to reading, language arts, mathematics, science, art, music, and drama.

INTERN TASK 4-1

Analyze each of the three approaches in terms of the following questions.

1. How would you describe the role of the teacher in each of the three approaches discussed?
2. Which of the three approaches might the beginning teacher find easiest to implement? Why?
3. What factors or conditions, besides the competence of the teacher, might make the use of one or another of these approaches advisable?
4. What relationship do you see between each of these approaches and (a) the teacher's philosophy of education, (b) beliefs about the major goals of social studies education, and (c) beliefs about the nature of children?

Discuss your responses with your field associate teacher and/or your clinic instructor.

MATERIALS OF INSTRUCTION: WHICH ONES AND FOR WHAT PURPOSES?

It is obvious that any approach the teacher selects will require the use of materials of instruction. What is not so clear is that instructional resources are used differently and to achieve different purposes in each of the three approaches. Instructional resources for social studies are plentiful today and most of them incorporate the newer trends in social studies education. The extent to which teachers use multimedia strategies varies, but only the most unimaginative teaching of social studies would have pupils use a single source of data, such as the textbook.

Instructional resources for the classroom are rarely self-instructing. They require the teacher to exercise professional judgment about how they are to be used and for what purposes. The effective use of any instructional material, therefore, depends on a professionally competent teacher. The factors that are critical in selecting appropriate learning resources for children are (1) the objectives to be achieved; (2) the age and maturity of the pupils; (3) the reading ability of the pupils; (4) the difficulty of the concepts imbedded in the subject matter; and (5) the extent of the background experiences of the pupils.

The following material is a summary of the most commonly used instructional resources in social studies teaching, along with a brief description of their nature and purpose.

1. *Textbooks.* Textbooks provide basic factual information about topics usually taught in the grade for which the book is written. They usually come in a series—that is, the publisher provides a book for each of several consecutive grades. Most have teacher's guides or teacher's manuals that accompany them in which the organization of the book is explained along with specific suggestions for teaching. Texts are usually written for the average reader. Some textbook series have a variety of supplementary materials that are available for purchase. Textbooks are usually provided by the school district on the basis of one for each child.

2. *Trade books.* Trade books are nontext library books that can be used for basic information or for enrichment. They may be factual accounts on a single subject, historical accounts, biographies, historical fiction, or standard literary works. They are valuable in providing rich detail, often affective in nature, that is not obtained in a straightforward factual account. They are usually secured through the school library or through the district instructional resources center on request by the teacher.

3. *Pictures and/or study prints.* These are among the most widely used visual aids in teaching social studies. They are available through a variety of sources ranging from commercially prepared study prints to personal collections by individual teachers. Many good pictures are included in regular textbooks. Pictures provide realism, which is helpful in building meanings of social studies concepts.

4. *Maps and globes.* Maps and globes are essential tools in teaching social studies in general and geography in particular. Basic map and globe equipment is ordinarily provided by the school district for each classroom. Special equipment and maps—such as miniature planetariums, product maps, and maps using unusual projections—can often be obtained for

short-term use from the district instructional materials center. Textbooks also include many good maps. Map companies provide maps and globes that have been especially designed for school use by children at various levels of maturity.

5. *Charts and graphs.* Charts and graphs are important tools in dealing with statistical data. They are often constructed by the children and the teacher in presenting information to the class. Many charts and graphs are included in social studies texts, especially in the middle and upper grades. Charts take several different formats, such as narrative, flow, and organizational. Informal charts may be experience summaries or data-retrieval devices. Line, bar, and circle graphs are often used in presenting social studies data. Both charts and graphs are more appealing to children and more easily understood if they use pictorial symbols.

6. *Filmstrips.* Filmstrips are of value in presenting information in a sequence. They are excellent where motion is not essential to understanding the ideas presented. Sometimes filmstrips are synchronized with a recorded message, resulting in a sound filmstrip. Easy-to-operate filmstrip projectors make them well suited for individual viewing by pupils. Filmstrips are usually available through the school librarian or from the district instructional resources center.

7. *Slides.* Slides (35-mm color) have the same use as pictures and study prints. They are not as widely used as filmstrips because they require more space for storage and can easily become lost. Because they are not locked in a fixed sequence, there is the problem of keeping them in the correct order for showing. To a large extent, filmstrips have taken the place of slides for school use.

8. *Films.* Films are valuable resources when motion is important to the presentation. With motion picture films, it is possible to achieve a high degree of realism. Usually, instructional films are 16-mm sound, but some 8-mm cassette films are also available. In almost all cases films must be secured from the district instructional resources center or obtained on a rental basis from a film lending library.

9. *Encyclopedias.* All classrooms need a children's encyclopedia such as *World Book* or *The New Book of Knowledge* for children to secure factual information on almost any

topic encountered in social studies. They are easy to use and children like them. They are an indispensable data source for social studies.

10. *Special references.* These include *The World Almanac,* atlases, the Yellow Pages from the telephone directory, catalogs, and other specialized sources of information. They are essential for obtaining factual data on out-of-the ordinary topics.

11. *Television.* Educational television programs provide basic information on social studies topics that may not be available through other sources. Programs are usually geared to the social studies curriculum of the local district, especially in large metropolitan areas. There are built-in problems of inflexibility and program scheduling—that is, the program may not be shown at the time it is needed by the class. Some of this can be overcome with videotape recording equipment. Television is unequalled for bringing current events to the classroom at the time they are occurring—inaugurals, international visitors of prominence, space program events, disasters, congressional investigations, and so forth.

12. *Field trips.* Field trips are useful in providing learning experiences it is not possible to achieve in the classroom. They provide pupils an opportunity to see social phenomena on a firsthand basis. Field trips usually are governed by local regulations and policies.

13. *Transparencies.* Transparencies have become popular in recent years because of the versatility of the overhead projector with which they are used. They can be used to show maps, diagrams, charts, and printed material. The overhead projector is itself a valuable tool; used in a semidarkened room, it has advantages over the conventional chalkboard in that the teacher can face the class while using it and does not have problems with chalk dust.

14. *Recordings.* Sound recordings of the disc type, as well as tape, are useful for social studies instruction to provide basic information, to reconstruct historical events, to record impressions, or to serve as an aid to reading. Easy-to-operate tape cassettes can be used to individualize learning for pupils.

15. *Simulation games.* These may be considered instructional resources or learning activities. They realistically reconstruct situations or events that are played by the pupils. In the process the participants learn concepts and skills relevant to the subject under study. Some commercially prepared simulation games are available; others can be prepared by the teacher.

16. *Classroom periodicals.* Classroom periodicals are used in connection with the current affairs program but provide information on many other social studies topics as well. A list of the most commonly used periodicals and the names and addresses of their publishers are provided in Chapter 8.

17. *Community resources.* The classroom must not be allowed to become a sanctuary, isolated from the rest of the community. The flow of people and data back and forth between the community and the classroom should be an easy and natural one. Community resources include persons who share information with the class, museums, art galleries, institutions of government public libraries, and many more. Some school districts have made surveys of community resources and list them in a curriculum guide.

INTERN TASK 4-2

Familiarize yourself with each of the learning resources discussed in this section. Pay particular attention to those resources that may not be found in the classroom itself. For example:

1. What films and filmstrips are available and how do you go about securing them?

2. What procedures does your school district require to be followed if children are to be taken on a field trip?

3. How complete is the district's collection of trade books and how are they obtained for use in the classroom?

4. Does the school have educational television facilities? If so, acquaint yourself with the program schedule, noting especially programs designed for social studies.

Discuss these matters with your field associate teacher, with your school librarian, and with the district learning resources specialist.

> ### *Field Associate Teacher Advisory*
>
> It is essential that the intern have firsthand experiences with the learning resources discussed in this section. Talk over with the intern local policies and regulations governing the use of these materials and equipment. As appropriate, provide the intern with an opportunity to use these resources in the teaching of social studies. Get help from the school librarian and the district learning resources specialist as needed.

INSTRUCTIONAL ACTIVITIES: WHICH ONES AND FOR WHAT PURPOSES?

The teacher exercises choices not only in the instructional materials to be used but also in the activities to be performed by the pupils. Teachers who use informal approaches will involve pupils in the decision making concerning the activities in which they will engage. Such negotiation is, of course, less common in structured approaches.

A frequent criticism of elementary school social studies education is that it does not provide a variety of learning activities. Children may be assigned material to read and questions to answer. When the assignment is completed, the teacher and pupils talk about the questions and content, after which another assignment of reading and questions is given. Reports by pupils similarly may depend on reading to secure data. Little is done to liven the program through role playing, art, music, or construction. The beginning teacher needs to develop competence and confidence in using a broad spectrum of learning activities. The reader should refer to Chart 2-1 on page 34 for a list of suggested activities and the purposes they serve. Also, the use of activities is discussed again in detail in Chapter 9.

INTERN TASK 4-3

Analyze the log of activities you prepared in connection with Intern Task 2-4. If you find that you are relying on a limited number of activities, ask your field associate teacher to assist you in devising ways to increase the number. You need to develop competence in handling pupil activities in each of the categories listed in Chart 2-1.

HOW DOES A TEACHER MAKE LONG- AND SHORT-RANGE PLANS FOR SOCIAL STUDIES?

For several years teachers have used a long-range planning format for elementary school social studies called the unit of work or simply the unit. Units of work are planned around some broad topic that is socially relevant and that makes it possible to develop informational learnings, attitudes, values, and skills. The topic of Canada, discussed in Chapter 3, is an example of a unit topic. The subject matter for units will typically cut across several of the conventional social science disciplines and may extend into related fields outside the social sciences—for example, into art, drama, literature, music, and science.

The way units are planned and taught varies greatly from one teacher to another. For one, the unit may be no more than a chapter or a section of the textbook that deals with a single topic. For another teacher, the unit may be a comprehensive study that incorporates learnings and activities from all the rest of the school curriculum. One teacher may structure the unit in advance by thorough preplanning; another may plan the unit as the study evolves. Two teachers working on an identical topic at the same grade level may have their classes deal quite differently with it. The same teacher might handle the same topic differently with different groups of children. Thus, we see that a great deal of individual teacher judgment and decision making go into the planning and teaching of social studies units.

Because of the variations in the way teachers develop unit plans, it is impossible to provide an outline that will suit all teachers. However, the one provided here includes most of the procedures incorporated in unit planning. Because it is a general outline, teachers will need to modify it to fit their particular individual preferences and situations.

Procedures in Preparing a Unit Plan for Social Studies

1. Select a unit title.
2. Survey available instructional resources.
3. State objectives to be achieved:
   a. Informational objectives.
   b. Skills objectives.
   c. Attitude and value objectives.
4. Select and organize subject matter.
   a. Identify main ideas to be developed and arrange them in the sequence in which they are to be presented. (See Chapter 3.)
   b. Indicate specific subject matter to be used to develop learnings and to achieve objectives.

   Note: The planning format suggested in Chart 4-1 can be used for this purpose.

5. Begin the study.
   a. Arrange the room environment appropriately.
   b. Plan for motivating and interest-arousing experiences for the pupils.
   c. Develop learning centers with relevant learning materials on hand.
   d. Prepare questions to generate interest in the topic.
6. Develop the study on an on-going basis.
   a. Provide exploratory experiences; help pupils identify problems; encourage hypothesizing and questioning.
   b. Involve pupils in information searches and data gathering.
   c. Discuss findings, test hypotheses, validate information, and apply what is being learned.
   d. Apply learnings through use of expressive activities such as illustrating, exhibiting, dramatizing, constructing, drawing, writing, and reporting.
   e. Summarize learning; come to conclusions; and identify new areas of inquiry.

7. Conclude the study.
   a. Summarize and review major ideas learned.
   b. Share learning with others: classmates, other classes, and parents.
   c. Transfer what has been learned to new situations.
8. Evaluate outcomes.
   a. Pupil evaluation and assessment of pupil achievement.
   b. Teacher evaluation and adequacy of the unit of study.

Short-range plans consist of a teaching trip-map that the teacher has in hand (perhaps literally in hand) at the time the teaching is done. Traditionally, these have been called lesson plans. These plans may cover the work of a class for a single period or may extend over a study sequence of a few days to a week or more. Today many teachers try not to break up their social studies teaching into discrete daily segments but plan for a continuous and sequential flow of teaching and learning from one day to the next. For this reason the format of short-range plans may change from day to day. Always, however, the teacher will need to anticipate what objectives are to be achieved, how the instruction is to begin and end, what the pupils will be expected to do, and what instructional materials will be needed. The following is an example of a daily teaching plan:

Topic:	Symbolic messages (valuing).	
Objectives:	Pupils will deduce certain information about a country from symbols placed on its coins.	
	Pupils will relate the symbols to basic values of their country.	
Resources:	At least one coin for each child,. preferably coins or facsimiles of coins, from several different nations.	
Procedure:	Teacher:	Boys and girls, for the past few days we have been studying the use of signs and symbols. At the close of our discussion yesterday we came to an important conclusion. What was it?
	Pupil:	We said that we could tell what people considered to be important to them by the symbols and signs they use on their buildings.
	Teacher:	Yes. Now today you will have a chance to test that idea in a slightly different way. Each of you will be given a coin to use. Study the coin carefully and see how many things you can tell about the country just from what you see on the coin.

Coins are distributed to the pupils. After they have had time to make their observations, ask the children what they have concluded. As these are presented, write them on the chalkboard. Have each pupil tell *why* the conclusion was made. Pass the coins about for other children to inspect. Items such as the following should surface in this discussion:

> These people believe in God.
> They want (or believe in) liberty.
> They are able to read their language.
> Men must be more important than women in this country.
> They construct large buildings.
> They speak more than one language.
> It is an old country.
> They have a queen (or king).
> They are a peace-loving people.
> They are proud of their wars and war heroes.
> They want people to be courageous.

Follow-up: Imagine that the United States is planning to issue a new coin and there is a contest to get the best design. You decide to enter the contest. The rules are these:

> 1. Write down three ideas that best describe what people in our country think are important to them.
> 2. Think of and draw symbols that could be used on a coin to show these three qualities.

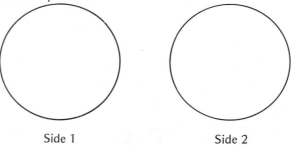

Side 1   Side 2

Figure 4-1. Teaching Plan.

WHAT SHOULD BE THE FORMAT OF SOCIAL STUDIES TEACHING PLANS?

The exact format used in planning for social studies teaching should be secured by the intern teacher from the field associate teacher with whom he or she is working because individual teachers vary greatly in their approach to instruction. One who uses structured strategies will plan differently from one who uses informal, open strategies. Consequently, it is impossible to provide a planning format that will be acceptable to all field associate teachers.

If the teacher's approach is structured to the extent that the main ideas of the topic under study are identified, a planning format of the the type shown in Chart 4-1 will be useful. In using this design, the teacher would need to define six to eight main ideas relating to the topic around which the subject matter and activities will be organized. This procedure could be combined with the more conventional unit format described on pages 90–91. Each of the main ideas could become one segment of the unit. If the teacher favors the use of behavioral objectives, these can be prepared for each of the unit components. That is, the teacher might write behavioral objectives that would define what the pupil would be able to do after completing the study of each main idea as developed by the planning design suggested in Chart 4-1.

INTERN TASK 4-4

Discuss teaching plans and how to prepare them with your field associate teacher. Make use of the planning format approved by your teacher education program and your school district. Do not engage in teaching social studies unless you have planned satisfactorily and your plans have been reviewed and approved by your field associate teacher.

Field Associate Teacher Advisory

In field-based programs the writing of behavioral objectives is usually regarded as a generic teaching skill and is taught to the interns prior to the time they are involved in special subject methods. The assumption here is that the intern is familiar with behavioral objectives and knows how to write them. If this is not the case, the intern should be instructed on the use and writing of behavioral and other objectives at this time.

(continued on page 96)

CHART 4-1. Social Studies Unit Planning

Unit Title _____ Date _____

Main idea to be developed:	Related skills:	Related attitudes and values:	Questions to stimulate reflective thinking:
Key concepts and terms:			

Text references:	Oral and written language activities:	Dramatic activities:	Construction activities:
Supplementary references:			
Audiovisual resources:			
Community resources:	Related curriculum activities (science, math, art, music):		

This form can be used in developing unit plans. Notice that it consists of three components: (1) the learnings to be achieved; (2) the references and resources to be used; and (3) the activities to be performed. A plan such as this should be developed for each main idea included in the unit.

SOCIAL STUDIES COMPETENCIES AND SKILLS

There is nothing inviolable about the particular planning formats suggested in this chapter. You should feel free to require the intern to use whatever format is approved for local use or with which you feel comfortable as long as it meets the requirements of the local teacher education program.

Planning is among the most important subskills involved in teaching. Thus, you should go over planning procedures with the intern in great detail and require him or her to prepare acceptable teaching plans *prior* to the teaching experience. The recommendation here is that the intern be held to a very strict discipline in the preparation of plans for teaching. Failure to do so is likely to lead to impromtu or off-the-cuff teaching of social studies.

CHECKING YOUR PERFORMANCE

Intern Task Checklist

Task 4-1. Analyzing three approaches. P. 83 _____

Task 4-2. Learning about local learning resources. P. 87 _____

Task 4-3. Analyzing the kinds of activities being used. P. 89 _____

Task 4-4. Developing teaching plans. P. 93 _____

Performance Checklist

In the field or in the clinic, the intern teacher has

1. Demonstrated an understanding of a highly structured approach, a moderately structured approach, and an informal approach to teaching social studies and has decided which is best suited to his or her teaching style and personality. _____

2. Identified three social studies textbooks and described the distinguishing features of each. _____

3. Identified and examined at least six trade books that are suitable for use in social studies units. _____

4. Selected a unit topic and identified the main ideas related to it. _____

5. Planned and taught a short sequence structured around the textbook adopted for the classroom. _____

6. Developed a short-range plan structured around a main idea using the format in Chart 4-1. _____

7. Developed and taught a lesson using a plan similar to the one in Figure 4-1 or using a lesson format approved by the local district. _____

8. Developed a unit using the format suggested on pages 90–91. _____

Field Associate Teacher Advisory

Tasks and performances should be checked off or initialed and dated by the appropriate local official, or the intern teacher can use the checklists for his or her own record.

Chapter 5

Teacher-pupil planning and decision making

Jack Rogers was unable to secure a teaching position at the time he completed his teacher education program because of an over-supply of teachers in the local area. Being determined to teach, however, he was able to get on the substitute-teacher list for a large school district. He hoped to establish his reputation as a good teacher, thereby enhancing his chances of being hired as a regular contracted teacher. Because he was competent and responsible—and eager—the substitute office called on him three to five days each week to fill in for teachers who were unable to report for duty.

The substitute teaching experience proved to be both frustrating and challenging for Jack. It also turned out to be a valuable professional experience for him in adapting himself to a variety of teaching situations. Even though he had good training and an excellent record as an intern teacher, he was never fully aware of the educational implications of individual differences in pupils and their teachers. Now each day placed him in a new teaching environment, and each day he was brought face to face with a new group of children. And how different these groups were! Some were responsible and cooperative. Others were disruptive and mischievous. Most groups were a mixture of both. Jack rarely met the regular teacher for whom he was substituting, but before long he felt he could tell a great deal about the teacher from the classroom environment and from the reactions of the children to him.

During his year as a substitute teacher, Jack became an astute observer of individual variations in children. Some differences could be predicted from the nature of the neighborhood in which the school was located. But what astounded him most of all were the variations

SOCIAL STUDIES COMPETENCIES AND SKILLS

among children in the same classroom. Reading abilities varied, as did interest in school, willingness to cooperate, language facility, writing ability, and motivation, all of which affected social studies achievement. Jack soon learned that if he was to function at all effectively as a teacher, he would need to become skillful in planning with the children and including them in decision making concerning the affairs of the classroom.

One evening as he was leafing through some of his notes from the previous year, he came across a list of basic competencies for social studies that had been provided by his clinic instructor. He was amused at how differently he interpreted them from the way he had a year earlier. "Yes," he thought to himself, "I'd say these are pretty basic all right!"

Basic Competencies—Social Studies

The intern teacher is able to

1. Identify types of individual differences found among pupils and can devise ways of working with pupils to take these differences into account.
2. Adjust teaching strategies to the learning styles, maturity, experience background, and personality characteristics of pupils in the class.
3. Encourage pupils to participate in planning and implementing the social studies program and permit choices in individual and small-group projects.
4. Help children develop a responsible concern for their own learning by securing their cooperation in the affairs and management of the class.
5. Obtain the cooperation of pupils in developing a suitable program of study for individual children.
6. Arouse a high level of interest in social studies topics, thereby encouraging pupils to participate enthusiastically in planning and study activities.

INTERN ADVISORY

After completing this chapter, together with related work in the clinic and appropriate classroom experiences in the field, you should be able to do the following:

1. Make an analysis of the abilities of the pupils in your class and know each one's learning strengths and weaknesses.
2. Develop and implement a social studies program that takes pupil differences (as defined in number 1) into account.
3. Arrange the physical layout of a classroom in a way that facilitates individual learning.
4. Involve pupils in cooperative planning activities.
5. Plan, organize, and develop a social studies learning center and listening post.
6. Negotiate study contracts with pupils in social studies.
7. Prepare individual learning packets on selected social studies topics.

HOW DO PUPIL DIFFERENCES INFLUENCE PLANNING AND DECISION MAKING?

The teacher in the foregoing vignette was sensitized to individual and group differences in children because of the nature of his assignment. The opportunity to develop such an awareness may not present itself when a teacher works with a single group of children in a self-contained classroom. Many conditions tend to mask important differences: children may be nearly the same age; they may come from neighborhoods that are relatively homogeneous with respect to socioeconomic status; and physical differences may not be great, especially in the lower grades. The way instructional materials are provided for schools—that is, the same textbook for each child—and a prevailing social philosophy of equality tend also to militate against the teacher's making a conscious effort to look for individual differences and to adjust instruction in accordance with them.

Most teacher education programs provide course work in educational psychology in which the nature and extent of human variation are developed. Consequently, there is no need to repeat such information here. Suffice it to say that after three quarters of a century of systematic study, we know that children who are randomly selected to form classroom groups are likely to vary substantially on all of those variables that relate to achievement in social studies: basic intelligence, reading ability, motivation, experience backgrounds, socioeconomic status, and so on.

Knowledge of and sensitivity to individual pupil variation by the teacher can serve as a detriment as well as an asset to pupil achievement. Used properly, such information and awareness should make it possible for the teacher to more nearly adjust the instructional program to the learning styles, maturity, experience backgrounds, and personality characteristics of individual children. Presumably, this helps ensure a successful performance by individual children. On the other hand, improperly applied, such knowledge and awareness can operate as a self-fulfilling prophecy. That is, the teacher observes the limitations of a child's characteristics, assumes that little can be expected of him or her, sets requirements accordingly, and the prophecy is fulfilled.

It is suggested that the appropriate procedure to follow in planning and decision making in social studies is the same as it is in any other area where improvement and progress are the objectives, whether this be athletics, music, painting, or dieting. This procedure always calls for a careful analysis of the subject's present performance. This may be called a diagnosis although that term has remedial connotations that do not necessarily apply. Perhaps the term *needs assessment*, often used in education, more correctly defines this process. In any case, it is usually a mistake to begin teaching someone something without first conducting a pretest or making an analysis of the individual's existing level of competence. With such information in hand, a teacher can begin thinking about what learning experiences the individual needs in order to progress.

The goal in good social studies teaching is to individualize learning as much as possible. This does not mean that pupils need to be taught individually on a tutorial basis. Neither does it mean that pupils must necessarily work alone. Much social studies teaching can, and indeed must, be conducted in large and small pupil groups and can also result in individualized learning. What we seek are programs that are personally meaningful to individual children (that is, the children perceive what they are doing as important, interesting, and worthwhile) and programs that enhance the potential for each child to achieve successfully objectives deemed to be important to social studies education. This means that even in classrooms in which there is a high amount of individualized learning, pupils may be working toward some objectives that are common to the entire group. How they achieve those objectives and the activities in which they engage, however, may be, and often are, different from one child to the next. It seems clear that if a teacher is to plan a program of this type, a great deal needs to be known about the pupils as individual learners.

INTERN TASK 5-1

Make a list of ten questions you might ask in making a needs assessment of pupils in social studies for the class to which you have been assigned. Discuss these questions with your field associate teacher. Then apply the questions to a sample of six individual children in your class.

HOW DOES ROOM MANAGEMENT RELATE
TO PLANNING AND DECISION MAKING?

An ordinary classroom can be converted into a tremendously stimulating laboratory for learning by an imaginative teacher. The general appearance of a classroom and its psychological appeal to children provide important clues to program building that stresses individualized learning. A key factor in classroom management is *flexibility*. We use this concept not only to describe the physical characteristics of the room, such as movable furniture and equipment, but also the programmatic variables. A few examples will illustrate what this means.

Deployment of Pupils. When a teacher has twenty-five to thirty pupils in a classroom, it is obvious that little can be done to individualize learning if they are taught on a whole-group basis all of the time. At the same time, it is not possible to teach each one on an individual basis for equally obvious reasons. Thus, ways need to be devised to deploy these children into smaller work groups at least part of the time in order to personalize and individualize assignments and activities. This need not be difficult to do. For example, children who are self-directed and have well-developed study skills can work on their own with little supervisory help from the teacher and should be allowed to do so. Others who read less well or who are socially less mature or are less responsible should be given more direct help and guidance by the teacher. Arrangements of this type can be achieved through the formation of subgroups within the class. In social studies it is recommended that such small groups be formed on an ad hoc basis rather than a permanent one.

Children can, and probably should, be grouped differently for information-gathering activities than for expressive activities. Those pupils who may need a significant amount of help from the teacher during information searches may function well without teacher assistance while they work on a construction activity or an art project associated with the unit. Some who need help in reading the social studies text may be able to work independently in using a sound filmstrip.

To generalize what is being described, we might say that children should be grouped in a variety of configurations for social studies instruction, ranging all the way from individual work by a single pupil to the whole class, working as a group. The deployment of pupils will vary from day to day, depending on the nature of the task and individual pupil need.

INTERN TASK 5-2

For each of the activities listed here, indicate which might best be handled (1) on an individual basis by the pupil; (2) in a small group of three to five pupils; (3) in a larger group of ten to fifteen pupils; (4) on a whole-class basis.

1. Practicing a skill that needs improvement.
2. Viewing a 16-mm sound motion picture film.
3. Engaging in dramatic play.
4. Discussing a news story.
5. Constructing a relief (three-dimensional) map.
6. Participating in a simulated archaeological dig on the school grounds.
7. Preparing a written report.
8. Doing research for a written report.
9. Engaging in role playing.
10. Using the encyclopedia.
11. Working in the learning center.
12. Completing a study contract.

Check your responses with your field associate teacher and/or your clinic instructor.

> ***Physical Arrangement of the Classroom.*** In order to move children about, as suggested in the foregoing section, the classroom environment must be appropriately arranged. Movable furniture and equipment are now found in most elementary school classrooms, making possible a number of seating alternatives. The guideline here is to arrange the environment in accord with the learning activities to be

performed. This may call for clusters of four or five children working in a group on one occasion or having all children seated in a semi-circle on the floor around the teacher on another. For independent study, pupils need to be arranged in a way that discourages inter-action with others. For this reason some teachers devise four or five study carrels for pupils that separate them from the larger group when they need or want to do individual study. For discussion situations, where a high degree of interaction is expected, children should be arranged to see each other, perhaps in a horseshoe configuration.

INTERN TASK 5-3

Arrange with your field associate teacher to visit four or five other classrooms in your school in order to see a variety of physical layouts. Notice, too, how, or if, these classrooms provide generously for bulletin board space, display areas, learning centers, resource and library centers, and project or construction areas.

Scheduling. Most schools expect teachers to operate their class-rooms on some kind of schedule. In elementary school self-contained classrooms, the teacher usually has a great deal of freedom in con-structing the schedule and in modifying it. Ordinarily, all that is required is that specific time breaks set by the school administration (such as lunch breaks, recesses, and dismissals) be observed rigidly. Beyond that, if scheduled "periods" run a few minutes overtime or a few minutes short, such matters are left to the teacher. This is im-portant in building flexibility into a program, because one cannot always predict precisely how much time will be needed for children to complete certain activities. Flexibility in scheduling also makes it possible for the teacher to combine other facets of the curriculum, such as language arts, music, art, or science, with social studies.

Pupil Involvement. Much of the social aspect of social studies can and should be taught to children in connection with everyday life in the classroom. What better way is there for a child to learn co-operation, decision making, care of equipment, discussion, and how to respect other's views than in the social setting of the classroom? Because most of these skills and values are learned best through direct participation, we are suggesting that there needs to be considerable pupil involvement in decision-making processes in the classroom. This not only gives children important practice in the use of these skills and values but provides them with a reason to identify psychologically with the group.

It is important to define the parameters of pupil decision making. There are some decisions about which children have nothing to say because they are policies established by some authority outside the classroom or by the teacher. It is, therefore, a mistake for the teacher to manipulate children by making them believe they are involved in such decisions.

INTERN TASK 5-4

Prepare a list of decisions made in your classroom in which children could legitimately participate. Now make a list of decisions in which children would not participate. Discuss your lists with your field associate teacher.

HOW DOES THE USE OF LEARNING RESOURCES RELATE TO PLANNING AND DECISION MAKING?

Much of the planning and decision making for social studies concerns itself with the use of multimedia. In previous chapters we have discussed the importance and availability of various learning resources. We now examine multimedia approaches from the perspective of individualizing learning.

One of the biggest obstacles to learning social studies in the elementary and secondary schools is the variation in pupils' abilities to get needed information: pupils cannot read well enough to find out what they need to know; or they do not listen attentively; or they lack the ability to sense abstract relationships. It follows, therefore, that anything the teacher can do to enlarge the scope of information sources, the more likely it is that social studies learning will be facilitated. The availability of a greater amount and variety of instructional materials in recent years has made this task easier for the teacher.

Reading Resources. It is impossible to do much about individualizing learning without taking into account the reading levels of the learners. Two facts are particularly relevant in this regard: (1) Reading continues to be an important vehicle for gaining information, perhaps *the* most important one beyond third grade, despite the widespread use of other valuable instructional resources; and (2) the range of reading ability is three to five years in classrooms in the early grades and five to ten years in the upper grades. To ignore the reading dimension is, therefore, to ignore the most critical element in planning and decision making in teaching and learning social studies. Because of the importance of the subject of reading, all of Chapter 7 is devoted to it, and consequently will not be discussed further here.

Learning Kits and Packages. The use of small packets of learning materials relating to specific components of social studies units have become popular in recent years. These kits may deal with a concept or generalization, with basic information, or with a skill. They consist of directions to the pupil along with study guide material, maps, pictures, charts, filmstrips, recordings, or whatever else the pupil will need in order to complete the required task. These kits may be packaged in file folders or in file-sized manila envelopes. Figure 5-1 shows what was contained in a learning kit prepared by a fourth-grade teacher on the subject of state parks.

Learning kits and packages may consist of a small collection of almost anything relevant to the topic under study. For example, samples of different kinds of fabrics might be included in a kit related to a unit on clothing. Specimen contracts, warranties, or advertisements could be assembled into a kit on consumerism. Often, museums put together artifacts into study kits that are available to schools on a loan basis. Instructional service centers may organize their collections of artifacts from different environments of the home state. In addition to kits and packages of this type and those assembled by the teacher, some are available through commercial outlets. These may include filmstrips, paperback books, and cassette tape recordings.

Learning Centers. Sets of learning kits and packages along with reference books, library books, audio and visual materials, artifacts, and other media may be placed in a single study area in the classroom called a learning center. The purpose of the learning center is to provide a study space for individuals or small groups of pupils in which they will have immediately accessible to them all the materials they will need in conducting inquiries or practicing skills. More than one learning center might be developed for social studies. For example, one center might include only machine-related audiovisual

SOCIAL STUDIES COMPETENCIES AND SKILLS

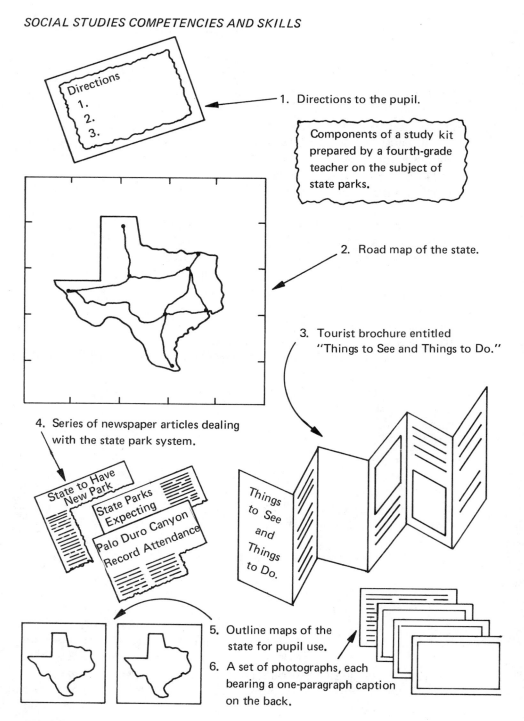

Figure 5-1.   Components of a Learning Kit based on the subject of state parks.

resources and another only printed and visual material. Learning centers should be so arranged that pupils can use them on their own anytime during the school day when they have study time. If the children can make use of learning centers without teacher assistance, they can engage themselves profitably while the teacher provides direct study help to others. Figure 5-2 provides an example of how a social studies learning center might be organized. Of course, this presents only one of several possibilities.

Listening Posts. As the name implies, these are stations in the classroom that consist of recorded material for pupil use. They provide a way for children to obtain information who may not be able to get it through reading. Children may follow the narrative in print while listening to the recording. Recordings can be prepared by the teacher or by pupils who read well, or they can be purchased from commercial houses. Dramatized accounts of well-known historical events as well as musical selections related to social studies units are available commercially.

Although some teachers believe that the use of recorded passages along with printed narrative improves reading skills, the research is not convincing on this point. Overuse of recorded materials as a substitute for reading may actually work to the disadvantage of building a child's ability to read social studies prose because of the failure to participate in the reading of social studies prose. If used in conjunction with other media in a balanced offering of information sources, however, recordings make a valuable contribution to data-gathering processes.

CAN ASSIGNMENTS AND TASKS BE "CUSTOMIZED" FOR INDIVIDUAL LEARNERS IN GROUP SETTINGS?

We have already explained that a teacher cannot be expected to provide individual tutoring in social studies on a daily basis when class sizes range from twenty-five to thirty or more children. Besides, many things that children should learn in social studies require them to be in group settings. For instance, group situations are essential if children are to be taught discussion skills, how to cooperate with others on a group project, or how to engage in a simulation game. Nonetheless, there are other types of learnings, activities, and projects that can be performed by pupils on an individual basis. Certainly

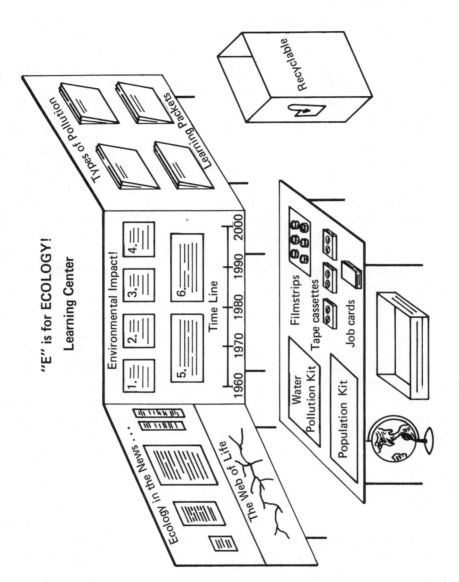

Figure 5-2. This is one of several ways that a social studies Learning Center can be arranged.

some of these assignments and tasks should be individually tailored and should be paced by the pupil. A few procedures for this purpose are discussed in this section.

Pupil Contracts. Some teachers find that they are able to provide tailor-made assignments and tasks by negotiating them with individual pupils. The agreement is formalized through the use of a contract that is signed by the teacher and the pupil. The contract simply states what the pupil is to do and when the assignment or task is to be completed. If contracts are used, it is important for the pupil to know precisely the extent of the obligation, the reward for finishing it well and on time, and what penalties may be attached to the failure to complete it. Once agreed to, the contract should be completed as specified. It is not a good practice to become lax about contract obligations. When this is allowed to happen, not only is the contracted work uncompleted, but the child may learn not to regard such agreements in a serious way. This learning could lead to unfortunate consequences if transferred to contractual agreements outside of school.

A teacher can prepare and have available contracts calling for a variety of assignments and tasks from which pupils can select those that most suit their needs, or the pupils themselves can propose a contract and negotiate it with the teacher. Both of these procedures have been used successfully. In the latter case, a greater amount of pupil initiative is required. This suggests that where pupils lack the maturity and judgment needed to put together a workable contract, the teacher will need to assist and encourage them. The tendency in pupil-initiated learning contracts is for the pupils to overcommit themselves. The teacher, knowing the capabilities of individual pupils, should be sure that the obligation is one that the pupil will be able to complete in the specified time.

The contract can, of course, take many forms. Teachers often design a contract to give it the appearance of an official document. (See Figure 5–3.)

Individually Paced Materials. Time is always a variable in completing assignments and tasks. Some children simply work more rapidly than others, regardless of the difficulty of the material. Traditionally, teachers have treated the length of time provided as a constant

SOCIAL STUDIES COMPETENCIES AND SKILLS

A Contract

I Do Hereby Agree to Do the Following
Activities in Social Studies.

1. _____

2. _____

3. _____

4. _____

_____
Pupil's signature

_____
Teacher's signature

Today's Date _____

Date Due _____

Figure 5-3. A sample Pupil Contract format.

and have required all pupils to complete the assignments at the same time. Usually this means that much of the work is carelessly done or not completed at all.

When assignments are individually paced, pupils are required to complete them at a specified level of quality and exactness, but they may, within reasonable limits, do so at their own speed. This procedure is the most useful in dealing with content or skills regarded as essential for everyone to learn at a certain level of proficiency. This means that a specific level of proficiency is indicated (also known as criterion level) and the child does not proceed to the next step in the sequence until that level is achieved. Often individually paced instruction is used in conjunction with behavioral objectives. It has obvious implications for evaluating pupil learning.

HOW CAN CREATIVE ACTIVITIES BE USED TO INDIVIDUALIZE LEARNING?

Learning can be individualized at the expressive, or outgo, phase as well as at the information intake phase. This makes possible a greater range of pupil options, thereby making the program more appealing and interesting to children. A child who may not be able to draw or sketch a map might be able to write an excellent essay. One who writes well may not do equally well in dramatic activities. Some pupils work effectively on individual projects, others do their best work in group enterprises.

It is a common assumption that when pupils are involved in creative activities, less in the way of "real" learning takes place. Traditional attitudes toward learning suggest that it must be accompanied by a hard-nosed discipline that is joyless. The feeling is widespread that if children enjoy what they are doing in school, it is prima facie evidence that the program does not amount to very much. The following interesting narrative describes a parent's attitude on just his point:

> At first we were quite concerned when we found out that Lori was to be placed in Mr. Allison's room the next year. His room had such a relaxed atmosphere about it, and he was very popular with the kids. We just assumed, I guess,

that a teacher who was so well liked by all the children could not be very effective in maintaining a disciplined environment for learning. I must say this assumption was wholly unfounded.

Mr. Allison was clearly the most creative, imaginative, and overall the most effective teacher Lori had during the seven years she attended that school. He always had the most unusual things going on in that room that would so hook the kids that they spent hours of unsupervised study on what they were doing. Schoolwork seemed to be a sheer delight, strange as that may seem. They analyzed advertising techniques in a unit on consumerism; they simulated law and justice procedures; they studied the effects of immigrant groups on American life and culture; there were art, poetry, music, and dramatic activities galore. Once they constructed a whole set of authentic models of Indian villages representing various tribes that inhabited this part of North American in pre-Columbian times. This involved the children in an incredible amount of research and information gathering in order to do the constructions. There were always games, puzzles, inquiries —tremendous interest grabbers. It was the only time I can recall that children had literally to be told to go home after school. If not, they would stay until dinnertime.

Mr. Allison convinced my husband and me that disciplined learning did not have to give the appearance of rigidity and drudgery. He seemed to embrace the philosophy that a teacher should obtain "maximum learning with minimum effort." But the "minimum effort" only seemed that way because of the tremendous motivating power of the creative activities he used. Actually, I have not seen children work any harder nor be more productive in their efforts than their year with Mr. Allison.[1]

How does a teacher develop this type of stimulating program for girls and boys in social studies? In part, this comes from an imaginative teacher who is able to capitalize on the natural interests and curiosities of children. The teacher encourages them to raise questions and to suggest ways of working. These, then, are converted into interesting study activities. This means that the teacher takes children into his or her confidence, helps them organize themselves

---

[1] An actual case reported to this writer.

to do the tasks, and provides the facilitating materials to make the activities possible. One rarely sees children doing creative activities of the type described in the narrative without also seeing a great deal of pupil involvement in planning and decision making. Part of the secret—if there is a secret—is that the teacher is able to release the creative capacities that are present in most groups of children but that often lie dormant because the children are told what they are to learn, how they will learn it, when they will learn it, and what the consequences will be if they fail to learn it.

The reader may not view himself or herself as a particularly creative or imaginative person and, therefore, will conclude that he or she could never be able to teach as Mr. Allison does. Such an attitude is self-fulfilling and an excuse rather than a reason for not engaging in imaginative and creative teaching. Not all teachers *should* teach as Mr. Allison—each of us should develop a personal teaching style that may be just as creative and imaginative.

In planning and decision making, perhaps we rely too much on books and aids. We are always on the lookout for "good ideas," "practical suggestions," or "how-to-do-it" formulas. Not enough time is spent on searching in our own storehouse of ideas, letting our own imaginations run free, and brainstorming for alternatives and possibilities. Professional reading and teaching aids are necessary, and there is little need to engage in exercises that reinvent the wheel, but at the same time there is no substitute for creative thought. Teachers need thinking time to mull ideas over in their minds, to rehearse procedures mentally, and to consider activities and strategies that make it possible to break out of the ordinary routines of teaching.

The second thing a teacher can do to develop programs of this type is to learn as much as possible about the psychology of children. Teachers like Mr. Allison are discerning observers of children's behavior. They really know what turns children on. They know how to ask questions and suggest possibilities that children find absolutely irresistible. They know enough about the behavior of children to be able to convert pupils' suggestions and expressions of interest into projects and activities that become a part of the instructional program. The truly professional teacher knows how to anticipate the responses of children and is skillful in monitoring the reactions of the children to his or her teaching.

SOCIAL STUDIES COMPETENCIES AND SKILLS

CHECKING YOUR PERFORMANCE

Intern Task Checklist

Task 5-1.   Listing questions used in making a needs assessment.   P. 102   _____

Task 5-2.   Deciding on size of group for certain tasks.   P. 104   _____

Task 5-3.   Visiting other classrooms.   P. 105   _____

Task 5-4.   Listing decisions in which pupils should and should not be involved.   P. 106   _____

Performance Checklist

In the field or in the clinic, the intern teacher has

1. Made an analysis of the abilities of a sample (six or more) of pupils in the class and knows their learning strengths and weaknesses.   _____

2. Developed and implemented a social studies program that takes pupil differences (as defined in number 1) into account.   _____

3. Arranged the physical layout of a classroom in a way that facilitates individual learning.   _____

4. Involved pupils in cooperative planning activities.   _____

5. Planned, organized, and developed a social studies learning center and listening post.   _____

6. Negotiated study contracts with pupils in social studies.   _____

7. Prepared three or more individual learning packets on selected social studies topics.

Field Associate Teacher Advisory

Tasks and performances should be checked off or initialed and dated by the appropriate local official, or the intern teacher can use the checklists for his or her own record.

Chapter 6

Encouraging inquiry

Lisa Markham and her field associate teacher, Sally Brooks, were discussing various aspects of inquiry teaching one day after school, and Sally advised, "It's important for you to know, Lisa, that inquiry teaching is a matter of some controversy in this district."

"But I don't understand, Miss Brooks. What can be controversial about teaching children to figure things out for themselves?" Lisa asked.

"It's not that simple," Miss Brooks explained. "Some parents feel that time spent on inquiry might better be spent on teaching children the three Rs. They also feel that inquiry procedures conflict with certain basic values that are taught in the home or in the child's religious training. Many believe that basic values should not be questioned; rather, that they should be inculcated in children."

"That's ridiculous," said Lisa. "Whether a person can read, write, or do math has little to do with the ability to solve problems and make decisions."

"I agree that it seems absurd," continued Miss Brooks. "But from the parents' point of view, it is a matter of priorities, with the three Rs ranking much higher than inquiry. Just recently I came across a newspaper article quoting a parent. Just a minute, I think I have it here. Yes, here it is. Let me read it to you.

To hell with values. They can inquire all they want to. There's plenty of hard data [to show that] a kid's basic values

> *are still shaped in that ultimate classroom, the home. But there are skills man developed over thousands of years, and they are not being communicated to my kids. My kids can't read, write or compute. And I'm mad.*[1]

In the same article a president of a publishing company adds,

> *We've asked children to think about problems the smartest people in the country don't have answers for. And we've given kids the impression their answers are as good as anybody else's, which they aren't. Because the kids don't have the basic fund of knowledge to think about some things. It's as if they sent you and me over to SALT and asked us to deal with the problem of strategic arms limitation. We don't have the information to make meaningful decision in that area.*[2]

Lisa listened thoughtfully. Then she said, "I guess I'd be mad, too, if my children could not read, write, or compute. But shouldn't we be able to do both? After all, you can't drill and practice _all_ day long. There is more to education than reading, writing, and arithmetic."

"Of course," continued Miss Brooks, "But we do need to be sensitive to values issues that might be offensive to certain groups. Also, we should be realistic about the kinds of inquiries we ask children to conduct. It seems farfetched for children to try to solve problems that baffle the best minds in the world. Some of what we have done under the label of inquiry has been silly. In such cases I think parents have a legitimate concern."

"Well, I can see I will need lots of help from you in keeping on the right track in my inquiry teaching," said Lisa, obviously concerned. "By the way, have I shown you the Basic Competencies our clinic instructor gave us dealing with inquiry teaching?"

"Yes, but we haven't discussed them," responded Miss Brooks. "Let's get together on them tomorrow. You should not be discouraged from using inquiry as a result of our conversation. You can be assured that I'll give you all the help I can."

[1] Chicago *Sun-Times*, "See dad. See mom. See them fume," by William Braden, October 19, 1975, p. 3.

[2] Ibid.

Basic Competencies—Social Studies

The intern teacher is able to

1. Understand and respect various ways of knowing.
2. Identify various inquiry skills and explain ways of teaching those skills.
3. Use different types of questions to elicit various types of thinking.
4. Identify problems and issues that can be used to initiate inquiries.
5. Locate and construct instructional materials that are needed in developing inquiry skills.
6. Develop an attitude of curiosity and independent thought in pupils.
7. Help children evaluate information and sources of information.

INTERN ADVISORY

After completing this chapter, together with related work in the clinic and appropriate classroom experiences in the field, you should be able to do the following:

1. Explain some of the issues surrounding inquiry teaching.
2. Identify intellectual skills that are associated with the inquiry process.
3. Conduct simple inquiry episodes with children.
4. Use appropriate questions to achieve specific purposes; use several different types of questions in teaching social studies.
5. Identify problems and situations that are well suited to the development of inquiry skills.
6. Explain how instructional materials are used in conducting inquiries.
7. Show by example what factors contribute to pupil interest in social studies.
8. Conduct instruction that provides pupils with experience in evaluating information and sources of information.

WHAT ARE SOME WAYS PEOPLE KNOW THINGS TO BE TRUE?

The major goal of inquiry-oriented teaching is to develop in pupils those attitudes and skills that enable them to be independent problem solvers. This means, among other things, that pupils need to develop a healthy skepticism about things and events in the world. Good problem solvers have a curiosity about what they see going on around them. They develop a questioning attitude. It is perhaps this element of inquiry that makes some parents have reservations about its use with young children. They would prefer to have their children accept certain beliefs and ideas as basic truths that are not to be questioned. The religious concept of faith is an example. Because of these conflicts, it is important for the intern to know that inquiry, based on scientific problem-solving procedures, is only one of several ways of knowing things to be true. Unfortunately, in school we sometimes teach as though this were the only way of knowing, and as a consequence we alienate those who do not share this view.

Perhaps the most common way of knowing something is by relying on an authoritative source. Our first and best teachers are our parents. As young children we perceive our parents as authoritative sources of knowledge. They protect and shelter us. They answer our questions about how things work. Because they seem to know so much and seem usually to be right in what they tell us, we learn to accept their explanations as true. As we grow older, we rely on other authorities—our teachers, scientists, books, doctors, historians, and so on. We simply do not have time to rediscover everything for ourselves, and even if we did, this would be an extremely inefficient use of our time. We can, we do, and indeed, we must rely on authorities for much of what we know about social and natural phenomena because we have no other way of getting such information.

The problem with the use of authority as a way of knowing is, of course, the credibility of the authority. We have to know enough about medicine, for example, to be able to differentiate between the wisdom of a competent physician and the bad advice of a quack. Sooner or later all of us discover that our parents are not a reliable source of information on all subjects. We also learn that not everything we read in books can be accepted as true, either—we need to know something about the credentials of the author before we can evaluate the validity of the account.

It should be immediately apparent that the potential for conflict between inquiry as a way of knowing and the use of authority is very great. Parents are understandably concerned if the school undermines their child's perception of them as authoritative sources of information. The conflict becomes even greater if parents perceive the school's teaching as jeopardizing the child's belief in God as the ultimate authority. This is most likely to happen in cases where the family accepts the meaning of Scripture literally. This issue surfaces even at the college level in connection with courses entitled "The Bible as Literature." If one regards the Bible as the literal word of God, treating it simply as a piece of literature would be disrespectful at least and possibly even blasphemous.

Teachers cannot ignore the fact that a large segment of our population believes that revealed truth is a legitimate way of knowing —that is, that God revealed truth to human beings either through written accounts (such as the Bible or the Koran) or through holy persons who were especially commissioned to make these truths known to others. It does not matter in the slightest what the teacher's personal views on this matter are; the fact is that seated in the public school classrooms of this nation are hundreds of thousands, perhaps millions, of children who, to some extent, are taught the validity of revealed truth, and to fail to take this into account in school instruction is a mistake.

Personal knowledge is still another way of knowing. We know something to be true simply because we believe it to be so. What we believe to be true may seem preposterous to someone else—we have no way of "proving" it in the scientific sense—yet we know it is true. Such beliefs may even be regarded as superstitions by others, and, therefore, such truths may not be shared except with intimates, if at all. Premonitions, extrasensory experiences, and clairvoyance are examples of personal knowledge regarded as true by the participants in such experiences.

We come finally to scientific problem solving as still another way of knowing. When this procedure is explained, it is usually presented as a five-step operation involving (1) problem identification; (2) hypothesis formation; (3) data gathering; (4) testing hypotheses in terms of evidence (or data); and (5) drawing conclusions based on the evidence. The process should not be conceptualized as a series of steps, however, but as a way of thinking that requires hard evidence or observable events to associate causes with effects. Conclusions based on scientific problem solving are accepted tentatively, based on information available at the time. This leaves the door open to the further refinement of explanations and conclusions—or even different explanations or conclusions—at a later time when more information may become available. This procedure stresses the *probability* of something's being true in terms of evidence rather than being true in the *absolute*, unchanging sense. This means that there are no areas closed to further investigation, obviously another point of conflict with those who embrace other ways of knowing.

Scientific problem-solving procedures are exceedingly powerful weapons in the battle against ignorance. It is no exaggeration to say that knowledge breakthroughs that have made possible modern science, technology, and medicine can be attributed to this system of thinking. So spectacular have been the achievements of scientific problem solving that critics suggest that science itself has become a god in the modern world. As a result, in recent years, the plea has been heard more frequently that more attention should be given to other ways of knowing. The demand for equal time by those who espouse the creation theory and oppose the evolution theory provides an example of this issue.

The purpose of this discussion of knowledge and knowing, although admittedly brief and incomplete, is to alert the intern to some of the complex issues surrounding inquiry teaching. Although this chapter is intended to promote inquiry procedures in the classroom, this is not to deny that there are other legitimate ways of knowing. It is the responsibility of public school teachers to help children develop ways of thinking that characterize an educated, rational citizenry. At the same time, teachers must be sensitive to the fact that there is so much about which we know so little; for many people, ways of knowing other than scientific problem solving appear to be more appropriate in dealing with those unknowns. The individual's right to embrace other ways of knowing must be respected.

Field Associate Teacher Advisory

In fairness to the intern it is important that you discuss any particular problems related to inquiry teaching that might be present in the local area. The beginning teacher should not be intimidated by local pressure groups; at the same time the intern must also understand that parents have a legitimate concern about their children's education. This would be a good time for you to discuss with the intern such matters as professional ethics, the right to teach and the right to learn, and the role of professional associations in coming to the defense of teachers who come under unfair attack. This must not be presented to the intern in such a way as to discourage him or her from engaging in inquiry teaching at all.

WHAT SKILLS ARE INVOLVED IN INQUIRY
AND HOW DO WE TEACH THEM?

In statements of educational goals and objectives, it is quite common to find the development of thinking abilities being given a high priority. Similarly, it is rare to find a teacher who does not claim to teach pupils to think. The problem, of course, is that there is often a big gap between intent and performance, resulting partly from a failure to understand how thinking skills are taught and learned. To admonish someone to think is of no value except as a way of telling the individual to pay attention and concentrate on the task at hand. More appropriate strategies for teaching those thinking skills that are associated with problem solving are those we call inquiry or investigation oriented.

The usual assumption is that the development of thinking skills flows naturally as a result of the increase of knowledge. The belief is widespread that if one is well informed, the application of that knowledge to the solution of problems will pretty much take care of itself. Consequently, educational programs often emphasize the accumulation of information rather than a concern with its application. If there is a concern for application at all, the feeling is that it should come later, after there has been a period of knowledge accumulation, in high school or college or as an adult. The research of the late Hilda Taba and others indicates that this procedure is based on faulty assumptions and that knowledge accumulation and knowledge application go hand in hand and are part of the same process we call thinking.[3]

The process of thinking consists of a series of subskills, and like any other skills, they must be practiced if they are to be applied with any degree of proficiency. These subskills can be identified as follows:

[3]Hilda Taba, "Implementing Thinking as an Objective in Social Studies," in *Effective Thinking in the Social Studies*, 37th yearbook, Jean Fair and Fannie R. Shaftel, eds. (Washington, D.C.: National Council for the Social Studies, 1967), pp. 25–49. The late Hilda Taba was Professor of Education at San Francisco State University.

1. Identifying problems and questions for study.
2. Making inferences and drawing conclusions from data.
3. Making comparisons.
4. Developing hypotheses.
5. Using evidence to test hypotheses.
6. Planning how to study a question or a problem.
7. Getting data from a variety of sources.
8. Predicting possible outcomes.
9. Deciding what evidence is needed in studying a problem.
10. Deciding what evidence is relevant to the study.

These skills must be incorporated in the on-going work of the class if pupils are to develop proficiency in their use. Occasional special lessons on inquiry are not in themselves adequate for building competence. Of course, not all of these subskills will appear in social studies lessons every day. During a period of a couple weeks, however, one should see balanced and systematic attention being given to them. Figure 6-1 illustrates how inquiry skills can be built into the regular work of the class.

HOW ARE INSTRUCTIONAL MATERIALS USED IN INQUIRY STRATEGIES?

Special instructional materials that are inquiry based are helpful, but not essential, to engaging children in inquiry. Any of the standard materials can be used as sources of information, including textbooks. What is different about inquiry, however, is the way these materials are used.

The usual assumption regarding instructional material is that it includes essential information that must be learned by the pupils. Nowhere is this more evident than in the use of textbooks. Textbook content often *becomes* the curriculum. Even today some elementary school teachers are required by their principals to "cover the textbook" during the year. Consequently, study exercises, discussions, reading assignments, and other activities are designed to get the pupil to learn the facts, concepts, and information included in the text. Examinations are then based on how well the informational content has been learned. In this way the instructional resources determine what the curriculum is to be.

LESSON 49 [4]

Learning outcome: Pupils relate the early growth and development of the Middle West to environmental influences and cultural adaptation.

Material used:

✓ Text, pages 158–164

Teaching strategy:

1. *Developing and testing hypotheses derived from maps*

The pupils develop hypotheses.

● Before pupils read about the settlement and development of the Middle West, they can anticipate what they will read by making inferences from maps of the region.

○ From the pattern of Indian removal shown in the map on page 158, pupils can readily hypothesize that the southern part of the Old Northwest was settled before the northern areas.

. . . use evidence to support a conclusion or a generalization or test a hypothesis and draw a conclusion.

○ They can readily develop a hypothesis about how settlers entered the region by noting the course of the Ohio River and noting, from page 120, the road and canal situation in the early days of Northwest settlement.

● Page 160 and page 161 down to "Poor land in the north" can then be read to test these ideas.

● The section on the natural environment of the Middle West, pages 158–159, and the paragraph about the northern part of the Northwest Territory, on page 161, should then be read.

● The reflective question on page 159 introduces, for the first time, the problem of westward-moving settlers meeting a natural environment different from that to which they were accustomed.

○ This is an opportunity to stress the generalization that people are capable of adapting their culture to new surroundings.

○ The reporter handling the question should see that ways of building homes and fences and ways of heating would have to be modified in a non-forest environment.

● The reporter who handles the reflective question on page 162 should use the map on page 121 to make clear how the Erie Canal encouraged the movement to the Old Northwest of immigrants who had entered the country through New York City.

. . . use non-textbook sources.

● Interested pupils might report on place names and other evidence that reflect the cultural mosaic of the Middle West.

2. *Reading for answers to specific questions*

● Reading of pages 162–164 can be guided by questions along these lines:

. . . use evidence to support a conclusion or a generalization or test a hypothesis and draw a conclusion.

○ "How did Robert and John Reid make a very important adaptation to the new natural environment they met in the Middle West?"

○ "A good location in relation to transportation routes and a rich surrounding countryside are essential if a city is to grow. How does Cincinnati illustrate this principle?" The reflective question on page 165 should be considered with this question about Cincinnati.

Figure 6-1. Lesson plan from a textbook teacher's guide.

[4] Bertha Davis, *Teacher's Guide for Lands of Promise and Its Related Media* (New York: Macmillan Publishing Co., Inc., 1974), pp. 63–64.

Inquiry teaching does not tie the curriculum that closely to the information sources. It encourages pupils to raise questions, to speculate, to hypothesize, and to define problems quite apart from the instructional resources to be used. We might imagine a teacher and a class together planning an inquiry into the subject of urbanism and the problems of city life. This planning session might take place without any reference to instructional resources. In fact, such a planning session could take place in another room where there are no instructional materials available. Let us say that initially the class decides to conduct some exploratory research on cities by assembling what information it can find on these questions:

1. When did cities first come into being? Why did they appear when they did?
2. What caused the growth of cities in modern times?
3. Are there limits as to how large cities can become?
4. Why are cities located where they are?
5. Why do some cities continue to grow larger while others become smaller and sometimes disappear entirely?

The class decides how it will divide these questions among its members and agrees to have its first progress report in two days. The problem now is to locate information relating to these questions. Their teacher has provided them with several good leads to information:

1. Their textbook has a unit entitled "People and Their Cities." This is a lengthy unit separated into four sections and totaling ninety-three pages.
2. A learning center has been prepared containing many materials on cities.
3. The librarian has been alerted that the class will be studying urbanism. As a result, a separate shelf of books has been assembled on cities and city life.

In a few minutes the class is dispersed and begins its information search.

This example illustrates that the pupils conducting the inquiry are making use of precisely the same instructional materials that they would use in a more conventional lesson. They are, however, using these materials as sources of data to respond to their own questions. This is quite different from regarding the informational content of the instructional materials as the curriculum and setting out to learn it.

The example cited showed a class using conventional instructional materials for purposes of inquiry. It would also be possible to show a class using materials that were designed for inquiry in traditional ways. We are forced to conclude that it is what the teacher does that determines the extent to which learning will be inquiry oriented and not the instructional materials used by the pupils.

WHY ARE QUESTIONS ESSENTIAL TO INQUIRY?

Questioning is a commonly used teaching technique that serves a variety of purposes. For example, many questions deal simply with procedural matters: Is everyone ready to move to the next step? How much longer do you think you will need in order to finish that project? What should you do after you get your materials? Such questions are important but do not deal directly with the substantive materials under study. The teacher uses them to clarify procedures, to determine whether pupils understand what they are to do, to find out whether additional explanation is required, to get feedback on the effectiveness of a demonstration or explanation, and so on.

Questions may also be used to check the child's comprehension of concepts, generalizations, or subject matter. Often such questions require the pupil to reproduce or recall information that has been read or discussed in class. Research of classroom-teacher behavior through the years shows that teachers use a high percentage of questions of this type. These questions are sometimes referred to as "low level" because they involve simple recall and memory rather than higher-order mental operations such as application, analysis, synthesis, interpretation, sensing cause and effect, or evaluation. These questions can be easily identified because they usually begin with who, what, when, and where. These questions are important, especially in checking comprehension or to ascertain that pupils are familiar with facts essential to the topic. The problem is that there is a tendency to overuse them, with a corresponding lessened use of other questions that do require higher-order thought processes. In terms of inquiry the most important questions to ask are those that require elaborative, reflective responses. These higher-level questions often begin, "Why . . .," "How . . .," "How do we know . . .," "Show that . . .," "If that is true, then . . .".[5]

These higher-level questions serve two general purposes relating to inquiry. One is that they trigger mental operations that are in accord with a problem-solving, discovery learning format. For example, what mental operations are involved if the teacher asks the question: What is the most important reason for a small population in the area? Before responding, the child has to (1) analyze the situation, (2) consider all of the reasons that might apply, (3) evaluate each in terms of its importance, and then (4) select the one considered to be most important. Mental operations of this type characterize higher-level, or reflective, questions. Simply recalling a "correct" response is not adequate—the information has to be processed intellectually: analyzed, synthesized, applied, interpreted, evaluated, and so on. Thus, appropriate questions are essential in building reflective habits of thought.

These questions also serve the purpose of teaching the child improved habits of study. If the only kinds of questions encountered are based on recall of factual information, the child learns to study in terms of such objectives. The child may not learn how to apply information or even to process it in terms of broader intellectual outcomes. For example, without such experience, a child may attach the same degree of importance to a trivial incident as to a major concept or a profound generalization. Also, problem solving requires the ability *to ask* appropriate questions, and pupils cannot develop this skill unless they encounter such questions in their study.

INTERN TASK 6-1

The following types of questions are used to promote inquiry. Add two examples to each of the types listed.

[5]Students familiar with the Bloom *Taxonomy* will recognize that the higher-level questions correspond to those based on objectives in the comprehension, application, synthesis, and evaluation categories; *see* Benjamin S. Bloom, Ed., *Taxonomy of Educational Objectives, Handbook I, Cognitive Domain* (New York: David McKay Co., Inc., 1956). For a comprehensive treatment of questioning strategies, the reader is referred to Francis P. Hunkins, *Questioning Strategies and Techniques* (Boston: Allyn & Bacon, Inc., 1972); Norris M. Sanders, *Classroom Questions: What Kinds?* (New York: Harper & Row, Publishers, 1966); John Jarolimek and Clifford D. Foster, *Teaching and Learning in the Elementary School* (New York: Macmillan Publishing Co., Inc., 1976), Ch. 8

1. Analyzing component elements.
   a. What land features are most important to the occupations of the people who live there?
   b. When the term *natural resources* is used in the selection what does it include?
   c. _____
   d. _____

2. Interpreting data.
   a. As you study the maps, what can you say about the number of people who live in this area?
   b. What do the types of homes in which people dwell tell you about their way of living?
   c. _____
   d. _____

3. Predicting outcomes.
   a. If everyone worked only four days a week, what businesses might be expected to grow?
   b. You have the population figures for the years 1900, 1920, 1940, and 1960. What do you think the population will be in 1980?
   c. _____
   d. _____

4. Probing for additional information.
   a. What else can you say about that?
   b. That's fine as far as you've gone, but what are some other reasons?
   c. _____
   d. _____

5. Clarifying meanings.
   a. What would be an example of what you mean?
   b. Are you saying that no immigrants came that year?
   c. _____
   d. _____

6. Verifying statements or conclusions.
   a. How can we be sure that is a true statement?
   b. Where would we look to find proof for what you are saying?
   c. _____
   d. _____

7. Applying information.
   a. Where would be the most reasonable place to build the highway?
   b. Why did the most important railroads and transportation routes run in an east-west rather than a north-south direction?
   c. _____
   d. _____

8. Sensing cause and effect.
   a. How might a winter frost in Florida affect the lives of people in northern cities such as Minneapolis, Milwaukee, Detroit, and Cleveland?
   b. If farmers make greater use of machinery and there is less need for farm hands, where do people in the rural areas find jobs?
   c. _____
   d. _____

WHAT TOPICS ARE WELL SUITED TO INQUIRY?

Almost any topic can be shaped to meet the requirements of an inquiry episode. However, topics that are to some extent controversial and problematic are best because they are consistent with the nature of inquiry. That is, there is clearly something to inquire about and the outcome may still be in doubt. Subject matter and topics relating to current affairs, law and justice, the environment, intergroup relations, economics, and geography are a few that lend themselves well to inquiry. As an example, the following case could be used as the basis for an inquiry into certain aspects of the legal and justice system:

Farmer Indicted in Elk-Killing Case

Kenneth Reed was indicted in Sheridan District Court Tuesday on five counts of killing elk, a protected species in this state. Reed, a local farmer, did not deny killing the elk, but said they were damaging the grain crop he needed to feed his dairy herd.

Reed said that the animals began damaging his crop in midsummer and that he had repeatedly asked the Fish and Game Department to do something about it. Through his attorney, Reed said that he had contacted the department "at least a dozen times" by telephone. He also said that he sent three letters to the department warning that if something were not done, he would shoot the animals. Reed insists that he was justified in killing the elk to protect his property.

It is expected that the case will come to trial this fall. If found guilty, Reed could be sentenced to one year in jail and fined $1,000 on each of the five counts.[6]

This case raises some interesting legal questions relating to the right to protect one's property. Because television programs often show individuals using firearms to protect their property or themselves, children may have distorted ideas about the legal aspects of protecting one's self or one's property. Some of the issues raised by this case are these:

1. Why might the person be found not guilty in this case even though the specific action—that is, killing the elk—is clearly against the law in that state? Why should such a finding *in one case* not be interpreted by citizens as encouragement to break the law any time they think it is unfair or does not apply to them?
2. How does the fact that Reed had contacted the Fish and Game Department several times, without any apparent results, have any bearing on the outcome of the case?
3. Do individuals have the right to "take the law into their own hands" when appropriate officials refuse to or are unable to take corrective action?
4. Would the outcome of this case most likely be different if the trespassers were people instead of elk?

In conducting inquiries of this type, it is helpful to use a format such as the following:

1. What are the *facts* of the case?
   What actually happened? When? By whom? To what and to whom? What needs to be established is what lawyers call the fact pattern.
2. What are the *issues*?
   What conflicts are evident in the case? What mitigating circumstances must be considered? What values are at stake?

---

[6]This is a fictitious case, although in 1975 in a case much like this one, a Minnesota farmer was found not guilty by a district court jury.

132

3. What *alternatives* can be suggested in resolving the case? Not only guilt or innocence, as in this case, but other forms of restitution or resolution and the consequences that flow from each.

INTERN TASK 6-2

Using the information provided in the foregoing section, search out a suitable topic for an inquiry episode and prepare it for presentation to the class to which you have been assigned. Before you get too far along in the development of this lesson, however, discuss your plans with your field associate teacher. When your planning is completed, use the episode with your class.

HOW DOES A TEACHER DEVELOP CURIOSITY AND INDEPENDENT THOUGHT IN PUPILS?

The development of an attitude of curiosity and independent thought stems from the teacher's ability to personalize learning for children. In recent years much of the literature on the pedagogy of social studies has dealt with the development of concepts, generalizations, and so-called big ideas. There is, of course, merit in this if we use concepts, generalizations, and major ideas as organizing frameworks. But perhaps our professional love affair with the general has caused us to lose sight of the motivating power of the specific. One cannot get very excited about a generalization! For instance, teachers often report that when they deal with justice and the legal system as abstract concepts, pupils are bored. When they begin asking such questions as "What would you do if you were falsely arrested for shoplifting or drug possession?" the pupils immediately come to life. Ideas simply mean more to us when we can relate them to ourselves.

Henry Steele Commager, writing on why the late Theodore Blegen was able to bring so much excitement to his writing about the history of Scandinavian people in Minnesota, made these comments:

> . . . In his histories something is always happening; his people are not statistical items, but poor Norwegian fishermen or cotters who sing mournful ballads, or Minnesota farmer-wives painfully writing letters home to the old country, or boys and girls in icy churches listening piously to sermons that no longer

have meaning to them. Theodore Blegen has the same feeling for history that animated Ole Rölvaag and Johan Bojer, the same interest in the poor and the forgotten, the women and children, the plain people with their hopes and disappointments, their concern for the weather and the crops, for school and church, their quiet pride in their new homes, their deep sadness for what they have given up, their endless wonder at what life has done to them and what it promises to do to their children in this New World.

. . . it is the individual experience that counts, and that, in the end, illuminates the experience of the race. . . . he never loses sight of the individual . . . whose experience is a microcosm of the experience of a large part of the human race.[7]

These remarks provide us with important clues about how to make inquiries exciting for pupils: Inquiries must deal with specific individual experiences that are significantly related to the lives of pupils. When the experiences are personal, they are perceived as being part of an exciting adventure in learning.

Of course, the classroom environment is important in developing an attitude of curiosity and wonderment. The kinds of questions that teachers ask also contribute. But the ability of the teacher to capture the imaginations of the children through their own experiences is most important. Notice how this is done in the following excerpt:

The starting points for meaningful classroom experiences may grow organically out of a particular experience the class has had; for example, a field trip, a classroom discussion, a conversation with a friend, or something as simple as an object a student brought to school to share. A group of nine- and ten-year-old-children in Fargo, North Dakota, turned a story they read together into a house-building experience. The story, about a class which built a clubhouse, prompted a similar idea—the class would build one of its own. Children greeted the idea with such enthusiasm that some visited a lumber-yard and arranged to get some old plywood. They developed rather elaborate plans which involved measurement and geometry. An architect demonstrated model making, which the children then tried. They viewed a variety of films on house building. A tape-recorded lesson taught them about

[7]Henry Steele Commager, ed., *Immigration and American History* (Minneapolis: University of Minnesota Press, 1961), pp. vii–viii.

tools—the lever, plane, and gear. Retired carpenters in the community provided additional demonstrations. Individual children pursued many different interests in relation to the house-building project. They wrote letters telling others of their experiences. They engaged in individual projects involving Indian homes, termites, trees, creatures who live in trees, homes around the world, workers who build homes, old and modern tools, skyscrapers, doll houses, and, of course, they built the 10′ × 8′ × 6′ clubhouse. They gave a party to thank parents and others who had helped, and presented their construction to the younger children in the school for use during recess.[8]

INTERN TASK 6-3

This section has included two excerpts, each of which speaks of the characteristics of situations that people find interesting and engaging. One is written about printed material for adults; the other about activities of elementary school children. Do you perceive anything that these two excerpts have in common? Discuss this question with your field associate teacher, and then decide if there is anything in these situations that you might apply to your own teaching.

HOW DOES A TEACHER HELP CHILDREN EVALUATE INFORMATION AND THE SOURCES OF INFORMATION?

There is much in our culture that encourages us to have faith in others and to trust our fellow human beings. Because of our tradition of using printed material, we attach high credibility to information found in books. Persons are often considered authorities on a subject when they have written and published a book on it. Conversely, there is also much in our culture that cautions us to be wary of what we hear and read. Our free enterprise system has long issued the warning of caveat emptor—"the buyer beware." Or, we see the familiar signs in out-of-the-way cafes and bars that inform us "In God We Trust—All Others Pay Cash." A person who believes everything he or she is told or what is read is a patsy; one who believes

[8]Vito Perrone and Lowell Thompson, "Social Studies in the Open Classroom," *Social Education*, 36 (4) : 460–464, 1972.

nothing is a skeptic. The first is easily duped and victimized; the other tends toward cynicism and distrust. Neither provides an acceptable model for children.

We are confronted here with a situation in which children need to develop a healthy skepticism about the information they find and about information sources, without at the same time destroying their confidence in legitimate data sources. In the middle and upper grades it is helpful to discuss this matter simply to build awareness of the need to validate information sources. This can be personalized through the use of case studies familiar to pupils—case studies of advertising claims, political rhetoric, confidence schemes, the work of fraud divisions in police departments, and so on. This discussion can and should be related to the need for dependable data sources in classroom inquiries. Even young children can understand that the use of unreliable data will lead to unreliable findings.

Pupils should also be given direct experience with data that are inaccurate either because they are out of date or because they are biased. In social studies it is easy to get accounts that are out of date because of rapid changes that have taken place in recent years. For example, earlier editions of textbooks or wall maps may be compared with present editions. Also, the use of two editions of a special reference, such as *The World Almanac*, to compare data, will underscore the need for current sources of information.

Familiarizing children with bias in accounts and teaching them how to detect it is more subtle and more difficult to handle. Nonetheless, middle- and upper-grade children can understand a few of the more obvious ways that bias can be introduced in source materials. This will alert them to the need to scrutinize such material with extra care:

1. The use of affectively toned descriptors. Examples include "a *stubborn* president," "*harsh* chemicals," and "*foot-dragging*" mayor.
2. The possibility of conflict of interest. Examples include oil or mining company instructional materials dealing with environmental problems and pollution; tobacco company research dealing with the effects of smoking on health; and labor union documents dealing with employment and wages.
3. The credibility of authorship. Examples include an authority in one field writing in another, as when a nuclear physicist

SOCIAL STUDIES COMPETENCIES AND SKILLS

writes on social welfare programs; and a layman or professional free-lance writer writing about a technical subject.

INTERN TASK 6-4

Develop a lesson that will provide your pupils with experience in evaluating information sources. If you are working with primary-grade children, this might take the form of evaluating the credibility of a popular television commercial with which they are familiar. With older youngsters, you might develop an exercise to sensitize them to bias in printed material. Have your plans reviewed by your field associate teacher, then teach the lesson to your class.

CHECKING YOUR PERFORMANCE

Intern Task Checklist

Task 6-1.   Framing inquiry questions. P. 128   _____

Task 6-2.   Identifying a topic suitable for an inquiry episode. P. 132   _____

Task 6-3.   Searching for common characteristics in interesting accounts
and experiences. P. 134   _____

Task 6-4.   Developing a lesson dealing with evaluating information.
P. 136   _____

Performance Checklist

In the field or in the clinic, the intern teacher has

1. Demonstrated an acquaintance with some of the issues surrounding inquiry teaching.   _____

2. Identified intellectual skills that are associated with the inquiry process.   _____

3. Conducted simple inquiry episodes with pupils.   _____

4. Used appropriate questions to achieve specific purposes; used several different types of questions in teaching social studies.   _____

5. Identified problems and situations that are well suited to the development of inquiry skills.   _____

6. Used instructional materials in conducting inquiries.   _____

7. Demonstrated the ability to interest pupils in social studies.   _____

8. Conducted instruction that provides pupils with experience in evaluating information and sources of information.   _____

Field Associate Teacher Advisory

Tasks and performances should be checked off or initialed and dated by the appropriate local official, or the intern can use the checklist for his or her own record.

The central role of reading in social studies

Dr. Restin, the clinic instructor, knew he had struck a sensitive nerve in his interns when he raised the issue of reading with them. One intern, obviously discouraged by the circumstances in which she was placed, spoke:

"I agree with the <u>Newsweek</u> story that kids have to be able to read in order to write. And it would be just an accident if a child learned to read in the environment in which I am placed. Just look at the situation. There are a hundred kids in this big, so-called open classroom. Three fourths of them do not have any idea of what they are supposed to be doing most of the time. The noise and commotion are unbelievable. Kids lounge around on the floor. They do everything but stand on their heads, and some even do that. We try to show a filmstrip and discuss it, but there are so many distractions that we spend half our time just trying to get the pupils' attention. I'm supposed to be learning how to teach, but instead I am being driven out of my mind by a madhouse of confusion. How can kids learn to read in such a place? Of course they can't and don't, and that's why parents and others are concerned."

"My situation is different from that," said another. "I am in a self-contained classroom, and the program is structured enough so that we do not have the management problems Cheryl talks about. But these children read so poorly that we simply cannot make use of the social studies texts. Why can't children be taught to read well *enough in the primary grades so that they can use their reading skills to learn in the middle and upper grades? Maybe the elementary grades should spend full time on reading and writing so that children can master those skills."*

Another intern picked up the discussion by saying, "It's strange, you know. I'm in a fourth-grade class and those kids seem to be able to recognize the words they read, but their understanding of what they read is zilch. It just may be that we spend too much time on the mechanics of reading and not enough time on having them get the meaning of what they read. I had a child read orally a whole page of her social studies text to me and she did so flawlessly. Yet she could not tell me a single major idea included in the passage. Weird!"

Dr. Restin moved the discussion toward a consideration of the relationship between social studies achievement and reading ability. He also had the interns discuss their understanding of the reading process. He stressed with them that reading was not simply "word calling" but was, instead, a highly complex intellectual process that involved the gaining of meaning from printed symbols. He lectured briefly on the implications of this for social studies. He concluded by saying:

"There must be a mutual relationship between reading and the various content fields such as social studies, science, and mathematics. You cannot assume that children learn to read during your reading classes and read to learn in the content fields. The problems children encounter in reading do not simply go away when they move from the reading group to social studies. Indeed, the problems will probably escalate because of the special reading skills required to handle social studies content.

"Your responsibility in social studies instruction, therefore, includes attention to those reading abilities and skills that are uniquely associated with social studies. The same applies, of course, to the other content fields. We need to improve substantially the ability of children to read because they live in a world that demands literacy. Literacy will not be achieved by eliminating social studies and science from the curriculum and directing attention to the three Rs. Instead, we should use these subjects as additional means for building a well-rounded competence in this most important of learning skills, reading."

Basic Competencies—Social Studies

The intern teacher is able to

1. Identify reading skills essential to social studies.
2. Develop a classroom climate that encourages and supports reading.
3. Conduct informal diagnostic reading procedures.
4. Adapt the text to the reading capabilities of pupils.
5. Select social studies reading materials in accordance with pupils' reading abilities.
6. Use social studies content to enhance general reading skills.

INTERN ADVISORY

After completing this chapter, together with related work in the clinic and appropriate classroom experiences in the field, you should be able to do the following:

1. Develop suitable teaching and practice exercises for each of the reading skills that are important to social studies.
2. Identify factors that contribute to a classroom climate that supports reading.
3. Devise diagnostic exercises based on social studies reading skills that provide information concerning the reading needs of pupils in your classroom.
4. Adapt and use the textbook to suit the varying reading abilities of pupils in your class.
5. Select and use trade books and other nontextbook materials to suit the varying reading abilities of the pupils in your class.
6. Improve children's reading skills through the use of social studies subject matter and instructional materials.

WHAT READING SKILLS ARE ESSENTIAL TO SOCIAL STUDIES?

A high percentage of all instruction relies on the pupils' ability to read. Additionally, in social studies much of this reading beyond the primary grades is tied to the textbook. Estimates indicate that 75 to 90 per cent of the pupils' school learning is structured around the textbook. When this is coupled with the fact that the readability of social studies textbooks is known to be difficult, it becomes clear why reading can be and often is a major obstacle to satisfactory achievement in social studies.

There can be no doubt that children nationally do not read as well as should be expected, considering the attention and resources that flow into efforts to teach them to read. June R. Chapin and Richard E. Gross indicate that,

> It is estimated conservatively that by the end of the sixth grade approximately 10 per cent to 25 per cent of all students are "seriously" below their grade level in reading—typically defined as two grade levels below normal. By other estimates, one-third of the elementary school children and one-fourth to one-third of the high school students are handicapped readers. Below-grade reading achievement for the disadvantaged is well documented.[1]

The same source cites the late Dr. James E. Allen, Jr., former U.S. Commissioner of Education, who presented the following evidence in support of the "right-to-read" program:

1. One out of four students, nationwide, has significant reading deficiencies.
2. In large city school systems up to half of the students read below expectation.
3. There are more than 3 million illiterates in our adult population.
4. About half of the unemployed youth, ages sixteen–twenty-one, are functionally illiterate.
5. Three quarters of the juvenile offenders in New York City are two or more years retarded in reading.
6. In a recent U.S. Armed Forces program called Project 100,000, 68 per cent of the young men fell below grade 7 in reading and academic ability.[2]

[1] June R. Chapin and Richard E. Gross, *Teaching Social Studies Skills* (Boston: Little, Brown and Company, 1973), p. 21.

[2] Ibid., p. 20.

THE CENTRAL ROLE OF READING IN SOCIAL STUDIES

The National Center for Health Statistics conducted a four-year study ending in 1970 and showed that of youngsters in the twelve- to seventeen-year age group, 4.8 per cent could not read adequately. The criterion of literacy in this study was the ability to read as well as an average fourth grader, a level probably too low to engage in functional reading as an adult. Clearly, this indicates that an alarming number of young Americans are not able to engage in what the clinic instructor, Dr. Restin, called "this most important of all learning skills."

Evidence of the type presented here cannot be explained away on the basis of changing school populations or that test scores show that children read "at least as well now as they did a generation ago." Such claims are contrary to the facts. Children should read significantly *better* today than they did a generation ago because more is now known about how to teach reading, and materials for teaching reading have become more sophisticated. We need to face squarely the reality that we have something of a national disaster on our hands in the teaching of reading, and all concerned need to make every effort to reverse the trend of the deterioration of reading ability among the young people of this country.

Reading problems arise not only in word analysis and decoding but in knowing what words mean, in processing information gained through reading, and in interpreting what is being communicated in print. This being the case, the content fields such as social studies and science should figure prominently in building reading comprehension abilities. Unfortunately, this does not always happen because of the mistaken assumption that the child comes to social studies already knowing how to read. Consequently, teachers do not perceive the teaching of reading as an essential component of the teaching of social studies and science.

The point of view being developed here is that the teaching of reading is an integral part of the teaching of social studies and that there are special reading skills that must be taught in the context of social studies subject matter. This is not to suggest that a systematic and sequential program of basic reading instruction is unimportant. Quite to the contrary. It is to say only that the basal reading program is not in itself adequate and that the teaching of reading must be of concern to the teacher whenever the child encounters reading in the entire school curriculum.

In addition to the usual basic reading skills relating to word analysis and simple comprehension, the following elements are critical to successful achievement in social studies:

In social studies, the capable reader

- Uses chapter and section headings as aids to reading.
- Uses context clues to gain meaning.
- Recognizes author bias.
- Adjusts speed of reading to purpose.
- Interprets what is read.
- Detects cause-and-effect relationships.
- Understands essential terms and vocabulary.
- Gains information from maps, pictures, and other illustrations.
- Uses various parts of a book as aids to reading.
- Is able to skim to locate facts.
- Distinguishes between fact and opinion.
- Compares one account with another.
- Recognizes topic sentences.
- Interprets quantitative data accurately.
- Obtains the literal meaning of material read.
- Relates what is read to reality.
- Uses reference aids and references to find information.
- Is able to locate a book in the library.

INTERN TASK 7-1

a. Select the social studies text for the grade to which you have been assigned and find a specific example in the book that illustrates the need for the child to be able to use each of the skills listed above.
b. Show by example how the reading skills listed above could be built into a primary-grade program even if a basic textbook were not used.

Check your responses with your field associate teacher and/or your clinic instructor.

Field Associate Teacher Advisory

Now is a good time to discuss the reading situation in your classroom with the intern, noting especially your views and perceptions of the relationship between reading and social studies. The comments of the interns in the opening narrative of this chapter might serve as the basis for such a discussion. Also, share with the intern any unique strengths or weaknesses in reading that are apparent in the class.

HOW DOES A TEACHER DEVELOP A CLASSROOM ENVIRONMENT THAT ENCOURAGES AND SUPPORTS READING?

Teachers who are successful in teaching children to read are those who perceive the ability to read as a matter of considerable importance and, in a variety of ways, get children to do a lot of reading. Children do not learn to read in three (or however many) groups during the reading period any more than one learns to play the piano during the hour lesson one has with a piano teacher once a week. The basal reading program provides only the basic instruction, which must be supported, reinforced, and practiced in between times. Thus, successful reading achievement occurs in an environment that encourages and supports reading throughout the school day.

In planning the reading environment it is not just a matter of surrounding the child with books. Books that are not of intrinsic interest to children or that are beyond their ability to read may discourage rather than encourage reading growth. The reading materials available to the child should be selected to achieve certain purposes, important among which are the development of pupil interest, pupil initiative, and pupil independence in reading. Teachers devise many interesting and imaginative procedures to achieve these purposes. For instance, classroom reading centers may feature books on specific subjects known to be of interest to the pupils. Classroom book clubs are organized in which children can share and exchange ideas about books. Books may be arranged to simulate a book store or a library. Magazines and periodicals are kept current to capitalize on the interest children have in emerging news stories. The classroom should present the children with many irresistible options to select reading materials of high interest to them.

When pupils find the reading to be tough going in social studies, the usual ways of dealing with this are either to (1) select simpler material, or (2) have the pupils get the data through nonreading sources, such as a tape recording. This sounds simple enough, but in actual practice it may be very difficult for the teacher to implement. First, in the middle and upper grades, where this problem is most prevalent, there may not be simpler material available that is relevant to the topic under study. In some cases it is almost impossible to simplify the narrative for a complex topic much below the fourth- or fifth-grade reading level without emasculating the prose of those concepts that are essential to the understanding of the topic. Second, data may not be available to the pupil in the classroom through nonreading sources. Thus, if these procedures are to be followed, the teacher must rewrite the material or place it on tape, neither of which can be done on a day-to-day basis because of the amount of time such tasks require. The use of nonreading material also has the disadvantage of taking the child farther and farther away from reading, thereby not providing opportunities to practice the very skill in which practice is needed.

Whether or not simpler materials can be obtained, the teacher will need to work with children individually or in small groups in directed study situations. This will ensure that children have had experience with essential content and will at the same time provide them with needed assistance in reading. In this way reading becomes a part of the total instructional effort in social studies. Specific techniques for this procedure are discussed later in this chapter.

HOW DOES A TEACHER LEARN ABOUT THE READING LEVELS OF PUPILS?

Elementary teachers in self-contained classrooms provide basic reading instruction to children, and, therefore, should be well acquainted with their reading levels. Unfortunately, however, teachers who may be sensitive to pupil differences in reading ability while conducting reading instruction may ignore those differences when it comes to social studies. Or, they conduct social studies instruction as if those variations in reading ability did not exist. Most elementary teachers have had good training in the teaching of reading, and although they are not expected to do intensive diagnostic work-ups on pupils, they should be able to make informal assessments of pupil performance in reading. We are assuming here, therefore, that through daily contact with pupils in the basal reading program, through standardized test data, and through observation, the teacher already has some understanding of the ability of individual pupils to apply word-attack skills and to comprehend what is read.

In social studies the teacher should regard diagnostic and instructional procedures as two essential components of the same process. Suppose, for example, the teacher wanted to teach a relatively simple skill such as learning to skim to locate facts. As an initial step, the teacher ought to prepare a diagnostic exercise that will indicate how well pupils are able to perform this skill. For example, an exercise such as the following might be devised:

THE CENTRAL ROLE OF READING IN SOCIAL STUDIES

Directions:

1. Open your book to the correct page.
2. Find the answer as quickly as you can.
3. Write your answer in the space.
4. You will have exactly twenty minutes to do the exercise.

(1) Page 117.   What does "VP" mean? _____

(2) Page 121.   The goods and services a worker can get in exchange for his money wages are called

_____

(3) Page 149.   The number of farm workers in 1870 was

_____

(4) Page 152.   The percent of women doctors in the Soviet Union is _____

(5) Page 192.   The cause of the crisis was _____

(6) Page 209.   The number of miles of inland waterways in the United States is _____

(7) Page 209.   The cheapest transportation in the United States is by _____

(8) Page 230.   Places in cities that have no business buildings are called _____

(9) Page 241.   Towns and villages outside large cities are called _____

(10) Page 246. The date San Francisco opened its new Bay Area Rapid Transit—BART—System was ___

_____

If a child cannot do this sample exercise, it may be that he or she cannot read well enough to know what the questions ask him or her to do. In that case the reading instruction must begin with attention to more fundamental skills and abilities relating to decoding and comprehension. However, if the child can read the questions but does not know how to locate the answers quickly through skimming, this skill can be taught and practiced. This sequence—diagnosis, instruction, and follow-up practice—can be applied to any of the social studies skills listed on page 144.

A few other sample exercises are these:

I. *Using Context Clues to Gain Meaning.*

Select the words that belong in the blank spaces in this paragraph from the list of words that follows the paragraph.

The work of the TVA was started by building _____ _____ . A _____ is a wall or bank built across a river to stop its flow. The _____ hold back the water so the rivers do not overflow their banks and cause floods. Lakes, or _____ , are formed behind the _____ . Water from the _____ is allowed to flow into the streams when the rivers are low. This makes them _____ at all times. Power plants were built at the foot of some _____ . These plants _____ , or make, electricity. The electricity generated in the plants supplies _____ and _____ to factories, towns, and farms for a two-hundred-mile area.

reservoirs	navigable	power
generate	dams	light
dam		

II. *Recognizing Topic Sentences.*

Open your book to page 57. This page contains four paragraphs. Read each paragraph and find the sentence that best tells what the paragraph is all about. In the spaces here, write down the beginning two words of the sentences you select.

Paragraph 1. _____   _____

Paragraph 2. _____   _____

Paragraph 3. _____   _____

Paragraph 4. _____   _____

III. *Understanding Terms and Vocabulary.*

Acronyms (AK' - row - nimz) are words that are formed from the first letter of each word in the full name of something. For example, USA is an acronym for United States of America. Acronyms are abbreviated expressions.

Use your text to find the full title of the following acronyms:

1. NATO _____

2. HEW _____

3. TWA _____

4. AFL–CIO _____

_____

5. UN _____

6. NAACP _____

7. DOD _____

INTERN TASK 7-2

Devise three or four appropriate diagnostic and/or practice exercises based on the social studies reading skills listed on page 144 and try them out with your class. Do not use those skills for which examples have been provided in the text.

HOW CAN THE TEXT BE ADAPTED
TO THE READING CAPABILITIES OF PUPILS?

As has already been noted, most social studies programs are structured around textbooks, and children often find texts difficult to read. Therefore, we will discuss in detail how the text can be adapted for use with children with varying reading abilities. For best results the teacher will want to use some combination of these strategies, rather than rely on a single approach.

Using Study Aids

Most social studies textbooks offer the reader a great number of study aids. Figure 7-2 shows the organizational format of a typical book. Left unguided, the child is not apt to make good use of these aids. It is recommended, therefore, that the teacher spend some instructional time on a regular basis acquainting children with ways that they can use the aids provided in the book to achieve more efficient use of it.

SOCIAL STUDIES COMPETENCIES AND SKILLS

The Efficient Reader is constantly on the alert for "editorial comment" in what he reads.[3]

Distinguishing Between Fact and Opinion

In a well-written newspaper, news stories tell what happened; editorials tell the newspaper editors' opinions about what happened. In books, there is no such sharp division. The reader, as you have already been told, must look for words that signal *here is an opinion,* or *here is a conclusion,* or *here is a judgment.* The reader must also be on the alert for opinions, conclusions, and judgments even when no signals announce them.

1. Skim page 539 starting with the sentence "Almost every Argentine . . . ." Where does the author begin to state conclusions?

2. On page 540, read the first sentence. That statement is
   _____ a judgment based on evidence.
   _____ an opinion.

3. Read all of that paragraph and the paragraph that follows. Which statement in those paragraphs would be most difficult to support with specific data?

4. Start reading on page 543 from the subhead "Paraguay under dictators." Where does opinion begin?

5. On page 544, look at the first sentence under "Uruguay's situation today." On what kind of evidence would an author base such a statement? In other words, are there ways of *knowing* when people are "less happy"?

6. On page 551, look at the paragraph beginning "Brazilians are proud . . . ." Which sentences are statements of facts that can be readily checked?

7. On page 552, look at the last paragraph. These sentences are judgments by the author. On what kind of evidence would such judgments be based?

Figure 7-1. Study exercise from a social studies textbook.

[3]Merle Prunty, Bertha Davis, and Ernest B. Fincher, *Lands of Promise* (New York: Macmillan Publishing Company, Inc., 1974), p. 532.

Using the Various Parts of the Book

The social studies text should not be read the way a storybook is read—that is, beginning on the first page and continuing until the book is completed. When a book is used properly, the child will turn to it to get a specific piece of information, to study a map, to look at an illustration, to find out how to pronounce a technical term, and so on. If a book is to be used in this way, the child must be familiar with its various parts and must know where to look in order to find the needed information.

It cannot be assumed that the child will learn how to make intelligent use of the various parts of a book through a single presentation. This skill, as is the case in most skills, must be taught, retaught, and practiced many times over a period of several years. Each time the presentation and application become a bit more sophisticated until the desired level of proficiency is attained. Many exercises can be devised to provide practice in using parts of a book. The following is an example of one:

In the left-hand column are listed the parts of your book. In the right-hand column are listed some things you might want to find out about. For each item in the right-hand column, tell what part of the book you would turn to first in order to get the information.

Parts of Your Book	You Want to Know
Title page	The meaning of "alliance"
Copyright page	The number of units in the book
Preface	How to say the word *anthracite*
Table of contents	When the book was published
List of maps	The population of the state of
List of illustrations	Maryland
Glossary	The date Lewis and Clark started on
Pronunciation key	their expedition
Appendix	What a prairie schooner looks like
Index	The route followed by the Mormons
	to Utah
	Whether the book tells anything about
	Mexico

SOCIAL STUDIES COMPETENCIES AND SKILLS

UNIT 3. LIFE WAYS AROUND THE WORLD ←——————————————

CHAPTER SEVEN – THE EARTH AS THE HOME OF MANY PEOPLE ←—————

How Do People Use the Earth?

Where Do People Live on the Earth?

How Are People Alike in What They Need? ←—————

How Are People Different in the Way They Live?

Soon the days become shorter. Often one can see birds flying south. Nearly every night the temperature drops below freezing. The *growing season* is over even though there may still be many warm days. The growing season is that time between the last killing frost in the spring and the first killing frost in the fall.

Finding the Main Ideas ←—————

Go back to the section called "How Do People Use the Earth?" on page 212. Which of the following is the main idea of that section?

a. All people must have certain things from the earth in order to live.

b. People who live in cities need the earth less than people who live on farms.

Understanding Key Words and Terms ←

Producer   Exchange   Culture

Use these words to complete the paragraph below

In every _____ people _____ goods and

services. How people _____ etc. . . .

Using What You Have Learned ←—————

On page 143 there are listed several fire hazards . . .

Getting the Facts ←—————

Skim the section "How Do People Use the Earth?" on page 212 and tell which of the following statements are true:

Thinking About What You Have Read . . . ←—————

Why do you suppose . . .

Figure 7-2. Typical organizational format of social studies textbooks.

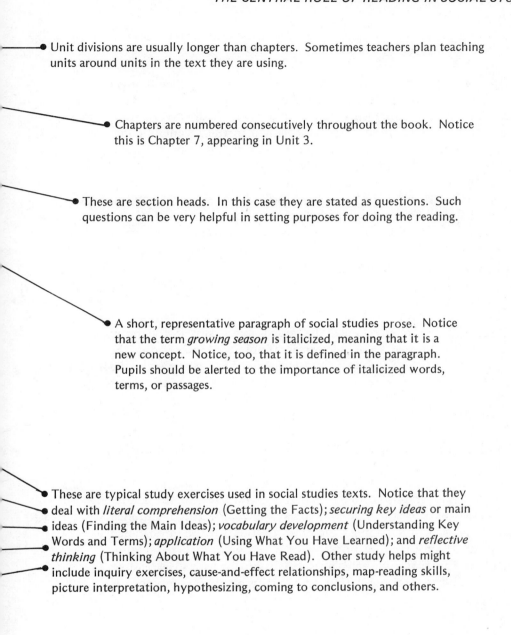

Unit divisions are usually longer than chapters. Sometimes teachers plan teaching units around units in the text they are using.

Chapters are numbered consecutively throughout the book. Notice this is Chapter 7, appearing in Unit 3.

These are section heads. In this case they are stated as questions. Such questions can be very helpful in setting purposes for doing the reading.

A short, representative paragraph of social studies prose. Notice that the term *growing season* is italicized, meaning that it is a new concept. Notice, too, that it is defined in the paragraph. Pupils should be alerted to the importance of italicized words, terms, or passages.

These are typical study exercises used in social studies texts. Notice that they deal with *literal comprehension* (Getting the Facts); *securing key ideas* or main ideas (Finding the Main Ideas); *vocabulary development* (Understanding Key Words and Terms); *application* (Using What You Have Learned); and *reflective thinking* (Thinking About What You Have Read). Other study helps might include inquiry exercises, cause-and-effect relationships, map-reading skills, picture interpretation, hypothesizing, coming to conclusions, and others.

Using the Organization of the Book.

Authors and publishers organize social studies texts in ways that will make it easy for the reader to make good use of them. Pupils need direct instruction to familiarize them with the organization of the text. Ordinarily this is explained in the teacher's guide that accompanies the book. At the beginning of the year, the book should be previewed to show the pupils how it is organized into units, chapters, sections, study aids, and so on. Then as the book is used, frequent reminders will help to illustrate how the book's organization can assist the reader in finding needed information.

Each series of social studies texts has its own unique organizational style. Figure 7-2 depicts a format that is representative of the scheme used by many social studies series.

Using Topic Sentences.

Reading comprehension can be aided materially if the pupil understands the use of topic sentences. Topic sentences bring the reader directly to the idea being presented. Other sentences in the paragraph simply elaborate on the main idea. If the reader cannot separate the main idea from the subordinate or supporting ideas, he or she may become lost in the detail and miss the significance of what is being presented. A little instruction and practice will, in most cases, prove to be beneficial in building this skill, thereby improving comprehension.

In children's material the topic sentence is usually the first sentence in a paragraph, although that is not always the case. Therefore, practice exercises should not always have the topic sentence come first. This will encourage the child to look for the importance of the idea rather than the position of a sentence in a paragraph. Being able to identify topic sentences assists writing as well as reading skills. A sample exercise relating to identifying topic sentences is given on page 148.

Using Picture Captions.

Pictures and illustrations elaborate concepts presented in the narrative but usually do not repeat exactly what is said in the text. Neither do picture captions simply tell what would be obvious to the reader only by looking at the picture. Thus, captions should call attention to some element or relationship in the picture or illustration that might be missed by the casual viewer. Often this is done by using a question or series of questions. In this way pictures and illustrations can provide the reader with a wealth of information. In teaching children how to use pictures and illustrations they find in their texts, questions such as these may be appropriate:

1. Exactly what is being shown in the picture?
2. What relationships are illustrated by the picture?
3. When was this picture taken? (recently, years ago, time of day, and so on)
4. How does the picture illustrate something we discussed in class?
5. What influences (causes or effects) can be detected in the picture?
6. What does the picture tell about the life-styles of the people?
7. How does the picture illustrate something valued by people?
8. How does the picture show conflicts between traditional and modern ways of doing things?
9. What does the picture show that illustrates the roles of men, women, and children in that society?
10. What characteristics of the culture are shown in the picture?
11. What can you say about the geography of the area shown by the picture?
12. What conversation might be going on between the persons in the picture?

Building a Social Studies Vocabulary.

Most social studies texts provide extensive study aids to assist with vocabulary development. This includes any or all of the following:

1. Contextual definition of words and terms.
   Examples: Thousands of persons in this city earn their living by *processing* food. Processing means preparing food for marketing.

   In recent years people have become concerned about *pollution*. Pollution comes about when something harmful is placed into the water or air.

2. Use of boldface type and/or italics.
   Examples: The things from which products are made are called **raw materials**. Three *raw materials*—iron ore, coal, and limestone—are found in the Midwest.
3. End of unit, chapter, or section exercises.
   Examples: Matching exercises.
   Selecting terms for incomplete sentences.
   Finding definitions of key terms in the text.
4. Glossaries.
   Examples:

Pig iron:	melted iron that hardens into bars
Pilgrim:	a person who travels to holy places to worship
Plantation:	a large farm that specializes in one crop
Polar regions:	areas in the high latitudes

5. Pronunciation guide.
   Examples: tropics   (trop′ iks)
   volcano   (vol-ka′ no)

Generally, it is better to clear up the meanings of critical terms before or during the reading of a selection rather than after the reading is completed. Many social studies terms have multiple meanings, and, therefore, *new terms and words should be introduced and explained in context rather than in isolation.* For example:

- He established the first *bank* in the region.
- The river overflowed its left *bank*.
- "You can *bank* on that," he said.
- Directly ahead was a big *bank* of snow.
- As he looked west, he could see a large *bank* of clouds.
- Just before crashing, the plane seemed to *bank* to the left.
- The assembly line consisted of a long *bank* of machines.

When terms that have multiple meanings are encountered in a passage to be read, only the meanings being used in the passage should be developed at that time and they should be developed in context.

Directed Study

Social studies texts are not designed to be self-instructing. The authors expect that teachers will direct the pupils' use of the book.

In this connection the teacher should study the teacher's guide in order to use the text in accordance with the way it was designed to be used. In general the following guidelines are important in directing the pupils' use of a textbook:

Preview Material to Be Studied. Work with the class as one whole group. Ask the children to open their books to the section or unit to be studied and leaf through it to get the general idea of the topic. Such a preview provides a good opportunity to call attention to the organizational format, important maps and illustrations, and terms that are critical to the understanding of the topic. Attention should also be called to the study aids included. The teacher may want to raise speculative questions concerning the content and encourage children to hypothesize about relationships that seem to be apparent to them. Perhaps especially interesting or highly motivating passages that are a few sentences in length can be read by the teacher, simply to set the tone of the material to be read. No attempt should be made to read the entire selection in detail at this point. That will come later. Now all that is wanted is an overview.

Attend to Word Difficulties. Clarify as matters of fact the meanings of words without creating the impression that some words are expected to be difficult. To call attention to difficult words may simply suggest to children that they *should* have a problem with particular words. The types of words that need attention in social studies can be grouped as follows:

- *Technical terms.* Words, terms, and expressions peculiar to social studies and usually not encountered when reading selections from other fields of knowledge. *Examples*: veto, meridian, frontier, latitude, longitude, legislature, polls, franchise, temperate, plateau, hemisphere, mountainous, wasteland, balance of power, capitalism, democracy, nationalism, civilization, century, ancient, and decade.
- *Figurative terms.* Metaphorical expressions; having a different connotation from the literal meaning usually associated with the word. *Examples*: political platform, cold war, closed shop, iron curtain, logrolling, pork barrel, open door, and hat in the ring.
- *Words with multiple meanings.* Words with identical spelling but whose meaning is derived from context. *Examples*: cabinet, belt, bill, chamber, mouth, bank, revolution, fork, court, assembly, and range.

- *Terms peculiar to a locality.* Expressions peculiar to a specific part of the country that are not commonly used elsewhere. *Examples*: truck, meeting, borough, gandy, draw, coulee, right, prairie, section, run, butte, and arroyo.
- *Words easily confused with other words.* Words that are very similar in general configuration. *Examples*: peasant for pheasant, alien for allies, principal for principle, longitude for latitude, executive for execution, and conversation for conservation.
- *Acronyms.* Abbreviated expressions. *Examples*: NATO, HEW, TVA, NAACP, CIO–AFL, and UN.
- *Quantitative terms.* Words and terms signifying amounts of time, space, or objects. *Examples*: shortly after, century, fortnight, several years later, score, and 150 tons.

Establish Purposes for Doing the Reading. When a child reads a storybook, the reading is ordinarily done simply for enjoyment. This contrasts sharply with reading a social studies book, which is intended to serve other purposes. The child may not understand this essential difference between the reading requirements of the two different types of materials. Consequently, in assigning material to be read from the social studies text, the teacher should specify the purposes for doing the reading. This will usually take the form of guide questions, many of which may be provided by the text itself in the way of study aids. For example, some texts use the question format for sections in the book, thus indicating to the reader what the narrative discusses in that section:[4]

How did Spanish influence in the Southwest start and grow?
How did Texas become a state?
How was Oklahoma settled?
How do people in the South Central states earn a living?

Some texts provide a list of questions at the beginning of sections, quite apart from the section title, that are intended to serve as purposes for reading. This is a better procedure than placing questions

[4]The reader will note that this text is organized in this way—that is, each of the section heads is a question that in turn corresponds to the competencies listed at the beginning of the chapters. These questions are intended to serve as purposes for doing the reading.

at the end of a section. A child should not have to read the selection before finding out why he or she was reading the selection in the first place. This kind of purposeless reading in social studies undoubtedly accounts for much ineffective reading. If the text does not provide questions to set purposes, the teacher must do so.

Questions to serve as purposes for reading should focus on the essential information presented in the selection to be read. They should not be discussion questions that require reflection. Such questions can be used later, after the material has been read and the essential content and concepts are understood. Compare how these two types of questions might serve as purposes for reading a selection:

1. Questions that *are* well suited for setting purposes for reading:
    a. What discovery brought many settlers to Colorado?
    b. To what nation did most of the land in this region once belong?
    c. Why is there little vegetation in many areas of the Rocky Mountain states?
    d. Name at least three ways in which dams help the people of this region.
    e. What are some important uses of copper? Where is copper mined?
    f. What are some of the places in the Rocky Mountain states that tourists like to visit?

2. Questions that are *not* well suited for setting purposes for reading:
    a. If pioneers of a hundred years ago could see the Rocky Mountain states today, what changes would attract their attention?
    b. How do you think the "mountain men" were helpful to the pioneers who came later?
    c. How might the West have developed if it had not been for the discovery of gold?
    d. Who do you think should be held responsible for the erosion of land during the Dust Bowl years?

Vary the Rate of Reading. Earlier in this chapter we discussed the skill of skimming a passage in order to find a specific fact. When doing such reading, the eyes of the reader race quickly over the page. No attempt is made to comprehend the details of the narrative. Indeed, in reading for the purpose of finding a specific fact, it would be inefficient to read every word and understand every detail. If, on the other hand, the pupil were reading a selection in order to arrange the ideas in degrees of importance, as in constructing an outline, the reading would have to be done slowly, deliberately, with careful attention to the details, and most importantly, with critical thought being given to the ideas presented in the selection. The tendency is to read everything at the same speed, but obviously the rate of reading must be governed by the purpose for which the reading is done.

The teacher can use the social studies text to devise performance exercises and tests that will provide pupils with practice in varying their rates of reading. If some children are reading too slowly for a particular purpose, they can be given practice to read more rapidly. If others are reading too rapidly, the practice exercises should demand a high level of comprehension that can be achieved only if the reading is done more slowly and thoughtfully. All of this can be and should be a regular part of the on-going social studies program of instruction.

INTERN TASK 7-3

Devise four practice exercises requiring differing *rates of reading* as follows:

1. Identify a purpose for reading a selection.
2. Select an appropriate text passage for such a purpose.
3. Develop follow-up questions that are based on the stated purpose.

Have these practice exercises approved by your field associate teacher and then use them with the class you are teaching.

Check Reading Comprehension. Varying reading rates and checking comprehension, of course, go hand in hand. The object is to read as rapidly as possible with a degree of accuracy and comprehension that is in accordance with the purposes for which the material is being read. Earlier in this discussion we stressed the importance of setting purposes prior to having children read if we expect them to read with understanding. Equally important is some type of follow-up check on the extent to which the material has been read accurately and with understanding. Naturally, the exercise that checks level of comprehension should be consistent with the purposes that were set for doing the reading.

Typically, textbooks provide questions to check reading comprehension. They are usually found in the study aids at the ends of sections, chapters, and units under such headings as "Finding the Facts," "Remembering What We Read," "Recalling Important Ideas and Facts," "Getting Important Ideas," and so on. If these exercises are not available in the text, or if the ones provided are for some reason not suitable for the particular class, the teacher should construct them.

Selective Use

In addition to making good use of the study aids and directing the pupils' study of the textbook, the teacher can also make selective use of the text in accordance with the reading capabilities of individual pupils. There is no reason for every child to read all of the narrative, study every picture, map, and illustration, and do every study exercise. Children who are capable, mature readers should not have to do the study exercises that are intended to assist the poor reader. These more capable readers should move on to exercises that involve application, interpretation, or analysis. In the texts these are usually called "Thinking It Over," "Sensing Relationships," "Applying What You Have Read," and so on. Having read the text with understanding, these pupils should move to other kinds of exercises, activities, and projects.

With the children who read less well, the teacher should make use of those text exercises that relate to reading skill building: vocabulary and concept development, literal comprehension, and securing basic information. This probably means that only portions of the text need to be read by the pupils. In some cases the basic information can be secured by reading only the topic sentences. In other cases the needed information can be obtained by making use of the visuals in the text. In classes where there are pupils who are having an inordinate amount of difficulty reading the material, the teacher should meet with those pupils as a group and direct their study of the text. If the number of pupils having such problems is large, they should be divided into two groups. In directed study situations of this type, it is expected that the teacher will be selective in what is treated, giving attention only to the most essential parts of the text.

What we are seeking is a diversified use of the text. Because each child has a textbook does not mean that the book is used by each in the same way. Neither does it mean that a book has no value for a child if he or she has difficulty reading it. Social studies textbooks are sources of data in which the information is presented in charts, maps, graphs, and pictures, as well as in the printed word.

INTERN TASK 7-4

Using the social studies textbook adopted by the class to which you are assigned, select one section and identify those portions you would use in working with slower-reading pupils. Also indicate how you would use the same section with more capable readers. Discuss your ideas with your field associate teacher and use them with the pupils you are teaching.

HOW DOES A TEACHER USE READING MATERIALS OTHER THAN THE TEXTBOOK?

Most of our discussion thus far has been structured around the textbook. The text, however, is not the only reading resource available to pupils and it may not even be the best one. Nonetheless, in dealing with reading social studies materials of any type, the principles discussed in connection with the use of the text apply: setting the purposes for reading, varying reading rates, clarifying terms and concepts, checking comprehension, and so on.

This writer is not aware of any elementary school social studies specialist who would suggest that a single textbook is in itself an adequate learning resource for a modern program in social studies education. There is today a wide range of materials in print that can and should be available to children in social studies. Here are some examples:

1. Classroom periodicals, such as those in the *Scholastic* series and *My Weekly Reader.*
2. Magazines.
3. Pamphlets.
4. Encyclopedias.
5. Trade books, including
   a. Informative accounts on such topics as trucks, trains, communication systems, homes around the world, the law, drug use, and so forth.
   b. Informative fiction in which historical events are reconstructed around a fictionalized plot.
   c. Biographies.
   d. History.
   e. Poems.

   f. Locally produced materials.
   g. Paperbacks.
6. Lyrics to songs and ballads.
7. Selected adult newspaper articles.
8. Free and inexpensive materials.

When using nontext reading resources, the teacher may want to place the material in a social studies or reading learning center in the classroom to make it easy for pupils to use on an individual basis. Much of it can be selected by the pupils if it is organized appropriately and is easily accessible. Professor Ann Bohler of Ball State University has prepared several study exercises for pupils based on nontext resources. One that she shares with her students is offered here:

Let's Visit the Past

Pretend that we can take a time machine to the past to visit one of the people we have studied, such as Benjamin Franklin or Dolly Madison. Who would you like to visit? What were this person's interests when about your age? Read one of the books in the learning center to get more information. Then complete the activity below. You are to pack a trunk with ten items to take with you in the time machine. What would you take? Why would you take them? Do you think your host or hostess would like them? Why or why not?

Name of host or hostess _____

Where and when he/she lived _____

His/her interests _____

What would you take? _____

  1. _____
  2. _____
  3. _____
  4. _____
  5. _____
  6. _____
  7. _____
  8. _____
  9. _____
 10. _____

Figure 7-3. A study exercise based on nontextbooks in a learning center. (Courtesy of Professor Ann Bohler, Ball State University, Muncie, Indiana. Used by permission.)

The nontext reading assignment may also be negotiated with individual pupils through a contract, as discussed on page 111. Still another way to get children and materials together is through the use of Task Cards. (See Figure 7-4.)

SIDE ONE

Find Out for Yourself

(If you cannot do any one of these, look for a clue on SIDE TWO of this card.)

1. Find the article on "Safety" in the *World Book.*
2. Into how many sections is the article divided? _____
3. Skim through the article to find these two facts:
   a. Where do most accidents happen? _____

   b. What do the letters *UL* on electrical wiring and appliances stand for? _____
   _____

4. Suppose you heard that someone had been killed in an accident in his or her home but you did not know what kind of an accident it was. You would be right most of the time if you guessed that the accident was a _____

   or a _____ or _____ .
5. Suppose you questioned the accuracy of this article. What is there about the article that might renew your confidence in its authority? _____
   _____

Figure 7-4. An example of teacher-prepared task cards.

SIDE TWO

CLUES

1. Select volume S–Sn. Look for the article according to the alphabet.

2. See the "Outline" at the end of the article.

3. a. Look under the section "Safety/Home."
   b. Look under "Safety with Electricity."

4. What does the article say about the major causes of accidental deaths in the home?

5. What group critically reviewed the article?

Elaborate study sequences can be structured around trade books, as is illustrated by the following excerpt from the *Teachers' Resource Guide* prepared by the Illinois Bicentennial Commission:

JOHNNY TREMAIN [5]

(Time: Flexible: Gr. 7–8)

RATIONALE

Johnny Tremain, by Esther Forbes, winner of the Newbery Medal in 1944, is the story of Boston in turmoil. Through the fictional characters, historic personages, historic events, and the times presented in this historical novel, young readers will gain insight into "rebellious Boston" and appreciation of the roles young people played in the struggle for independence.

OBJECTIVES

To allow students the experience of sharing literature related to the Revolutionary period; (in the era of individualization of reading, this can be a new experience for the group to read the same book; it can also be a stimulating activity.) to gain appreciation of good prose writing through reading the historical novel; to create awareness of the causes of the Revolution and the reasons for Boston's being a significant center of protest by reading *Johnny Tremain;* to gain insight into the lives and activities of young people in this historic period while discussing the story.

STRATEGY

Time should be spent in introducing the author to the students. As an introduction and as a motivational factor the teacher can read the trial scene or use excerpts from the record, if available. Then the teacher should establish the setting of the book. (Alternative methods of reading are students reading individually or participating in oral interpretations, reading selected passages; teacher/librarian reading selected sections to the group.)

Other activities for in-depth study for interested students follow:

(1) Have students prepare a large map which depicts Boston, Concord, and Lexington. (Include location of places important in the story, i.e. route taken by Revere, Dawes, and Prescott.)

(2) Give a Reader's Theatre presentation.

(3) Have students dramatize certain events such as Johnny's visits to the Lyte home, the trial, and meetings of the Sons of Liberty.

(4) Teach students to appreciate the culture of the period such as **(a)** poetry—"Concord Hymn," R. W. Emerson; **(b)** music—"Yankee Doodle," "Tea Tax Song"; **(c)** painting—"Spirit of '76," "Boston Massacre."

(5) Involve students in research activities such as the life and activities of historic personages in *Johnny Tremain;* "Sons of Liberty"; battles of the war; the continental soldier; historic account of Paul Revere's ride vs. "The Midnight Ride of Paul Revere" by H. W. Longfellow; apprentices in colonial America.

EVALUATION

Should reveal the following: Have the students reacted favorably to this project? Have they indicated enjoyment and challenge? Has there been reinforcement in the understanding of the role Boston played in the struggle for independence? Have they identified with any of the literary characters in the book? The assessment of the project can be direct and informal. Students can respond in writing.

MATERIALS NEEDED

(1) Books: Paperback copies of *Johnny Tremain* for each student; regular edition of *Johnny Tremain; Paul Revere and the World He Lived In,* Esther Forbes; *Songs of '76: A Folksinger's History of the Revolution.*

(2) Recordings: "Johnny Tremain" (Miller-Brody. Available in cassette); "America's Fight for Freedom in Story and Song" (O'Neill).

(3) Pamphlets: *Boston,* Know Your America Series, Doubleday; *Boston Tea Party,* Know Your America Series, Doubleday.

(4) Periodicals: *American Heritage* (selected issues containing the series, "Men of the Revolution" and "Battles of the Revolution"); *American History Illustrated,* October, 1971, and April, 1972.

(5) Visuals: "American Revolution: The Cause of Liberty" and "American Revolution: The Impossible War" from *American Heritage* series of color films; maps of colonial Boston and environs; slides and filmstrips of historic sites in Boston and surrounding area.

Figure 7-5. A study exercise based on a trade book.

---

[5] Illinois Bicentennial Commission, *Teachers' Resource Guide* (Chicago: Rand McNally & Co., 1975), p. 23.

INTERN TASK 7-5

Select a trade book suitable for use in the grade to which you have been assigned. Prepare a study sequence similar to the *Johnny Tremain* example. You may use the example as a model for the development of your own material. Discuss your plans with your field associate teacher; then use it with the pupils you are teaching.

HOW CAN SOCIAL STUDIES CONTENT BE USED TO ENHANCE GENERAL READING SKILLS?

In this chapter we have repeatedly stressed the importance of reading as a learning skill in social studies. We also have indicated that the teaching of reading skills must be an essential component of the social studies program. Reading competence can be enhanced through the social studies in at least three ways:

Directed Study Strategies

These strategies have already been discussed in this chapter in the section dealing with the use of the textbook. They are a carefully guided program of instruction that focuses on the content of the topic under study. The purpose is not so much to improve reading directly as to make certain that the pupils understand the basic content they are studying. Nevertheless, when this happens, the reading ability as well as social studies achievement is enhanced, resulting in an important positive side effect for the pupil.

Diversified Materials Strategies

These strategies are based on the availability and use of a wide range of reading materials with the thought of matching appropriate materials with the reading abilities of individual pupils. These approaches are of necessity highly individualized, which makes them attractive to pupils and teachers. The concern in this case is to provide each child with a manageable reading task that is related to the topic under study. The accommodation to reading ability variation is made through custom tailoring the reading material with particular attention to conceptual and structural complexity. The use of highly motivating, interesting materials makes reading them an irresistible temptation; in the process the child's reading skills are improved.

Improvement of Reading Strategies

This set of strategies, as opposed to the prior two, improves reading skills through the use of social studies materials and content. The social studies content is not regarded as unimportant, but the teacher does not attach the degree of importance to it that is assigned to the ability to read. The social studies curriculum, therefore, is an extension of the basic reading program. There is much to be said for this approach, particularly as it applies to the primary grades. In fact, one might argue that both the basic reading program and the social studies program would be improved if there existed a close functional relationship between these two basic curriculum areas.

SOCIAL STUDIES COMPETENCIES AND SKILLS

CHECKING YOUR PERFORMANCE

Intern Task Checklist

Task 7-1. a. Finding examples of reading skills used in the text. P. 144 _____

b. Building reading skills into the primary grade program where a textbook is not used. P. 144 _____

Task 7-2 Devising diagnostic and/or practice exercises based on social studies reading skills. P. 149 _____

Task 7-3. Devising practice exercises requiring differing rates of reading. P. 160 _____

Task 7-4. Adapting the text to varying pupil capabilities. P. 162 _____

Task 7-5. Developing teaching plans based on a trade book. P. 166 _____

Performance Checklist

In the field or in the clinic, the intern teacher has

1. Developed suitable teaching and practice exercises for a selected number (three or four) of the reading skills that are important to social studies. _____

2. Identified in conversation or in writing factors that contribute to a classroom climate that supports reading. _____

3. Devised diagnostic exercises based on reading skills that are essential to social studies. _____

4. Adapted and used the textbook to suit varying reading abilities of pupils in the classroom. _____

5. Had experience in selecting and using trade books and other non-textbook materials to suit the varying reading abilities of pupils in the class. _____

6. Used social studies subject matter and instructional materials to improve pupils' reading skills. _____

Field Associate Teacher Advisory

Tasks and performances should be checked off or initialed and dated by the appropriate local official, or the intern teacher can use the checklists for his or her own record.

Chapter 8

Space and time dimensions of social studies: concepts and skills

"I am amazed at how many things you are able to teach in connection with current events," Nadine Jackson said to her field associate teacher, Carole Robb. "Just today, on that Africa thing, the children were using maps and graphs, they were associating present events with the past, and they were analyzing news stories in a thoughtful way. You were even able to project their thinking into the future when you asked them to speculate on what they thought the situation might be like fifty years from now, when most of the present leaders will have been replaced."

"You are a perceptive observer, Nadine," Ms. Robb responded. "It's nice to have things turn out the way one plans them—at least once in awhile! The fact is there is so much we need to teach in social studies, all of which is important, that we simply have to find ways of doubling up—getting extra mileage so to speak, from the things we do. I have found that skills that are essentially tools for learning and for handling data often can be effectively taught along with the subject matter. Skills and concepts such as those associated with reading maps and globes, interpreting graphs and charts, and orienting children to time and chronology can be very effectively applied in connection with current events."

"You shouldn't give me all that much credit for my observation skills, Ms. Robb. It just happened that our clinic instructor was discussing the need to attain multiple objectives simultaneously in the last clinic session. As a result, I was alerted to look for what I saw

170

SOCIAL STUDIES COMPETENCIES AND SKILLS

you doing so well this morning. A week ago it might all have gone
over my head. But what I don't understand is how you can get a
sequentially planned program this way. It seems to me to be a pretty
chancy way to develop a program. Aren't the risks of omitting important skills increased when you teach them this way?" Nadine asked.

"They certainly would be," said Ms. Robb, "if we relied entirely
on this way of teaching them. What I do is to combine the kinds of
teaching you saw this morning with direct teaching of these skills.
I don't ask pupils to apply the skills as you saw them doing unless the
skills have actually been taught beforehand. Sometimes news events
also provide an opportunity to introduce and teach a new variation of
a skill. I use this skills chart we developed in the district as a guide to
ensure that all important skills are taught during the year. That
provides for the sequential and systematic development you were concerned about."

Carole Robb showed the intern, Nadine Jackson, the skills chart
adopted by the district. It was prepared by a committee of teachers,
with the help of a specialist, and was based on a sequence developed
by two authors for a yearbook of the National Council for the Social
Studies. Nadine Jackson could see how the local committee was
influenced by the NCSS statement as it identified the following skills
as those that "are a major responsibility of the social studies":
(1) reading social studies materials, (2) applying problem-solving
and critical-thinking skills to social issues, (3) interpreting maps and
globes, and (4) understanding time and chronology.[1]

It was evident, too, that Ms. Willis, the clinic instructor, believed
these skills to be essential to social studies education because they
were reflected in the list of basic competencies she provided the
interns:

Basic Competencies—Social Studies

The intern teacher is able to

1. Explain the significance of the time and space dimensions
   of social studies education.

---

[1] Eunice Johns and Dorothy McClure Fraser, "Social Studies Skills: A Guide to Analysis and Grade Placement" in *Skill Development in Social Studies,* thirty-third yearbook, ed.
Helen McCracken Carpenter (Washington, D.C.: National Council for the Social Studies,
1963), p. 311.

2. Identify map and globe skills that are an essential part of the social studies program.
3. Plan for, locate, and use learning experiences and learning resources to teach map and globe concepts and skills.
4. Help children develop a sense of time and chronology.
5. Make use of current affairs to teach social studies concepts and skills.
6. Teach children to read and interpret data presented in the form of graphs, charts, and cartoons.

INTERN ADVISORY

After completing this chapter, together with related work in the clinic and appropriate classroom experiences in the field, you should be able to do the following:

1. Describe social studies teaching situations in which dimensions of time and space are essential to understanding the ideas being presented, and explain the significance of time and space to social studies education.
2. Identify six broad categories of map-reading skills and provide two examples of each.
3. Identify five learning activities appropriate for a grade of your choice that could be used in teaching map and globe skills and list learning resources needed to carry out each activity.
4. Conduct a teaching episode that involves instructional attention to time and chronology.
5. Plan and teach a lesson based on a current news event.
6. Plan and teach lessons that require the use of skills associated with graphs, charts, and cartoons.

WHY ARE TIME AND SPACE ORIENTATIONS AN ESSENTIAL PART OF SOCIAL STUDIES EDUCATION?

Suppose someone came into a roomful of people and announced, "There has been a disastrous earthquake!" What would be said by the others present? One can predict with a high level of confidence that the next things to be said would be,

"Where did it happen?"
"When did it happen?"

Only after these questions were answered would there be an interest in whether anyone was injured and the extent of the damage. Events hold little meaning for us unless we know the *place* and the *time* of their occurrence. Consequently, in social studies we find ourselves constantly making references to *where* something happened and *when* it happened. Such references to time and place may be specific, such as Lexington, Massachusetts, April 18, 1775; or they may be general, such as "a long time ago, in the area where three continents meet." These definite and indefinite references to time and space also involve *quantitative* concepts:

Space	*Time*
A great distance	Soon thereafter
Forty miles	A long journey
1,500 acres	Three decades
Largest continent	Four centuries earlier
55,000 square miles	A fortnight later
23½° north latitude	A four-hour interval

Both definite and indefinite references to time and space can be bothersome for children. For example, if children read that Columbus's ship, the *Santa Maria,* was 98 feet long, such a reference to distance probably will mean something different to every child in the class. It might be conceptualized as a distance ranging from one not greater than the length of the classroom to one of several city blocks. When there is such confusion over a relatively simple and definite reference to distance, one can only speculate on the misunderstandings that must abound when we use such references as the following:

A township was to be a square, six miles long on each side. Each township was to be divided into thirty-six sections. A section, therefore, was one mile square and had 640 acres in it.

The research that has been conducted on time, space, and quantitative concepts in social studies confirms that children often misunderstand them. The tendency is to overestimate the ability of children to handle such concepts. As a result, maps often are used that are more complex than they should be in view of the maturity of the children using them. Also children may make and use time lines that they really do not comprehend. Because children so easily verbalize quantitative concepts such as decade, century, thousands, hundreds, several miles, many years, and 10 per cent, the assumption is that they are understood. Research on this subject indicates that such assumptions are often in error.

When the abstractness of these concepts is reduced, they are made meaningful to children. We try, therefore, to provide children with a concrete reference to space and time, preferably one that is a part of their experiences. This is why current news events provide such a good vehicle for teaching some concepts and skills. The children read about current happenings in the classroom periodical or hear and see them reported on radio and television news. Thus, finding places on a map is a natural extension of everyday experiences.

The social studies curriculum operates within a matrix that might be represented very simply as follows:

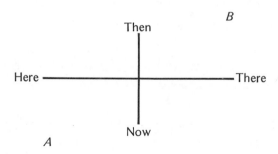

Experiences that could be charted at point *A* would be the least abstract and would usually be found in the early grades. Experiences at point *B* would be most difficult to make concrete for children because they are remote not only in space but also in time. Because many children today have firsthand experiences that acquaint them with places beyond their immediate environment, it is not as necessary to confine the social studies program to the local area as it once was. There can be more movement from the near at hand to the faraway even at early grade levels. This is more difficult to do with the time dimension, however. The reality of events of the past needs to be tied to the present, again calling attention to the importance of using current news events.

There are many instructional aids that can help one deal with these complex concepts, provided one has the skills to use them. For example, globes and maps are indispensable tools for working with space and spatial relationships. Time lines and charts can make time and chronology meaningful. Graphs and tables can make some types of quantitative relationships easier to comprehend. It is imperative, therefore, that the social studies program teach children how to use these tools.

INTERN TASK 8-1

a. Identify an event currently in the news that might be suitable for use with the children you are teaching. Then identify space, time, and quantitative concepts that relate to that event. Explain how you would teach them.
b. Select ten pages at random from an elementary school social studies textbook. Identify all the space, time, and quantitative concepts you find on those pages. Comment on how well you think the meanings of these concepts are developed in the text.

WHICH MAP AND GLOBE SKILLS ARE ESSENTIAL TO THE SOCIAL STUDIES CURRICULUM?

Maps and globes are vehicles for representing space symbolically. The essential features of all maps and globes are a gridwork, color, scale, symbols, and a legend that explains the symbol system used. The ability to read and interpret maps and globes, like conventional reading, is a summarizing skill in that it represents a composite of several subskills. These subskills can be inferred by making an analysis of the behavior of someone reading a map who is skillful at it. Fortunately, this will not be necessary because it has been done by specialists several times and always with somewhat the same results. One list that has been widely used by school districts throughout the nation in developing their map and globe skill sequence appears in two yearbooks of the National Council for the Social Studies:

1. Ability to orient the map and to note directions.
2. Ability to recognize the scale of a map and to compute distances.

3. Ability to locate places on maps and globes by means of grid systems.
4. Ability to express relative locations.
5. Ability to read map symbols.
6. Ability to compare maps and to make inferences.[2]

Directional Orientation

In order to deal with directional relationships on maps and globes, the child must first understand them in reality. The easiest directions to use are those that express relative location, such as close to, near, over here, and over there. These can be learned in the primary grades. The cardinal directions are also learned in the primary grades by having them pointed out and by referring to places that are known to children as being north of, east of, south of, and so on. Placing direction labels on the various walls of the classroom helps remind children of cardinal directions. They can associate east and west with the rising and setting of the sun. They can learn how a compass is used to find direction. While on field trips, children should be given practice in noting directions, observing especially the directions of streets and roads. Gradually, pupils learn the purpose of the poles, the meridians of longitude, and the parallels of latitude in orienting a map and noting directions. When maps with unfamiliar projections are introduced, pupils should be taught how to establish correct directional relationships on them.

Using Map Scales

In making a map the cartographer tries to reproduce as accurately as possible that portion of the earth being represented. Because globes are models of the earth, they can show the earth more correctly than can maps. No map can altogether faithfully represent the earth simply

---

[2]This list was developed by Professor Clyde F. Kohn for the 1953 NCSS yearbook. It is cited and elaborated on by Dean Lorrin Kennamer, "Developing a Sense of Place and Space," in *Skill Development in Social Studies,* ibid., pp. 157 ff. The chart in the appendix of that yearbook provides a list of related subskills along with a suggested curriculum sequence.

because the earth is round and maps are flat. The flattening process inevitably results in some distortion.

Scaling is the process of reducing everything in the same amount. In working with children in the primary grades, scaling should be done in the relative sense. Some things are larger or smaller than other things and the maps should show their *relative* size as accurately as possible. For example, a 50-foot high tree in the schoolyard should be about five times larger than the 10-foot-tall playground set. On conventional maps, three types of scales are used:

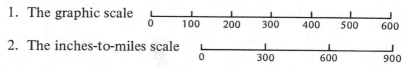

1. The graphic scale

    0   100   200   300   400   500   600

2. The inches-to-miles scale

    0   300   600   900

3. The representative fraction   1:250,000.

Of these, the graphic scale is the easiest to use and can be taught at about fourth grade. The inches-to-miles scale is more complex, but it can also be taught in the middle grades. The representative fraction is usually considered beyond the scope of the elementary school program.

Locating Places

The ability to locate places on maps and globes comes with a familiarity with these devices cultivated over a period of several years. Children first learn to locate places that are known to them on simple maps and layouts that they make in the classroom. In the early grades, too, children can learn the names and shapes of some of the major geographic features, such as continents, oceans, the equator, and the poles. The commercially prepared maps and globes designed for the lower grades are quite plain, having only a few features shown. Gradually, children increase their repertoire of known places they can find on the map and globe because of frequent references to the location of important cities, countries, rivers, mountains, and other physical features.

In the middle grades, children are taught to use coordinates to locate places. Local highway maps are well suited for use in teaching this skill because they deal with an area familiar to the children.

One set of lines of the gridwork—perhaps the north-south lines—is identified with letters; the other set of lines is numbered. The teacher can have the children (this is usually done in fourth grade) find several places located on or very near to a north-south line, say D. Then several places can be found on an east-west line, say 7. If the teacher is clever enough to pick two coordinates that intersect on a major point of interest, the children will discover that some city or other important feature is located at the point where D and 7 intersect. This experience provides readiness for the use of meridians of longitude and parallels of latitude in locating places on wall maps and the globe. At this stage, children are mature enough to understand why reference points such as poles, the equator, and the prime meridian are essential in locating places on a sphere.

Reading Map Symbols

Maps use symbols to represent real things: Dots of varying sizes stand for cities of different populations; color is used to represent elevation; hash marks stand for escarpments; and lines are used to show boundaries, coastlines, and rivers. Naturally, the reader will not comprehend the messages of maps unless he or she knows what these symbols represent. The child begins to learn their meanings early in the elementary school social studies program. The development of this subskill closely parallels that of locating places on maps.

Map and globe symbols vary in their abstractness. Indeed, some simple maps for children in the primary grades use symbols that are pictorial or semipictorial. These symbols either look like the object being represented or provide a strong clue as to its identity. It would not take much imagination, for example, to differentiate water areas from land areas on a globe simply on the basis of their color.

The instructional sequence to be followed in teaching the symbol system of maps is to move gradually from pictorial and semipictorial symbols on maps made by the children to the abstract symbols used on conventional wall maps, globes, and maps that are included in the textbooks of the middle and upper grades. It is essential that children learn to consult the map legend or key in order to confirm which symbols are being used. In most cases children in the middle and upper grades will be dealing with maps that use conventional map symbols, but special purpose maps such as those showing vegetation,

SOCIAL STUDIES COMPETENCIES AND SKILLS

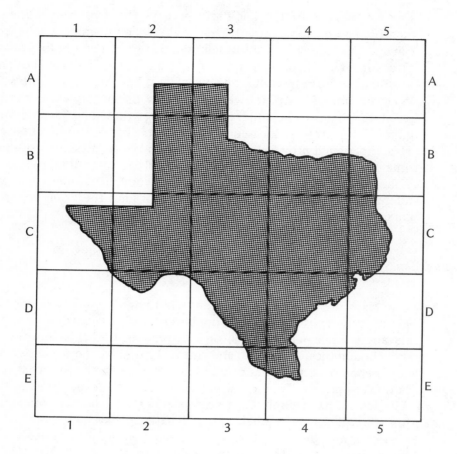

Figure 8–1. Middle-grade pupils can learn to use a grid in locating places by using road maps that have coordinates of the type shown on this map. Test your own memory of place locations by responding to these questions:

1. What major city is located at C,1?
2. What major city lies near the intersection of the squares A,2; A,3; B,2; and B,3?
3. Describe the location of Houston by using the coordinates provided on this map.

Check your answers by consulting a map of Texas that shows cities.

rainfall, population density, and so on, often use symbols that are unique to the particular map.

It is always a good idea to make generous use of photographs of the areas shown on a map in order to help the children associate the map symbol with what the place actually looks like. Similarly, when children go on field trips, they should be encouraged to observe carefully the appearance of landscapes and other features that are shown on maps. In time they will be able to visualize the reality that the abstract map symbols represent.

Figure 8–2. Pupils can be introduced to the concept of symbols through pictorial representations that they encounter in real life, such as the ones shown here.

Understanding Relative Location

Understanding relative location is an interpretive skill that requires information beyond that provided by the map itself. It has to do with thinking about how places relate to each other in terms of political, cultural, religious, commercial, or historical perspectives. It has nothing to do with how close or how far away places may be in the absolute sense. For example, the non-Asian people, and even many Asians, of the British Crown Colony of Hong Kong feel closer to Great Britain (10,000 miles away) than they do to the People's Republic of China (less than twenty miles away) because of political, economic, and cultural ties.

Relative location may also be thought of in terms of the amount of time required to get to a place using the kind of transportation available. This is commonly expressed nowadays in ordinary conversation and small talk as people say, "It takes me thirty minutes to get to work," or "I'm about two hours from Washington." Distances that now take two hours to traverse would have taken two days a hundred years ago and two weeks or even more at the time of the founding of the Republic. Increasingly, we reckon distances in terms of time. Consequently, places may be thought of as being remote or near in terms of how difficult it is to get to them. Air crash survivors stranded in the High Sierras in the dead of winter, no more than fifty miles from Fresno, California, might be as far away from civilization in the relative sense as they would be if they were on the moon.

Comparing Maps and Making Inferences

Comparing maps and making inferences is also an inferential skill because to some extent the reader has to project what he or she already knows on the map data. In this process the map reader discovers relationships among the sets of data presented by different maps. In the middle elementary grades, teachers often have children compare vegetation maps with rainfall maps. They also have them compare maps showing the location of important resources, such as iron and coal, with maps showing the location of industrial centers, population densities, and so on. It is quite common to find special-purpose maps of the same region in the children's textbooks, making comparisons easy. These provide excellent settings for inquiry exercises, as the children can study the data presented on two or more maps, make predictions or hypotheses about these data, and then go on to the next step of verifying or rejecting their speculations.

Children in the late middle and upper elementary grades should study maps based on different projections and compare the shapes and sizes of known areas with those same areas as shown on the globe. This will familiarize them with the concept of distortion, which, in greater or lesser amounts, is present in all flat maps. Pupils should learn why distortion occurs and what cartographers have done to minimize its effect.

INTERN TASK 8–2

For each of the six skills discussed in this section, suggest one specific learning experience that could be used with the children in the classroom to which you have been assigned. Check these with your field associate teacher, and, if approved, try to incorporate them in your teaching experience.

Field Associate Teacher Advisory

Map and globe skills provide good substance for first experiences in teaching because the objective can be made highly specific and clear and the presentation can be nicely packaged in a single class period. Encourage the intern to do some teaching of map and globe skills as a part of the regular social studies unit or in connection with current events.

HOW DOES A TEACHER PLAN FOR, LOCATE, AND USE LEARNING EXPERIENCES AND LEARNING RESOURCES TO TEACH MAP AND GLOBE SKILLS?

Children develop skill in map and globe reading in settings where teachers know which variations of the skills are to be taught at each level and where there is some method of accountability for such teaching. Regrettably, this does not occur as often as it should, and, as a result, the systematic teaching of these important skills becomes vulnerable to neglect. If we depend only ·on incidental references to maps and globes as a way of having children learn these skills, it will only be a fortunate accident if children become proficient in their use.

As a first step in developing a program of instruction in maps and globes, therefore, the teacher must determine which variations of the essential skills will be taught during the year. Naturally, it is helpful if the school district provides this information in a curriculum document as was done by the district cited in the vignette at the beginning of this chapter. If such a document is not provided, the teacher should develop his or her own list of skills to be taught, looking for guidance to such sources as the textbook teacher's guide, the appendix of the thirty-third yearbook of the NCSS,[3] curriculum documents from other districts, or college methods books in social studies. The summary on pages 182–185 is an example of material that could be used for this purpose.

A SUMMARY OF MAP AND GLOBE SKILLS

Elementary school pupils should develop map and globe skills associated with the following concepts and generalizations.

1. Primary grades.
   • A map is a drawing or other representation of all or part of the earth.
   • On maps and globes, symbols are used to stand for real things.
   • The earth is a huge sphere.
   • A globe is a small model of the earth and is the most accurate representation of the earth.
   • Half of the earth is called a hemisphere.
   • The earth can be divided into many hemispheres. The most common ones are the Eastern, Western, Northern, and Southnern Hemispheres; land hemisphere and water hemisphere; and day hemisphere and night hemisphere.
   • Any part of the globe can be shown on a map.
   • Large bodies of land are called continents.
   • Large bodies of water are called oceans.

---

[3]Ibid., pp. 313 ff.

- Directions on a map are determined by the poles; to go north means to go in the direction of the North Pole, to go south means to go in the direction of the South Pole.
- North may be shown any place on a map; north is *not* always at the top of a map.
- The North Pole is the point farthest north on the earth; the South Pole is the point farthest south.
- The scale on a map or globe makes it possible to determine distances between places.
- Maps are drawn to different scales; scale ensures that all objects are made smaller in the same amount.
- Maps and globes use legends, or keys, that tell the meaning of the symbols used on the map.
- The cardinal directions are north, south, east, and west; intermediate directions are northeast, northwest, southeast, and southwest.
- All places on the earth can be located on maps and globes.
- Different maps provide different information about the earth.

2. Intermediate and upper grades.

- The larger the scale used, the larger each feature appears on the map.
- The same symbol may mean different things from one map to another; the legend tells what the symbols stand for.
- The elevation of land is measured from sea level; some maps provide information about elevation.
- Physical maps can be used to determine land elevations, slopes of land, and directions of rivers.
- Parallels of latitude can be used to establish east-west direction and are also used to measure distances in degrees north and south of the equator.
- All places on the same east-west line (parallel of latitude) are directly east or west of one another and are the same distance north or south of the equator.
- All places north of the equator are in north latitudes; all places south of the equator are in south latitudes.
- The Tropic of Cancer and the Tropic of Capricorn are lines of latitude lying north and south of the equator. The part of the earth between them is known as the tropics.
- The Arctic and Antarctic Circles are imaginary lines that define the polar regions.

- The low latitudes lie on either side of the equator; the high latitudes surround the poles; and the middle latitudes lie between the low and high latitudes.
- Parallels of latitude, parallel to the equator, get shorter as they progress from the equator to the poles.
- Knowing the latitude of a place makes it possible to locate its north-south position on the earth.
- Meridians of longitude can be used to determine north-south direction and are also used to measure distances in degrees east and west of the prime meridian.
- The zero or *prime* meridian passes through Greenwich, a suburb of London.
- Meridians of longitude are imaginary north-south lines that converge on both poles.
- Meridians of longitude are *great circles* because they divide the earth into two hemispheres.
- The shortest distance between any two places on the earth follows a great circle.
- West longitude is measured to the west of the prime meridian from zero to 180°; east longitude is measured to the east of the prime meridian from zero to 180°.
- All places on the same north-south line (meridian of longitude) are directly north or south of each other and are the same distance east or west of the prime meridian.
- The latitude and longitude of any place determine its exact location on a globe or map.
- Longitude is used in determining the time of day at places around the world. The earth rotates through 15° of longitude every hour; the earth is divided into twenty-four time zones.
- An imaginary line through the center of the earth, running from pole to pole, is called the earth's axis; the earth rotates on its axis from west to east.
- Night and day are the result of the rotation of the earth.
- Maps and globes provide data about the nature of areas by using color contour, visual relief, and contour lines.
- All flat maps contain some distortion because they represent a round object on a flat surface.
- Different map projections provide different perspectives on the sizes and shapes of areas shown.

- Globes give such information as distance, direction, relative and exact location, and sizes and shapes of areas more accurately than flat maps can.
- Maps and globes often use abbreviations to identify places and things.

Map and globe reading skills are learned through direct teaching and by application in situations where the skill is normally used. In many instances these processes can be combined. Let us say, for example, that pupils in a fifth-grade class read that "Permafrost is a condition found only in the high latitudes." The teacher can use this encounter with *high latitudes* to teach map reading in connection with that concept. That is, class time can be taken to teach the meaning of *high, low,* and *middle latitudes* on maps and globes, and the teaching would occur in what we refer to as a functional setting. We urge teachers to teach as many map and globe skills as possible in this way, rather than isolate the skills from their relevant subject matter. After direct teaching there must be a generous application and use of the skills if proficiency is to be developed and maintained.

Because these skills are *developmental*, one cannot expect to teach them once and assume that they have been learned. Most skills are introduced early in the grades and then are retaught, reviewed, or expanded later on. We expect that children will show increased proficiency and maturity in their use of these skills each year that they are in school. Such development comes through continued teaching and use, not automatically through the natural process of maturation.

Representing space and distance symbolically, as maps and globes do, means that the concepts and skills are at least once removed from reality. A square with a cross on it, placed on a map, may stand for a church but is obviously *not* a church. Even a three-dimensional model that looks exactly like the church it stands for is still *not* a church, but only something that represents one. *Any* symbol we use is an abstraction, and we have a voluminous amount of research that speaks to the complexity of understanding abstract concepts. Therefore, in teaching map and globe skills, we try constantly to relate these abstract concepts to the reality of the child's experience by

1. Observing local landscapes and geographic features, preferably from a high point of vantage.

2. Using pictorial and semipictorial symbols, especially at the lower grade levels.
3. Using three-dimensional models of the areas mapped; using blocks and models to represent buildings.
4. Making maps of the local area with which pupils are familiar.
5. Making generous use of pictures, films, and filmstrips of the areas shown on maps.
6. Relating aerial photographs (angle shots rather than perpendicular ones) to maps of the same area.
7. Comparing areas shown on the wall map with the same area shown in a picture.
8. Developing descriptive words (adjectives) that apply to a particular area shown on a map.
9. Making use of current events that relate to the area shown on a map.
10. Visiting places shown on the map, such as the airport, harbor, park, and downtown area.

Teaching map and globe skills does require some amount of special resources and equipment. Every classroom should have a globe along with wall maps appropriate to the curriculum content of the grade. Outline maps are needed in the middle and upper grades. It helps to have available a three-dimensional relief map of the United States and of the home state. Additional equipment might include charts showing conventional map symbols, slated maps and globe, and special-purpose maps showing vegetation, historical development, and natural resources. When children engage in map making, they will need to have available essential construction materials: boxes, blocks, butcher paper, black tape, tracing paper, colored pencils, pens or crayons, paints and brushes, papier maché, plaster, salt and flour, or other modeling material.

Regular social studies unit work and the current events program provide natural settings for teaching map and globe skills. Children can use maps to record their data or observations as they study unit topics. They can analyze the relationships they detect in maps. They can use maps as a means of communicating ideas and findings to their classmates. It has been said that maps are the constant companions of geographers, and the same might be said about children as they engage in the social studies program. Maps and globes are not only tools that children are supposed to learn how to use but are in themselves sources of data when children use them to identify associated phenomena and make conclusions and inferences based on them.

SPACE AND TIME DIMENSIONS OF SOCIAL STUDIES: CONCEPTS AND SKILLS

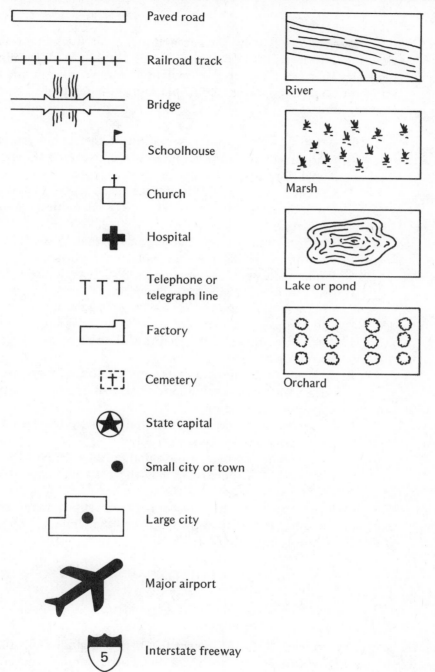

Figure 8–3.   Examples of standard symbols used on maps.

SOCIAL STUDIES COMPETENCIES AND SKILLS

What follows is a list of map and globe activities that will provide the intern with a few examples of the kinds of learning experiences that can be used to stimulate children's interest and at the same time teach important concepts and skills relating to map and globe reading.

1. After an on-the-spot observation of the school grounds or the immediate vicinity, the pupils construct a three-dimensional floor map of the area.
2. Children and teacher locate the place where stories about children in other lands take place or where news events are occurring.
3. Children find pictures in magazines that illustrate various landforms: plains, plateaus, hills, and mountains.
4. Pupils make maps of the same area, such as the local county, using different scales for each map.
5. Children trace great circle air routes on maps and on globes and compare the two.
6. The class compares the shapes of known areas on different map projections.
7. The group develops a classroom exhibit of maps found in current newspapers and periodicals and compares them with conventional maps and globes.
8. The class develops an illustrated glossary of concepts and terms associated with map reading.
9. The teacher secures an outdated political map of the world (1940–1950 vintage) and has the class compare it with a current political map of the world.
10. The class illustrates *mis*conceptions about maps such as "north is at the top of the map" or "the climate is temperate in the Temperate Zone."

INTERN TASK 8–3

Using the summary on pages 182–185, select five map and globe skills that you think would be appropriate in the social studies curriculum of the grade to which you have been assigned. Discuss your choices with your field associate teacher.

HOW DO CHILDREN DEVELOP A SENSE OF TIME AND CHRONOLOGY?

There is much in the cultural tradition of the urban, industrialized Western world to remind one of the importance of time. Airlines, trains, and buses operate on time schedules, as do places of business, factories, churches, public institutions, sports events, and television programs, to name just a few. Benjamin Franklin said, "Remember that time is money," this being one of several such proverbs that equate time with economic gain. When we speak of persons making "wise use" of their time, we usually mean that they are busy at something perceived to be "productive." Because time is such an important commodity in the lives of most of us, we have little tolerance for time wasters and loafers.

In spite of the substantial amount of research that has been conducted on the ability of human beings to deal with time concepts and chronology, much about this phenomenon remains shrouded in mystery. There can be no question that one's perception of time grows out of cultural conditioning. There are few cultures in which people are as compulsive about punctuality as are Americans. To some extent, one's time orientation relates to one's social-class membership, but research suggests that human beings vary greatly in their ability to understand time concepts. Circumstances also condition one's perception of time so that in some cases we say that "time flies," whereas in other settings time seems to drag on endlessly.

In writing for the thirty-third yearbook of the NCSS, Alice W. Spieseke identifies seven elements of time and chronology that relate to childrens' development and provides suggestions for teaching each one:

1. Mastering the telling of time by the clock.
2. Understanding the days, weeks, months, and years as expressed by the calendar.
3. Establishing a framework for time relationships.
4. Developing a meaningful vocabulary of definite and indefinite time expressions.
5. Coping with time concepts in reading and listening situations.
6. Relating dates to personal experience and to life span.
7. Placing related events in chronological order.[4]

---

[4]Alice W. Spieseke, "Developing a Sense of Time and Chronology," in *Skill Development in Social Studies,* ibid., p. 178.

Spieseke is careful to point out that this sequence represents degrees of difficulty but should not be regarded as an arbitrary grade placement of these elements. The sequence reminds us that the development of time concepts is a gradual process that extends over a period of several years. Dealing with time in the historical sense of placing events in chronological order represents a fairly mature level of dealing with time. Little wonder, therefore, that elementary school children have difficulty in handling time concepts of this type.

Children, of course, learn much about time relationships through ordinary living outside of school. Undoubtedly most children would learn how to tell time, would learn the days of the week and months of the year, and would become familiar with terms ordinarily used in referring to units of time, such as noon, midnight, afternoon, and morning, even if these were not taught in school. The school program can ensure that these skills are correctly and are adequately learned, however, and can provide children the opportunity to practice using them. A few lessons with a simulated clock, supported by practical application in noting when things happen in the schedule of activities during the day, will be adequate to teach most children how to deal with clock time. It is rare to find a mentally competent grown person who cannot tell the time of day. In any case the increased use of digital clocks should eliminate entirely any problems in reading clock time.

The main thrust of the school program should be, therefore, on those aspects of time and chronology that are not likely to be learned outside of school. This includes (1) the more technical language of time and chronology, such as century, decade, fortnight, fiscal year, calendar year, generation, score, millennium, A.M., P.M., B.C., and A.D.; (2) placing events in chronological order; (3) developing an understanding of the time spans that separate historical events. References to *indefinite* units of time, such as many years ago, soon thereafter, several years had passed, and in a few years, need special attention because they are apt to mean almost any amount of time to young children. Definite references to time can more easily be made meaningful by associating them with units of time that are known to the children: their own ages, the length of time they have been in school, when their parents or grandparents were children of their ages, and so on. The teaching or these relationships can and should take place within the context of social studies units, especially those that focus on history, and in connection with current news stories.

Time lines are often used to show how related events are arranged in chronological order and to show the relative amount of time that separates them. Though widely used, experts are not in agreement as to the value of time lines in clarifying time and chronology for young children. Children can develop the concept of representing time on a continuum by first charting events that they experience on a firsthand basis. This helps them arrange the events in the correct sequence. They can make time lines that show things that happened to them yesterday, today, or are being planned for tomorrow. The amount of time included on the line can gradually be expanded to cover several months and then years. Time lines are more interesting to children if events are shown pictorially, rather than simply as dots and dates. With middle- and upper-grade children, frequent use can be made of time lines in connection with historical studies of their home state and their nation. Such time lines need not stop with the present date but may be projected into the future, thus illustrating that time is continuous and that the present stands between the past and the future.

INTERN TASK 8–4

Engage your class in one or more of the following activities:

1. Discuss the meaning of some indefinite reference to time that the class has encountered recently in social studies or current events.
2. Develop a simple time line with your class using pictorial symbols.
3. Direct the study of the class to a time line in their textbook.
4. Have the class discuss situations in which they think "time flies" and others in which they think time "moves at a snail's pace." Encourage them to identify reasons for this difference. Are the situations the same for all pupils?
5. Have the class think of as many popular expressions or proverbs as they can that have to do with time. Conduct this activity for a period of days and as expressions or proverbs are suggested, place them on the bulletin board. Have children make drawings to illustrate them. Discuss this in terms of the importance of time in our lives.

HOW CAN CURRENT NEWS EVENTS BE USED TO TEACH SOCIAL STUDIES CONCEPTS AND SKILLS?

Some of what children in school today are reporting as current news events will be studied by their counterparts twenty-five, fifty, or a hundred years from now as history. Current events are a small part of the flow of human events that comprise the seemingly timeless story of human beings, the earth, and the universe. The purposes of teaching current news events in schools are (1) to promote interest in current affairs and news developments, (2) to promote the growth of critical thinking skills associated with the evaluation and analysis of news stories, and (3) to help children relate school learning to life outside of school.

Participatory democracy requires a citizenry informed on current public issues. It would be unreasonable to expect adults to have these skills without an opportunity to learn them. In this way the study of current news events can and does contribute directly to important citizenship training.

In order to achieve these goals, elementary school teachers usually provide time for children to report news items and to discuss them. In this connection the classroom often has a news bulletin board on which news stories are posted that have been brought to school by the teacher and the children. This can be combined with a world map that is used to identify where the news stories are taking place. Most classrooms also use a children's weekly news periodical. The most widely used children's news periodicals are

Scholastic Book Services
904 Sylvan Avenue
Englewood Cliffs, N.J. 07632
  Let's Find Out, K
  News Pilot, 1
  News Ranger, 2
  News Trails, 3
  News Explorer, 4
  News Citizen, 5
  Newstime, 6
  Junior Scholastic, 6–8

Xerox Education Publications
Education Center
Columbus, Ohio 43216
  My Weekly Reader, K–6
  Current Events, 7–9

The Civic Education Service, Inc.
1733 K Street
Washington, D.C. 20006
  Junior Review, 6–9

The extent to which current events programs and social studies programs are related depends on individual teachers. Some teachers separate the two programs almost entirely, whereas others build much of their social studies around current news happenings. Perhaps the best arrangement is some midposition that ties current affairs into the social studies program but at the same time does not make current events the social studies curriculum.

Current events programs should be characterized by a series of pupil-involving activities that relate to news stories. These should include using round table and panel discussion; preparing displays illustrating news stories; making charts, graphs, or maps that relate to news events; dramatizing news events; drawing cartoons to illustrate the news; conducting mock radio or television newscasts; and developing a classroom newspaper. News stories provide excellent settings for teaching thinking and inquiry skills. The current events program should involve children in learning how to deal with controversial issues appropriate to their age and maturity.

News stories that deal with controversial issues can be found in all communities, large or small. Here are some examples:
Whether to

- Relocate an airport because of complaints of jet noise during landings and take-offs.
- Allow an area to be rezoned for a shopping center.
- Permit freeway construction through a residential or farming area.
- Close an elementary school—or any other public service or facility.

- Build an athletic stadium.
- Allow a golf course to be built in·or near a city.
- Pass a dog leash ordinance.
- Allow animals to be used for medical research.
- Allow certain forms of gambling.
- Restrict trash burning.
- Construct a new hospital, school, courthouse, water tank, or television or radio tower.
- Build another bridge across the lake connecting the city with the suburbs.
- Designate certain buildings as having value for historical preservation.
- Allow controlled spraying of crop and forest land.

The created news story that follows illustrates one such controversial issue. As you read this news story, based on an actual incident in the Puget Sound area, think of (1) the issues it presents, and (2) what possibilities it holds as a teaching vehicle for pupils in the middle or upper grades. At the conclusion of the story, a few teaching suggestions are provided.

Whale Capture Creates Wail

Six killer whales are being held inside the Aqua Life, Inc., nets at Cook Inlet while Bill Holberg decides which ones, if any, will be kept for aquarium exhibits. Hundreds of people watched the capture from boats and shore yesterday afternoon.

The huge mammals swam slowly round and round inside two purse seine nets today, surfacing to "blow" for only moments. They stayed under for five minutes at a time. A large bull whale and a small calf that escaped the capture were nowhere to be found.

Governor Reconsidering

Meanwhile, a political storm was gathering over the capture operation. The governor today interrupted his skiing vacation long enough to say that he was "reconsidering" the state's position on making the inlet a sanctuary for killer whales. The state's senior senator in Washington said that a declaration of support for the governor for a whale sanctuary would clear the way for protection of the sea animals. Earlier efforts to get support from state officials for the idea were unsuccessful. The senator also said, "Apparently this man [Holberg] had a valid permit. But there aren't going to be any more. This is the end!"

Depth Charges Used

An assistant to the State Game and Fisheries Director, Jack Binns, watched the capture from about fifty feet away. Binns said Aqua Life, Inc., boats used "sonar, radar, and 'depth' charges" to drive the whales into smaller and smaller coves and finally into the nets. He said he watched three men in power boats racing across the water atop the whale school, "dropping 'depth charges' as fast as they could light them. I've never seen anything so disgusting in all my life," he said today. "This ought to be stopped right now."

A federal enforcement officer who supervised yesterday's operation said, "there is nothing in the permit that prohibits the use of such explosives."

Use of Charges Denied

Many citizens complained about the capture operation. An automobile dealer from South Harbor said he saw an airplane dropping "tomato can"-size cannisters that apparently exploded as the plane herded the whales. Bill Moss, veterinarian for Aqua Life, Inc., said no such charges were used. He said the whale chasers used "firecracker"-type explosives thrown from boats to herd the whales. Holberg himself was aboard the Aqua Life, Inc., boat, *KANDU,* and was unavailable for comment.

Court Action Threatened

Environmentalists and others bitterly opposed the capture of the whales. Fred Russell, president of the state's largest environmental protection group, PROTEX, demanded that the whales be released. He said his group was prepared to take the matter to court if necessary to prevent Aqua Life, Inc., from keeping the creatures. "This is an outrage," he said, "and we are not going to sit by and let it happen."

Russell cited a Canadian biologist who found that only about sixty-five killer whales remain in the Straits of Georgia and Juan de Fuca and in Puget Sound. Earlier data had placed the number of whales at about three hundred.

Overlapping Jurisdiction

The power to create a whale sanctuary rests with the federal government, but federal law says the governor of a state that contains the sanctuary may veto its creation. This overlapping of jurisdiction sometimes creates confusion or results in no action being taken.

Until today, federal officials thought the governor opposed creation of a killer whale sanctuary in this area. The governor's staff said that no record could be found of the governor's ever having opposed such a proposal.

The senior senator renewed his call for a sanctuary, something he has advocated since 1974. There is no reason to believe that the governor will oppose the creation of the killer whale sanctuary.

How can a news story of this type be used for social studies instruction? Here are a few suggestions:

1. Use the strategy discussed on pages 131–132 in making an analysis of this situation—that is, (a) have the pupils identify the *facts* of the case; (b) have pupils identify the *issues* in the case; and (c) have pupils identify *alternative solutions* to the problem and list the consequences of each alternative.
2. Use this story as a springboard for an in-depth study of endangered species. More than five hundred kinds of animals are listed as rare or in danger of extinction, including Indian tigers, Asiatic lions, snow leopards, eagles, grizzly bears, alligators, and some butterflies. Pupils should get into the values question of whether or not an animal has to be "useful" in order to be protected.
3. Have pupils study the roles of federal, state, local, and volunteer groups in decision making regarding issues of the type presented in this story. This should get them into local and state regulations concerning the conservation of natural resources and environmental contamination. It should also confront the matter of what individual citizens or groups of citizens can do when they see something happening that they believe to be unconscionable, even if legal.

4. This story provides an excellent setting for the study of the issue of capture of wild animals for use in circuses and zoos. Should zoos be allowed at all? Do animals benefit from zoos?

5. This story can provide the basis for the study of the web of life and food chains—that is, how changes in the population of one animal change the number of another animal on which it feeds. This can be coupled with a study of wildlife management, hunting and fishing regulations, and the concept of *open season.*

6. Study the lives of individuals who have dedicated themselves to the preservation of wildlife and other natural resources: John Muir, Jack Miner, Gifford Pinchot, and local environmentalists.

7. Develop this news story into a role-playing activity in which the issues are highlighted and satisfactory resolutions played out.

8. Have pupils in committees develop "position statements" to represent the point of view of the various principals in this controversy: the whale hunter, the governor, the president of the environmentalist group, an irate citizen, the director of Aqua Life, Inc., who would receive the captured whales, and so on.

9. Use the story to build interest in developing a social-action project dealing with ecology or conservation. A second-grade teacher in Wisconsin reports the following activities that were developed in such a project:

   a. The children helped others become aware of the problems faced by endangered wildlife by sharing their research findings with their family, friends, schoolmates, clergymen, and neighbors.

   b. They wrote letters to state and federal officials to urge their support of legislation designed to protect wildlife.

   c. They presented programs that dealt with the potential threats to wildlife by land developers, trappers, poachers, snowmobilers, hunters, pesticide programs, campers, and so on.

   d. They compiled a list of guidelines and distributed them to each pupil in the school, explaining ways individuals can help. These are some of the guidelines:

      (1) Refuse to shoot birds and other wild creatures "just for the fun of it."

(2) Refuse to participate in cruel and senseless "chases" of wild animals on snowmobiles, in cars, on bikes, on foot, or in boats or planes.

(3) Refuse to destroy animal homes.

(4) Refuse to disturb baby birds and animal babies in their nests.[5]

These suggestions provide interesting extensions of a news story. Of course, no one class would engage in all of them; indeed, it is unlikely that more than one would be used. Perhaps the teacher could create others even more suitable than those provided here. The point of this list is simply to illustrate the wide range of possibilities that inhere in well-selected current news stories. They provide the excitement of controversy, they are relevant to the current stream of human events, they deal with public policy issues, and they lend themselves exceedingly well to social action projects.

INTERN TASK 8–5

Select a news story of particular local interest and one that is mildly controversial. Develop a short teaching sequence based on the content and issues of that news event. Use the suggestions presented in this chapter in developing your plans. Check your plans with your field associate teacher, and, if approved, implement your plans in the classroom where you are teaching.

HOW ARE CHILDREN TAUGHT TO READ AND INTERPRET GRAPHS, CHARTS, AND CARTOONS?

Because of the widespread use of graphs, charts, and cartoons in social studies materials and in printed material outside of school, it is imperative that citizens develop the skills needed to read and interpret them. Just leafing through a daily newspaper or a weekly news magazine reminds one of how commonly these graphics are used and how powerfully their messages are conveyed. Citizens today are "digest" oriented. They do not have the time or the inclination

---

[5]Marsha Gravitz, "You and Me in the Classroom" *Instructor,* 82 (8), April 1973, 43.

to wade through a mountain of narrative that explains social events or conditions. They want to see these ideas in summary form and in stark relief. Besides, the complexity of social data, much of which is in statistical form, lends itself well to a graphic format.

Graphs are used to illustrate relationships among quantities. These relationships may be spread over a period of time, thus showing trends. The most commonly used graphs are some variation of the *bar graph*, the *pie* or *circle graph*, and the *line graph*. Any of these graphs may include pictorial representations, thereby making them more interesting to young children and making the content less abstract. For instance, with primary-grade pupils, stick figures can be used to represent children in a bar graph showing the number of pupils absent from class each day. It is easy to visualize the relationships of the parts to the whole in a circle graph, but to construct one accurately requires the ability to compute percentages, usually not possible in the elementary school grades. Modern elementary school textbooks make liberal use of graphs in presenting data, but pupils need to be instructed in how to read and interpret them. Because graphs can be designed to present distorted pictures of data, children in the middle and upper grades should be taught how bias is introduced in a graph.

Children can learn much about graphs and how to read them by constructing their own graphs. Such pupil-made graphs can be used in making oral or written reports and for bulletin board displays. In making graphs accuracy in the presentation should be emphasized rather than artistic perfection.

Like graphs, charts are widely used to present ideas in a vivid and forceful way. Formal charts are often designated as follows:

1. Narrative chart: Tells a story; shows events in sequence. (Example: how plywood is made, stages of the development of civilization, how to use the telephone, or the development of homes)

2. Tabulation chart: Lists data in table form to facilitate making comparisons. (Example: data placed in tabular form to show infant mortality rates, illiteracy rates, or per capita income among nations of the world)

3. Pedigree chart: Shows events stemming from a common origin. (Example: a family tree, the development of a political party, or the history of language)

SOCIAL STUDIES COMPETENCIES AND SKILLS

Number of Days the Sun Was Shining at 12 O'Clock Noon for the First Five Months

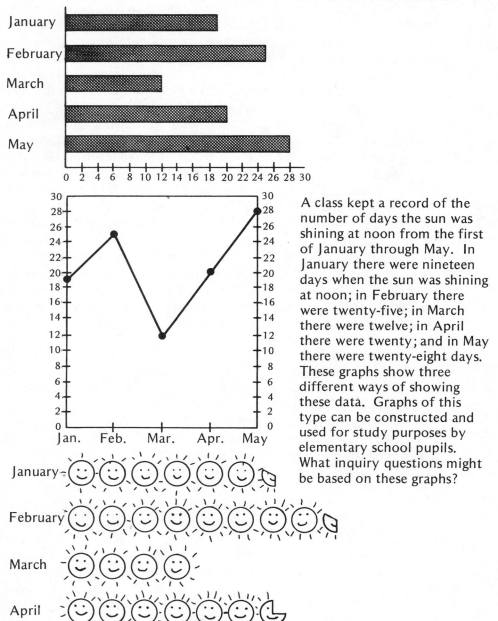

A class kept a record of the number of days the sun was shining at noon from the first of January through May. In January there were nineteen days when the sun was shining at noon; in February there were twenty-five; in March there were twelve; in April there were twenty; and in May there were twenty-eight days. These graphs show three different ways of showing these data. Graphs of this type can be constructed and used for study purposes by elementary school pupils. What inquiry questions might be based on these graphs?

Figure 8-4. Examples of graphs and data suitable for use with elementary school children.

4. Classification chart:	Groups data into various categories. (Example: the various types of restaurants, types of personal services available, or different modes of transportation)
5. Organization chart:	Shows the structure of an organization. (Example: the three branches of government, the structure of a corporation, or the organization of a city government or a school district)
6. Flow chart:	Shows a process involving change at certain points. (Example: how raw materials are transformed into finished products, the break of bulk in shipping as at a harbor facility, or how scrap iron is converted into a usable raw material)

The frequent use of formal charts in children's books provides a good basis for inquiry learning. In the process children not only learn how to read and interpret the chart, but broaden their substantive knowledge and build their understanding of associated concepts.

Informal charts are those the children and the teacher make in the classroom. These may be experience charts in which the class records what it has been doing. Such charts may have to do with unit plans, methods of work, or standards for evaluating reports, discussions, or general conduct. In conducting information searches, pupils may construct data-retrieval charts on which they will record their findings. Data-retrieval charts provide a good way of storing data in summary form for use at a later time. They are also excellent devices for comparing and contrasting observations.

CHART 8-1. Data Retrieval Chart[6]

Our Next-Door Neighbors		
Analytical Concepts	Canada	Mexico

Geographical features
  Size
  Climate
  Physical features
  Natural resources		

[6]This use of data-retrieval charts was developed by the late Hilda Taba and her associates in connection with curriculum development in social studies.

SOCIAL STUDIES COMPETENCIES AND SKILLS

CHART 8-1 *(Continued)*

Analytical Concepts	Canada	Mexico

History
  Native people
  Foreign influences
  Relations with U.S.
  Type of government today		

Economic development
  Main occupations
  Average per capita income
  Exports		

Population
  Ethnic groups
  Density
  Major cities
  Levels of education
  Religious groups
  Language		

This cartoon appeared in the *Seattle Post-Intelligencer*, Seattle, Washington, on Wednesday, March 10, 1976. Reprinted by permission of Robert D. McCausland, Editorial Art Department, *Seattle Post-Intelligencer.*

The cartoon on page 202 reminds us how much the reader must bring to such illustrations if they are to have meaning. To someone who was not familiar with the whale capture controversy described in the story on pages 194–196, this cartoon would not convey the meaning intended.

This illustration also depicts some of the techniques used by cartoonists—techniques that give their messages such power. In this case human qualities of emotion are ascribed to the animal. Sometimes cartoonists ascribe animal qualities to human beings, usually to show such characteristics as slyness, ugliness, greed, cunning, and so on. Animals are used to represent national groups—the American eagle, the Russian bear, the British lion, the Chinese dragon, and the donkey and the elephant of our own political parties.

An important characteristic of cartoon messages is that symbolism is used in a variety of ways *to present a single point of view.* There is no opportunity for rebuttal. Cartoonists use familiar situations, exaggeration, satire, and caricature. Sometimes cartoons present stereotypes of human groups that conflict with the humanistic attitudes and values social studies programs often aspire to achieve with children. For instance, cartoons that show the people of Africa as cannibals, or the native American people as feathered savages, or all government officials as crooks or philandering scoundrels do little toward helping build attitudes of respect toward such groups or the institutions they represent.

Cartoons are an important part of the message system we use to deal with social issues. Often a cartoon cuts directly to the heart of an issue, and, in an instant, communicates an idea with such force that the point could hardly be missed. But as the whale cartoon shows, understanding and interpreting the message of this medium require a sophisticated understanding of the issues involved. The cartoon clarifies them and puts them into a different perspective for the viewer. Cartoons are not intended to provide new information, but rather a different way of thinking about what is known. Consequently, cartoons used with elementary school children should be based on content and concepts clearly within the realm of those children's understanding and experience.

INTERN TASK 8-6

Demonstrate that you can incorporate graphs, charts, and cartoons in your teaching of social studies by making some use of them in your regular social studies work in the classroom. Discuss your ideas for the use of these devices with your field associate teacher prior to putting them into practice with the class.

SOCIAL STUDIES COMPETENCIES AND SKILLS

CHECKING YOUR PERFORMANCE

Intern Task Checklist

Task 8–1. a. Identifying news stories that would be suitable for classroom
use. P. 174 _____

 b. Identifying quantitative concepts used in textbook narrative.
P. 174 _____

Task 8–2. Suggesting learning experiences to teach map reading skills.
P. 181 _____

Task 8–3. Selecting map and globe skills for a particular grade level. P. 188 _____

Task 8–4. Implementing a time and chronology activity. P. 191 _____

Task 8–5. Planning and teaching a sequence based on a current news
event. P. 198 _____

Task 8–6. Planning for and using graphs, charts, and cartoons. P. 203 _____

Performance Checklist

In the field or in the clinic, the intern teacher has

1. Identified situations in which dimensions of time and space are essential to understanding the ideas being presented. _____

2. Worked with children in the classroom on samples of the six broad
categories of map-reading skills. _____

3. Defined and implemented learning activities to teach map and globe
skills, using appropriate instructional resources. _____

4. Taught social studies sequences that involve attention to time and
chronology. _____

5. Planned and taught lessons based on a current news event. _____

6. Planned and taught lessons that require the use of skills associated
with graphs, charts, and cartoons. _____

Field Associate Teacher Advisory

Tasks and performances should be checked off or initialed and
dated by the appropriate local official, or the intern teacher
can use the checklists for his or her own record.

Chapter 9

Getting the most out of group work

As a part of the general orientation to teaching, State University schedules a series of presentations by local and state school officials for the interns. These lectures come at about two-week intervals throughout the year and deal with a variety of topics of professional interest, such as professional ethics, applying for a position, school finance, and so on. The speakers are usually well received by the interns, not unlike veterans of military engagements sharing the wisdom of their experiences with the new recruits who, in the rapture of the moment, imagine themselves hitting the beaches in some distant land. Because these lectures are perceived by the interns as coming from persons associated with "the real world," and deal with "practical things instead of theory," the credibility of the presenters is usually unquestioned.

On the occasion to which we now direct our attention, the person making the presentation was Dr. Patrick Giovani, a capable assistant superintendent for curriculum in one of the large suburban school districts. The thrust of his message had to do with the need to develop programs based on broad educational goals. "This can only be done at the classroom level," he said. "All of us, and especially those closest to the children, namely the classroom teachers, need to keep in mind the kind of society and world in which these children are now living and in which they will continue to live for the foreseeable future. That world is not one of people living alone in isolated cubicles and interacting with computer consoles. If anything, it is *just the opposite—it is a social world. This was emphasized very strongly by Harvard Professor of Sociology Daniel Bell in a bicentennial essay for* Time *magazine:*

> *A postindustrial world, because it primarily involves services— doctor with patient, teacher with student, government official with petitioner, research team with experimental designer— is largely a game between persons. In the daily experience of a white-collar world, nature is excluded, things are excluded. The world is entirely a social world—intangible and capricious— in which individuals encounter and have to learn how to live with one another. Not, perhaps, an easy thing.[1]*

Dr. Giovani went on to explain that intergroup relations are more important than ever now because of the growing awareness of ethnic diversity. He made a humorous personal reference to his own ethnic heritage, an interesting combination of Irish and Italian, as clearly apparent by his name. He reminded the interns of the persistent tendency of otherwise intelligent people to kill each other because of differences in religious beliefs, even though all major religions have strong injunctions against the taking of human life. Dr. Patrick Giovani was a spellbinder, no question about it! Besides, what he said seemed to make eminent good sense. "Why is it," he asked rhetorically, "that we expect children to learn to live and work with each other when we don't teach them the skills, subtleties, and intricacies of group life? How can a child learn to work in a group if he or she always works individually, singly, in isolation from others?" A simple yet profound notion.

Miss Willis, the clinic instructor responsible for social studies, had more or less expected something along the lines of "basic education," "fiscal accountability to the community," and "behavioral objectives" from the assistant superintendent. She was nearly floored by the thought that a person of such prestige and influence in the local educational community had the courage—finally—to strike a blow for social education. Needless to say, Miss Willis made the most of this windfall of unexpected support for the social values of education with her interns in subsequent clinic sessions. She focused on the Basic Competencies identified in the teacher education program.

---

[1] Daniel Bell, "The Clock Watchers: Americans at Work," Bicentennial Essay, *Time*, Vol. 16, No. 10 (Sept. 8, 1975), p. 57.

Basic Competencies—Social Studies

The intern teacher is able to

1. Identify skills relating to group work.
2. Teach group-work skills in the context of social studies units.
3. Deploy children in a variety of configurations for instructional purposes in social studies.
4. Use a range of activities in teaching concepts, skills, and values.
5. Conduct dramatic play, role playing, and simulation game activities.
6. Engage children in social-action projects.

INTERN ADVISORY

After completing this chapter, together with related work in the clinic and appropriate classroom experiences in the field, you should be able to do the following:

1. Conduct social studies instruction in groups of varying sizes.
2. Use social studies activities to teach social and group-work skills to children.
3. Make use of a variety of activities in teaching social studies.
4. Explain the nature and purposes of dramatic play, role playing, and simulation games.
5. Use dramatic play, role playing, and simulation games in teaching social studies.
6. Engage children in social-action projects that relate to social studies.

WHAT SKILLS ARE INVOLVED IN GROUP ACTIVITIES?

It would be unthinkable to expect children to make use of such study skills as getting information from maps, looking up words in a dictionary, or finding an article in an encyclopedia without having provided some instruction in these skills. One would not expect children to learn these skills on their own through trial and error, even though some children could learn them in this way. But when we come to social skills or skills that involve the dynamics of groups, instruction proceeds as if children either already were proficient in these skills or that they will pick them up simply through participating in group activities. It must be stressed that children learn group-work skills in group settings, not by working alone. It should also be emphasized that simply providing the opportunity for group involvement is not enough. This must be preceded by or accompanied by instruction as to how an individual is supposed to function in a group setting. The assistant superintendent cited in the introduction to this chapter was correct in calling our attention to the fact that human beings are social creatures, and, consequently, the social values of education are enormously important in terms of the over-all goals of education.

In Chapter 1 the goals for social skills and for group-work skills were identified as follows:

1. Social skills.
   a. Living and working together, taking turns, respecting the rights of others, and being socially sensitive.
   b. Learning self-control and self-direction.
   c. Sharing ideas and experiences with others.
2. Group-work skills.
   a. Working together on committees and assuming various roles in small groups such as serving as chairperson, secretary, or group member.
   b. Participating in a group discussion or leading a discussion.
   c. Participating in group decision making.

Each of the goals listed involves numerous subskills. For example, in "participating in a group discussion," an important and frequently used skill, the individual would need to

1. Listen attentively when others speak.
2. Assume responsibility for contributing ideas.
3. Prepare adequately and be able to support ideas with factual evidence.
4. Be open-minded, respect and accept the contributions of others, but think independently.

5. Remain objective and not become overly emotional.
6. Speak loudly and clearly enough for all to hear.
7. Avoid being offended when ideas or suggestions are not accepted by the group.
8. Avoid dominating the discussion; make contributions concisely and briefly.
9. Ask for the clarification of any ideas not understood; ask for evidence to substantiate statements.
10. Recognize the problems caused by communication in arriving at group decisions or in discussing a controversial issue.
11. Assume responsibility for moving the group toward its goal; help keep the group from becoming sidetracked from the central issue.
12. Have confidence in the ability of the group to come to a satisfactory decision and support the decision of the group once it has been made.

Or, to cite another example of relevant subskills, a person who is "learning to live and work with others" will

1. Demonstrate a growing awareness of responsibility for one's own behavior.
2. Be aware of how one's behavior affects others.
3. Make others feel their contributions are appreciated and needed.
4. Enjoy the company of others; interact with persons of all races, cultures, and religions in positive ways when there is an occasion for such interaction.
5. Be sensitive to the views and feelings of others.
6. Be actively concerned about defending the rights of others.
7. Feel a responsibility to be involved in group planning and decision making; cooperate with others in achieving common goals.
8. Accept, value, and respect diversity among human beings as part of the reality of the human condition.
9. Demonstrate in a variety of ways a caring concern for others.
10. Have positive feelings of confidence about oneself.

The social and group-work skills that we promote and teach are value based. We do not want to train our children in human relations skills that run contrary to our commitment to the rights of individuals, consideration for others, humaneness, human dignity, freedom of choice and conscience, and so on. In human relations training we do not deliberately set out to teach our children to apply different rules to "us" than to "them." This is not true of all societies. An obvious example is found among some Gypsy groups even today, where children are taught that it is not right to steal from fellow Gypsies, but that there is nothing wrong with stealing from non-Gypsies. What is being discussed here should not be confused with the rights, privileges, and prerogatives that result in preferential treatment of in-group members as a consequence of residing in a particular territory, being of a certain age, occupying a position of importance, and so on. Such preferential distinctions are found everywhere. We are speaking here of the way people relate to each other simply as human beings.

All societies develop idealized types, or general models, of what human beings are supposed to be like and how they are supposed to deal with fellow human beings. The Soviet Union has a very elaborate system in its preschool establishments, its common schools, and its Pioneer program, to train young people in the ideas and skills needed for life in a collective society. In our own nation we stress individual rights and responsibilities as opposed to those of the collective or of the state. It is a profound fact that societies everywhere shape their young people as social creatures to conform to the values of that society. This is why cross-cultural studies of educational practices must deal fundamentally with the basic values of the cultures studied.

INTERN TASK 9-1

Identify specific subskills (pupil behaviors) that might be used as standards in teaching children to function in each of the following group settings:

1. *Whole class.*
   a. Contributing to class planning.
   b. Brainstorming for new ideas on a subject.
   c. Discussing a controversial topic.
   d. Holding a formal class meeting.
2. *Small group.*
   a. Making a plan of action.
   b. Working as a committee *member.*
   c. Working as a committee *chairperson.*

HOW CAN GROUP WORK SKILLS BE TAUGHT IN THE CONTEXT OF SOCIAL STUDIES?

A major over-all purpose of social studies education is to teach, promote, and practice democratic social behavior. Therefore, of all the curriculum areas, social studies provides the best and most natural vehicle for teaching social and group-work skills. Good social studies programs will include many activities that place children in situations in which they must plan and work with each other, strive toward common goals, and interact with others. Such activities may be used to achieve many worthwhile educational purposes, not the least of which is the development of social and group-work skills.

Precisely what situations can be used to teach and promote such skills? Here are a few examples:

1. *Informal sharing with one another.* Children show each other what they are doing and explain it—as, for example, a picture drawn to show something associated with the unit. They may bring items from home to share with their classmates. Reporting news items provides another possibility for cooperative sharing. As a follow-up to most classroom activities, such as viewing a film, engaging in dramatic play, or a field trip, it is essential that children share their ideas and perceptions with each other.

2. *Construction.* Construction activities in social studies are usually cooperative endeavors in which children must think, plan, and work with each other. The constructions might include model communities, Indian villages, relief maps, Conestoga wagons, dolls representing national groups, looms, boats, airplanes, and others.

3. *Experimentation.* This might include experiments with growing things, mainly plants, and the essential requirements for plant growth; earth-sun-moon relationships and the changing seasons; soil erosion; effects of pollution, and others. Most often experiments of this type will involve small groups of children working together.

4. *Listening.* Listening skills should be taught in both large-group and small-group settings. Listening is half the communication process, an essential skill in human relationships. Learning to listen while others are speaking—listening to reports, to a discussion, and to a presentation as part of a large audience in an auditorium—is important.

5. *Discussion.* One of the most important and frequently used teaching techniques is discussion. It could involve the entire class in the discussion of some aspect of the unit under study, or it could be a round table discussion, a panel discussion, a buzz group, or a brainstorming session. Some form of discussion is used on a daily basis in most social studies programs.

6. *Role playing and dramatic play.* Role playing and dramatic play are excellent processes for sensitizing pupils to problems relating to human interaction. They can be used to reenact events, to obtain a better understanding of concepts, or to call attention to social values such as honesty, integrity, consideration for others, and so on.

7. *Simulation games.* These are a variation of role playing but tend to be structured around a particular objective and follow a standardized set of procedures. This activity, as with role playing, must include a group of children working cooperatively. Simulation games might be used to explain an economic concept, race relations, the replay of a historical event, the conduct of a moot court, or a mock legislative body.

8. *Art activities.* In group situations these might involve the construction of murals, dioramas, or displays relating to the unit. It could also include making stage props or scenery and backgrounds for a dramatic activity.

9. *Music activities.* Folk dancing and folk games provide excellent opportunities for group activity. Singing musical selections or listening to other groups present musical programs suggests other possibilities for teaching social and group-work skills.

10. *Field trips.* It is essential that attention to social skills and group-work skills accompany a field trip. The entire group depends on each member to accept responsibility for the success of the trip. This activity not only involves the interactions of the pupils with each other and with their teacher, but also with the individuals or groups hosting the field trip.

11. *Committee assignments.* Much social studies work of pupils takes place in small, task-oriented groups. These might include committees that have various room responsibilities or responsibilities in connection with the study of the unit topic. Being able to function on a committee as a member or as a leader involves skills that obviously have high transfer value to life outside of school.

12. *Cooperative planning.* This could take place in large-group or small-group settings. Pupils can plan many of the specific learning tasks that are a part of the unit study. They can list questions and organize them. They can decide on ways of working—that is, in committees or individually—types of activities, and so on. On a daily basis pupils can evaluate their progress and plan for the next steps. All of these activities involve cooperative group efforts.

HOW DOES A TEACHER DEPLOY CHILDREN IN A VARIETY OF CONFIGURATIONS FOR SOCIAL STUDIES?

There is no doubt that a teacher's management problems can be reduced if children are kept in one large group, separated from one another, and taught in a more or less formal setting. Unfortunately, however, from the point of view of social learning, there could hardly be a less desirable arrangement. Of course, some group process skills can be taught and learned even in that setting. For example, children will discuss what they have read and will share ideas with each other. This involves showing consideration for others, taking turns, and listening attentively to what others are saying. It is important to learn all of these skills. But the skills of small-group endeavors cannot be learned in such a setting. Consequently, the teacher will want to use a combination of individual work, small-committee work, mid-sized groups (perhaps ten to twelve children), and whole-class instruction. This means that children will be shifting from one configuration to another, and this usually means greater potential for management problems.

Even though there are some risks to management in using a variety of grouping modes, the teacher is urged to use such formats. If it is properly handled, the teacher should have little difficulty in implementing variable group-size instruction. The following suggested procedure will help ensure a smooth transition from large-group to multiple-group instruction:

1. Take your time in starting small-group work. Wait until you have management procedure and routines well established with the children.
2. Get to know the children well enough so that you know the work habits, capabilities, and special needs of individuals.

Identify those children who seem to be independent, self-directed, and responsible in their work. These are the ones who should be selected for the first small-group assignments.

3. Select a task for this small group that is well defined, and one that the group is certain to accomplish successfully.
4. Provide individual work assignments for the remainder of the class. While they are working, meet with the small group, explain what they are to do, and designate a leader.
5. Have the needed learning resources readily available to the small group during this initial experience.
6. Supervise the work of the small group as needed. Answer questions, clarify, and redirect their efforts if necessary.
7. As their work progresses, have them share what they are doing with the remainder of the class. Involve them and the class in developing standards for small-group work.
8. Repeat the procedure with other groups, one at a time. As the children become accustomed to the procedure, you will be able to have more than one group functioning at the same time. Gradually, over a period of a couple months, you should be able to have the entire class working productively in small groups that require a minimum of supervision.
9. Evaluate group work frequently. Involve children in such evaluations using teacher-pupil-generated standards. Refine and add to the list of group-work skills. Monitor closely the behavior of children who are not as self-directed and as responsible as others. This is critical because the behavior of a few irresponsible children, if left unattended, can damage good work habits of the entire class. Sometimes these problems can be alleviated simply by moving a child who is having difficulty to another group. Or the child may be assigned to the group for only part of the work period. It is a mistake to remove such children from group activities altogether because it is precisely in the group where they must learn the skills and habits they obviously do not have.

WHY SHOULD A TEACHER USE A VARIETY OF ACTIVITIES IN THE SOCIAL STUDIES?

It has long been said that variety is the spice of life, and therefore a program with many activities should be more interesting and exciting than one that uses only a few activities. And perhaps that would be reason enough in an area of the curriculum as important as social studies. After all, we cannot expect children to grow into adults who are socially and politically active and concerned if they have been subjected to boring social studies programs for several years as children. However, there are other reasons that should be mentioned too.

As was noted in Chapter 1, in social studies we are concerned with both *product* and *process* learning outcomes. Product outcomes are those that come about because of the learner's encounter with the subject studied. They deal with the substance of the topic, developing an understanding of the facts, concepts, generalizations, and information inherent in the topic. Process learning outcomes, on the other hand, are achieved as a result of the way the subject is studied. This speaks to the value of multiple-activity programs. They make it possible for the children to learn important values and skills because of the nature of the activity itself. Group work is a case in point. Working together cooperatively involves children in a process through which they learn and apply many important human relations skills.

Somewhat the same relationship obtains between activities and process outcomes in teaching various aspects of thinking. A child applies different modes of thought in puzzling through a construction activity or making a mural from the ones he or she applies when reading something from the text or from a library book. Role playing and simulation games call into play different intellectual processes than writing a report does. Thus, to stimulate various aspects of thinking, it is necessary to provide appropriate activities to engender those modes of thought.

Activities can also give concrete direction and purpose to a child's learning. A child may not understand why it is necessary to secure information about an airport terminal, but if the class is going to construct a model of one in the classroom, the child can understand why it is important to have accurate information about it. Naturally, the teacher has more far-reaching and significant purposes in mind than simply having the class produce a replica of a farm, a pioneer village, a harbor, or a pueblo. But for the young child, far-reaching and significant purposes are often not understood unless they are tied to concrete activities in which the child will be directly involved.

Social studies education often deals with complex procedures, abstract concepts, and generalizations. "Doing" activities make these abstractions and complexities easier for children to understand. For example, the concept *division of labor,* although simple enough for an adult to understand, may be very difficult for a young child. However, young children can be taught to understand this concept through dramatic play or simulation games where a division of labor is involved. Or children may find the procedures involved in getting a letter from a sender to a receiver easier to understand than a verbal explanation if they can see the steps in the procedure in operation at a post office.

Social studies activities serve purposes even beyond the ones discussed here. Certainly they encourage the initiative and inquiry of pupils. They help pupils apply factual information to concrete situations. They provide numerous opportunities for thinking, sharing, planning, doing, and evaluating. They enhance the creative talents of children. Finally, they provide a way of relating various facets of the school program to each other. That is, in a social studies activity children may be required to read and write (and, therefore, spell and handwrite) and to speak in discussions and oral reports. They may deal with quantitative concepts and mathematics. They may be engaged in science, art, music, and perhaps even physical education. The activities of the social studies, therefore, can serve very well as the coordinating and/or integrating center of the entire school curriculum.

INTERN TASK 9-2

Identify specific purposes that could be achieved through the use of these activities:

Painting a mural

Role playing a story dealing with sex-role stereotyping

Weaving on a hand loom

Churning butter

Listening to musical recordings of a historical period

Playing a simulation game called Freeway Location

HOW DOES A TEACHER GO ABOUT INVOLVING CHILDREN IN DRAMATIC PLAY, ROLE PLAYING, AND SIMULATION GAMES?

Before discussing this question, it is essential that the meanings of these three activities be understood in terms of their use here:

1. *Dramatic play.* This is the unstructured and spontaneous enactment of situations in which players assume the roles of the characters and improvise a dialog as the enactment unfolds. Through dramatic play children relive the actual experiences of others. Kindergarten children playing house is an example of dramatic play. Children operating a miniature shopping center in their classroom are similarly engaging in dramatic play.

2. *Role playing.* This is the enactment or re-enactment of a situation in which the players assume certain roles, are confronted with a problem involving a moral or value dilemma, and one that requires players to make a decision. Role playing is more structured than dramatic play. It is problem oriented and the alternatives available to the individual players are usually defined within specified limits. The consequences that flow from each choice are not always predictable.

3. *Simulation games.* These are attempts to re-create certain aspects of reality for the purpose of gaining information, developing attitudes and/or values, or developing a skill. Insofar as is practicable and feasible, the "real thing" (that is, the actual situation) is replicated in a simulation game. Military war games, for instance, are well-known simulations. Individuals and groups play the roles of friendly and hostile forces, officers, troops, and whatever else is needed to promote reality. There are rules that must be followed and there are winners and losers. Not all games are simulations. The child's game of jacks for example is not a simulation—that is, it is not a representation of reality. Because most simulations used in school have gaming characteristics, many authors use the terms *games* and *simulations* interchangeably or combine them into *simulation games.*

There are a few general principles that apply to the use of any of these three teaching techniques:

1. They should be used for educational purposes, not simply to entertain the children or to break the monotony of a dull social studies program. In order to meet this requirement dramatic play, role playing, and simulation games must clarify or expand concepts and generalizations, provide new insights or perspectives, engender feelings, and provide an opportunity to learn or practice a skill. They should not be used only because they may be fun for the children and they seem to be the "in" thing to be doing.

2. All three of these techniques require careful planning and skill development if they are to be used effectively. This means that in all likelihood the first few times a teacher and a class try them, there will be some problems. Given the opportunity to learn and practice the skills involved, both teachers and children grow into these procedures over time.

3. The follow-up—the discussion and evaluation that follows the activity or, in simulation games, the *debriefing session*—is essential if learning is to be promoted. As far as this writer is aware, all specialists in the field of educational games and simulations agree on this point. Quite clearly, without a discussion and follow-up critique, pupils may leave the experience with misunderstandings of what actually happened.

4. These techniques should be perceived as an integral part of the social studies program. They should be used as one more avenue for learning rather than something tagged on to or even apart from the mainstream of the social studies program.

5. Authorities seem to be less sure about the value of these techniques in terms of cognitive gain than they are about their impact on the affective dimension of learning. Their value in promoting affective learning seems to be well documented. Even in the case of the space program, for instance, the astronauts undoubtedly had all the knowledge they were going to have about conditions on the moon's surface prior to participating in a simulated walk on the moon here on earth. However, the simulation gave them a "feel" for what it was like to find oneself in such an environment.

Dramatic Play

Most children engage in dramatic play spontaneously as a natural part of the growing up process. Young children will play house or play school on their own and will mirror the behavior of the adults close to them in dramatizing those roles. Given some encouragement and the opportunity to do so, therefore, the teacher will have little difficulty getting young children to participate in dramatic play.

Dramatic play as used in social studies, however, is not the same as when three six-year-olds play school on the back patio at home. These children are simply having fun. They can do almost anything they like in the roles they assume. This kind of dramatic license would not go unchallenged in social studies. For instance, in social studies these children might learn that the teacher is not allowed to deal with pupils in a high-handed way. They would learn that the teacher cannot do anything he or she pleases, even though it may seem that way to six-year-olds! They would learn that if the teacher wants to do something, it might be necessary to check with the principal or with the parents. Issues similar to this often come up in dramatic play. There will be children who want to ride their motorcycles into areas reserved for spectators, drive their buses without regard to other vehicles, bring their boats into the harbor whenever and however they wish, or fly their airplanes without regard to others. It is precisely these situations that indicate where additional information on a topic is needed by the children.

Some teachers use dramatic play in the early stages of unit study. They arrange the classroom with a variety of props and artifacts relating to the topic and encourage the children to examine them and to think of situations in which the props might be used. After the children have had an opportunity to browse through the material, the teacher calls them together and they share their ideas with each other. With the help of their teacher, they plan to dramatize some of their ideas. Often this experience builds an awareness of the need for additional information if their dramatic representation is to be performed with any degree of accuracy. They will need to do some research on the topic. This leads them into planning the next steps in their study: identifying questions that need to be answered, listing things they will need to know, and forming hunches and hypotheses for inquiry. This procedure is much like the one used in connection with constructions and the two activities, construction and dramatic play, are often combined. Children use their constructions as settings in which to engage in dramatic play.

As the information base becomes greater and there is a better understanding of the essential concepts and procedures, the subsequent dramatic play episodes will become more elaborate, more extended, and more accurate. The sequence of engaging in the play, evaluating it, getting additional information through research, and refining and replaying is recycled continually throughout the unit or for as long as the children are challenged by the activity.

Dramatic play can also be used to help children develop an appreciation for the human experience involved in the material they are studying. This can be achieved through the use of story material. The story may be fictional if the setting itself is factual. In re-enacting the story the children develop a sense of empathy for the principals who were a part of the experience related by the story.

Often stories used for this purpose are read to the children by the teacher. Usually the story is too long to be re-enacted in its entirety, and so certain episodes are selected. The teacher should, of course, help children plan the play and help them decide where the episode will begin, where it will end, and who will play which role. Before beginning the play the details and the sequence of the story should be reviewed. Exercises of this type are useful, also, in building the skills of dramatic play: creating a dialog, acting in believable ways, and staying in a role. The episodes can be played, cut, discussed, and replayed, perhaps with another set of actors.

Role Playing

In role playing the object is to focus on a problem involving human relations. It is up to the players to make a decision concerning a satisfactory solution to the problem. Because these situations require making choices between conflicting values—both of which are prized or neither of which is wholly acceptable—the decision making is always difficult. Moreover, there may be more than one satisfactory solution to the problem, depending on one's value orientation and perspective. Thus, these situations can be played, cut, critiqued, and replayed with a different set of actors. Each group could create a different solution to the problem.

What kinds of situations lend themselves to role playing? They should be realistically lifelike, involving a human dilemma with which pupils can identify. The situation must be problematical and involve decision making, otherwise there would be no point in doing the role playing. The Shaftels, in their book *Role Playing for Social Values: Decision Making in the Social Studies,*[2] provide numerous short problem stories for role playing grouped around such themes as honesty, fair-mindedness, rules for everyone, prejudice, feelings of rejection, and others. The teacher is advised to make use of these because they are designed especially for role playing. Of course, the teacher can also create original stories for this purpose too.

The following is an example of a story that could be used for role playing.

> *Directions:* This is a story about a boy who wanted something very badly. Just as he was about to get the opportunity for which he had waited so long, something happened that upset his dreams and plans. But maybe you can think of a way to help him recover what he seems to have lost.
>
> The story I am about to read is not finished. Listen to it carefully and think of ways to finish it.

"You're Outta' Luck!"

> Any person who could play ball at all well could find a place on one of the Little League teams. But to be selected for the Mustangs was something really special. They did not always finish as champions, but each year they came close. The team seemed to have a tradition and spirit that none of the other teams had. If you played with the Mustangs, you were recognized as the best. The players would come and go, but each year the magic of the Mustang team lived on.
>
> For as long as he could remember, Mark Carr wanted to be on the Mustang team. In past years he had not been selected. This would be his last chance to make it because it was his last year in the program. He was older now and had more experience than when he was turned down in the past. He knew he was a better first baseman than most boys three or

---

[2]Fannie R. Shaftel and George Shaftel, *Role Playing for Social Values:* Decision *Making in the Social Studies* (Englewood Cliffs, N.J.: Prentice-Hall, Inc., 1967).

four years older than he. Besides, everyone knew that Mark Carr had one of the best batting records of anyone in the league. All winter long he looked forward to the opening of the season because he knew this would be the year he would become a Mustang!

In order to make the team, one had to get through the tryouts. That wasn't easy, but it was almost as hard to sign up for tryouts. Only twenty-four players were taken in each try-out period, and there were only three periods. Mark had been sick on the other two tryout days and this Saturday was the last chance for him to sign up. Even though he was up early and at the field long before the sign-up was to begin, there were already eight ahead of him in line. Competition was going to be tough, no question about that. He stood around for two hours waiting for 10:00 when the signing was to begin. By 9:45 A.M. the line was completely filled, with a few extra disappointed boys hanging around who had come too late to get into the group of twenty-four. Mark was really glad to have been there as early as he had in order to be the ninth in line, certain to be selected for the tryout.

Just as the signing was to begin, an announcement came over the PA system, "Mark Carr, report to the officials' booth for an important message. Mark Carr, report to the officials' booth."

"Oh, no. Not now!" Mark said to himself. Then the announcement came again, "Mark Carr, report to the officials' booth immediately."

He had to go to the officials' booth, that was certain. But what about his place in line? "Don't worry about it, Mark, I'll hold your place," said his friend Eric, who was next in line. "They won't be starting for a few minutes anyway. You'll be back by then."

"O.K. Thanks. Tell them I'll be right back," he said and ran to the officials' booth.

At the officials' booth, Mark had to wait to get the mes-sage because a couple angry parents were arguing with the person in the booth, Mr. Jackson, about their son's eligibility. "Come *on*," Mark thought. After a long wait, he finally got up enough courage to interrupt by saying, "Please, Mr. Jack-son . . ."

"Oh, I'm sorry, Mark," said Mr. Jackson. "It's urgent that I talk to you about your medical examination card. I'll be with you right away." Then he continued arguing with the parents.

"Medical examination?" Mark wondered to himself. "Hurry, Mr. Jackson. *Please* hurry!"

It was more than a half hour before Mark was able to straighten out the problem about his medical examination card. Besides, it wasn't his fault that the information was not complete. If Dr. Oliver's secretary had read the directions before filling out the card, there wouldn't have been any problem. He ran back across the playing field where the Mustangs were signing up players for tryouts. The last boy to sign up was just walking away.

"Hi, Mark. Where were you this morning?" He recognized the voice of Mr. Banneker. "We were expecting you to sign for tryouts today. Looks to me as if you're outta' luck now."

Because both the actors and audience participate in role playing, the whole group needs to be involved in planning. It is important to stress that the audience are participants, not merely spectators. They will discuss and critique the enactment, and members of the audience may move into actor roles in re-enactments. Dr. Fannie R. Shaftel suggests the following steps in guiding role playing:

1. Warming up the group (a readiness activity).
2. Selecting role players.
3. Preparing the audience.
4. Setting the stage (ascertaining knowledge of role and situation).
5. Role playing: the enactment.
6. Discussing and evaluating.
7. Re-enacting and further enacting.
8. Reviewing and generalizing.
9. Decision making.[3]

Role playing should be perceived as training in the analysis of social issues, human relationships, or social interaction. In this context the quality of the acting must always be a secondary, or even a minor, consideration. Role playing deviates from its basic purposes when it becomes primarily a training program in play acting.

---

[3]In Lavone A. Hanna, Gladys L. Potter, and Robert W. Reynolds, *Dynamic Elementary Social Studies, Unit Teaching,* 3rd ed. (New York: Holt, Rinehart & Winston, Inc., 1973), pp. 261–264.

Simulation Games

In dramatic play, and to some extent in role playing, the actors are required to improvise and to create their own solutions to problems unencumbered by a strict set of rules. This is not true in a simulation game. Here the players are bound by certain rules; there are rewards for doing some things and penalties for doing other things. Winners and losers are determined by the outcome of the game. Children might, for example, engage in dramatic play representing transactions on the stock market. In a stock market simulation game, however, there would be more stringent rules about how the game is to be played; and when the game is concluded, perhaps some players would be wealthy and others would have lost everything. Presumably their successes would be determined to some extent by the wisdom of the decisions they made while the game was being played.

Simulation games have become popular with teachers in recent years, even though there is not agreement among experts about their educational value at the elementary school level. Nonetheless, an increasing number of simulation games are available commercially. The following are examples of the types of materials on the market:

1. *Gold Mining Camp:* This game simulates the economic problems of an 1850 gold mining camp. Economic concepts such as supply and demand, profits, needs, wants, and others are included. Designed for lower elementary grades. Available through Georgia Environmental Curriculum Studies Project; 128 Fain Hall; University of Georgia; Athens, Georgia 30602.

2. *Gold Miners and Merchants:* Designed to complement Gold Mining Camp. The pupils' buying and selling goods lead to an understanding of selected economic concepts: profit-loss-savings, scarcity-surplus, and supply-demand. Designed for lower elementary grades. Available through Georgia Environmental Curriculum Studies Project; 128 Fain Hall; University of Georgia; Athens, Georgia 30602.

3. *Survival Game:* Pupils select a specific environment in which they want to work—desert, polar region, or tropical rain forest. Then they are presented cards on which there are problems created by that environment. The job of the players is to maintain their survival by dealing with the problems.

To be used at about fourth grade with five pupils. Available through EDCOM Systems Inc.; 145 Witherspoon Street; Princeton, New Jersey 08540.

4. *Market:* This game involves consumer and retailer teams. Retailers try to make a profit; consumers try to gain points. There are three marketing periods in which consumers and retailers interact. Consumers try to get the best buys; retailers try to make the highest profit. Designed for sixth graders. Produced by Industrial Relations Center; University of Chicago; 1225 East 60th Street; Chicago, Illinois 60637.

5. *Kikuyu Games:* Actually includes two games, both based on the life styles of the Kikuyu tribe of Kenya. One deals with the settlement patterns of the tribe. The other simulates the Kikuyu market place in which players develop concepts of bartering. The games are called Githaka and Market Place, respectively. Designed for upper elementary grades. Available through CBS Learning Center; Princeton, New Jersey 08540.

In addition to games such as these, there are many simulation games that are included as integral parts of social studies textbook programs now on the market.

In her book *Games for Growth,* Alice Kaplan Gordon makes the following suggestions to teachers who plan to use simulation games:

1. If possible, play the game through with other teachers or friends.
2. Become acquainted with the physical components of the game.
3. Thoroughly read the materials provided for the teacher's use.
4. Modify the game, if necessary, to meet particular needs of the class.
5. Decide the basis on which roles will be assigned. Try to include bright and slow students on the same teams.
6. Distribute copies of the rules, and profiles and scenarios where they are used, to each student the day before play.
7. Arrange the components of the game in the classroom.
8. Brief students on
   a. the purpose of the game.
   b. the roles of individuals or teams, and objectives.
   c. the physical layout of the room.

    d. the first move.
   This phase should not exceed fifteen minutes.
9. During play, circulate among groups or individuals and offer suggestions where desirable, answer questions when necessary. Try to involve the student in answering his own questions and arriving at solutions.[4]

A teacher may want to construct his or her own simulation game, perhaps with the help of the pupils or of a colleague. The following suggestions may prove useful:

1. Decide what instructional purpose is to be served by the game. That is, what objective or objectives are to be achieved through the use of the simulation game?
2. Select real-life situations that can be used to illustrate or dramatize the objectives. Prepare a narrative, or scenario, that describes the situation and makes explicit the problem, conflict, issue, or process to be simulated.
3. Establish the sequence of events and decide how much time will be required or allowed for each.
4. Decide which players will be involved, how many there will be, and how they are to be grouped.
5. Make clear what the specific objectives of individuals or teams are to be. How are success and/or failure experiences to be recognized and recorded? What resources (votes, play money, political support, food, and so forth) will players have for trade-offs and bargaining?
6. Decide how individuals or groups will interact in order to register wins or losses.
7. Clarify the role of the teacher in
   a. Introducing the game.
   b. Playing the game.
   c. Debriefing the game.

---

[4]Alice Kaplan Gordon, *Games for Growth* (Palo Alto, Calif.: Science Research Associates, Inc., College Division, 1970), p. 112.

Intern and Field Associate Teacher Advisory

The intern cannot possibly learn to use dramatic play, role playing, and simulation games without actually having the experience
of working with these techniques on a direct, firsthand basis.
It is crucial, therefore, that the intern and the field associate
teacher plan together in arranging for intern involvement in
these techniques in the classroom. It is recommended that the
initial experiences be with simple dramatic play, moving then to
guiding some role playing and finally to simulation games. It
will be helpful if the field associate teacher is able to demonstrate
the use of these techniques for the intern. If that is not possible
or feasible, perhaps the two of them can handle these sessions
cooperatively. In any case the intern should not complete the
program without direct experience with these important techniques in teaching elementary school social studies.

HOW CAN ELEMENTARY SCHOOL CHILDREN BECOME INVOLVED IN SOCIAL-ACTION PROJECTS IN SOCIAL STUDIES?

Engaging in social action means that pupils apply some of what
they learn in the classroom to life outside. This may mean some activity or project in the school, usually beyond their own classroom, or
something entirely removed from the school itself. The reader should
be reminded that in its statement of curriculum guidelines, the National Council for the Social Studies referred to social participation as one
of the four essential components of social studies education. In this
context social action, or social participation, is a criterion by which a
social studies program is to be judged. Thus, it is clear that an involvement in social action by pupils is more on the order of a mandate
than an option.

Social-action projects ought to be consistent with the maturity
of the children doing them. Children are not ready to deal with the

great social issues of our time—war and peace, labor relations, political corruption, abortion, race relations, and organized crime, to name a few—when they are not able to get along with one another on the playground and in the lunchroom, when they leave their school looking like a disaster area each day, and when there is a high incidence of vandalism in the school. The appropriate place to begin social action is with projects that address themselves to these problems. Pupils ought to apply social action to those problems that are immediately around them. Often, the simpler the activity, the better. For example:

> Teacher: "Boys and girls, would you please look around the room to find one thing that you would like to change that would make our room a more attractive place in which to work. Don't do any more than think about it just now. (Pause.) Now, what would you like to change?"

> As ideas are suggested and accepted, pupils can immediately make the changes. If more than one child comes up with the same idea, teams of children can be assigned to do the task.

This same project could be done outside on the school grounds. A variation of it could be extended into a home or neighborhood project. Clean-up campaigns often are popular social-action projects, perhaps because they are the easiest to do and there is a continuing need for them.

Children who are actively involved in applying their learnings to social-action projects are almost always ones who have imaginative, concerned teachers. That is, it is the teacher who provides the leadership and encouragement for such activities. Here are a few social-action projects that teachers report are successful:

- Collecting and refurbishing used toys and donating them to Goodwill Industries for redistribution.
- Collecting food for the Neighbors in Need Program.
- Making party favors for elderly persons in a local retirement home at times of major holidays.
- Collecting books for the local library's used book sale.
- Studying and publicizing places in the local area that may be safety hazards.

- Preparing store window displays dealing with an issue of local interest.
- Studying the ethnic heritage of the local community and preparing a display showing something about the history and contributions of various groups.
- Making a survey of one's home to look for safety hazards or fire dangers and correcting them.
- Sponsoring a bicycle safety program in school.
- Volunteering to do babysitting free to mothers on Election Day.

INTERN TASK 9–3

Develop an appropriate social-action project that could be performed by your class. Discuss your idea with your field associate teacher. If approved by your field associate teacher, have your pupils implement the project. Report the success of the project to your fellow interns in the clinic.

SOCIAL STUDIES COMPETENCIES AND SKILLS

CHECKING YOUR PERFORMANCE

Intern Task Checklist

Task 9-1. Identifying subskills to serve as standards for group work. P. 210. _____

Task 9-2. Relating specific purposes to activities. P. 216. _____

Task 9-3. Developing and implementing a social-action project. P. 229. _____

Performance Checklist

In the field or in the clinic, the intern teacher has

1. Conducted social studies instruction in groups of varying sizes. _____

2. Used social studies activities to teach social and group-work skills to pupils. _____

3. Made use of a variety of activities in teaching social studies. _____

4. Demonstrated in conversation or in writing that he or she understands the nature and purposes of dramatic play, role playing, and simulation games. _____

5. Made use of dramatic play, role playing, and simulation games in teaching social studies. _____

6. Engaged pupils in at least one social-action project related to social studies. _____

Field Associate Teacher Advisory

Tasks and performances should be checked off or initialed and dated by the appropriate local official, or the intern teacher can use the checklists for his or her own record.

Chapter 10

Evaluation procedures and processes in the classroom

The local weekly newspaper had been opened neatly to page B–2 and placed on the table in the teachers' lounge where its message could not be missed when the teachers came in for their midmorning break.

Are Schools Accountable for Cost and Quality of Education Today?[1]

Somebody is accountable.

Johnnie can't read or write, as newspaper and magazine articles relate, but the cost of his education is increasing. There is a widespread movement to reject this educational failure by the refusal of state legislatures to maintain present levels of funding for the schools. The call to return to "basic education" grows louder each day.

The local legislature is concentrating on bills that would set up a statewide testing program of student achievement, that would specify probationary periods for teachers deemed not competent, that would determine statewide standards of teacher evaluation, and that would set forth hearing procedures.

Some educators have described the accountability issue as a red herring to detract attention from the real issue, funding. One legislator said the funding issue and the accountability issue were a trade-off: schools will get funding if they accept accountability laws.

---

[1] Adapted from an article by Gail Loiselle in *Northshore Citizen,* Bothell, Washington, February 26, 1976, p. A–2.

Reasonable expectations of education must take into consideration some facts about the good old days of the three R's.

In 1776, only about 15 per cent of the population was literate. This literate minority left their eloquent records while the illiterate majority left none, except for marks on legal papers.

In 1890, only 7 per cent of all eligible young people were in high school. Life was still largely rural.

In 1920, for the first time, the majority of the population were urban inhabitants, no longer down on the farm with its simpler life. More than half of all eligible youths were in high school. Schools were still traditional, dedicated to an academic format that is less expensive.

In 1975, less than 30 per cent of the population was rural. More homes had a radio and/or a television set than a subscription to a newspaper. Of all eligible youth, 94 per cent were in high school, one result of child labor laws and mandatory schooling designed to control the labor pool.

The aim of education has changed from academic achievement for personal benefit to acculturation for social benefit. The shift is from educating the mind to educating the whole person. The expansion of the curriculum into sports, music, art, home economics, woodworking, mechanics, driver's training, and business machines involves a greater outlay of funds than for a strictly academic curriculum.

In essence, the wonderful world of the past did not ever exist, except as remembered by those who weren't there.

This article reflects the concerns of citizens in communities all over the land. The article might have appeared in any newspaper in the United States. It tells us that more and more parents and patrons of the schools are asking the simple question: Are our kids getting the quality of education we are paying for? This is a cost-benefit question. But who can answer such a question when the costs of everything are skyrocketing, when school populations are changing from what they were in the past, when the nature of society itself is changing, and when the outcomes of education are as intangible as they are.

From the perspective of the classroom teacher, accountability means doing all that one can with the time and resources available to ensure that each child progresses at a rate commensurate with his or her potential. This is what is required to be professionally responsible, quite apart from what accountability local school districts may require.

*Accountability carries with it the additional responsibility of convey-
ing information concerning pupil progress to parents and other concerned parties in forms that objective observers would regard as valid
and reliable. In order to do this, a careful and systematic evaluation
of pupil performance on a day-to-day basis is critical. In social studies
education, the following are basic competencies that the intern teacher
must develop in order to do this job:*

Basic Competencies—Social Studies

The intern teacher is able to

1. Explain the various ways evaluation relates to instruction and to learning objectives.
2. Construct and use informal techniques and devices to
   evaluate pupil achievement in the social studies in the
   areas of
   a. Cognitive gain.
   b. Attitude and value change.
   c. Skill growth.
3. Select and use standardized tests relevant to elementary
   school social studies education.
4. Report pupil progress to parents.

INTERN ADVISORY

After completing this chapter, together with related work in the clinic and
appropriate classroom experiences in the field, you should be able to do the
following:

1. Provide a rationale for the use of evaluation as it relates to teaching.
2. Construct and use the informal evaluative techniques and procedures
   discussed in this chapter. More specifically, you should be able to construct and use at least one procedure for evaluating objectives dealing
   with each of the three categories of outcomes: (a) cognitive gain, (b) attitude and value change, and (c) skill growth.
3. Administer a standardized test to a class.
4. Report pupil progress to parents, using whatever form is adopted by the
   district in which you are teaching.

WHY IS EVALUATION AN INTEGRAL PART OF TEACHING?

Evaluating learning progress is an indispensable part of the teaching process because (1) it helps clarify objectives for learners—it helps them know what is important to learn; (2) it provides feedback to the learners, thereby keeping them informed about their progress or lack of it; (3) it informs learners if and how they are deficient in order that they can improve; and (4) it informs the teacher of the extent to which pupils have achieved desired outcomes. Additionally, evaluation is essential in reporting pupil progress to parents and informing the public about the effectiveness of school programs.

Evaluation takes many forms and occurs at several levels. Many school districts have some type of testing program that provides information about pupil achievement. Some states use statewide standardized testing. For several years there has been a national effort to secure information through testing about the educational attainment of students and young adults. Closer to the classroom, evaluation takes place many times each day as the teacher observes children at work and makes judgments about their behavior, their study habits, and their work products. Children themselves form opinions about the quality of their work, and this is yet another form of evaluation.

In this chapter we will deal with classroom evaluation of pupil learning as it occurs on a day-to-day basis. What we are concerned about are those techniques, procedures, and settings in which *judgments* are made concerning activities in the classroom: What do the children need to learn? How can observed deficiencies and/or limitations in pupil abilities be accommodated? Is the instruction proceeding too rapidly? Too slowly? How well have concepts been learned? Is additional practice required on some skill? Are the small-group activities productive? How might they be improved? How can the noise level in the room be reduced? Why isn't this class more interested in what we are doing? These are examples of the hundreds of questions teachers ask themselves as they watch the work of their classes. These questions involve evaluation of the type we are most concerned about.

Tests, of course, have a place in the program of evaluation in the classroom too. Many teachers make some use of examinations that are published by commercial firms and marketed nationally. There is also need for well-constructed tests that the teacher makes. Teacher-made tests in the elementary school should serve all of the purposes discussed in the opening sentence of this section. Tests have the advantage of providing a written record of the child's responses; impressionistic reactions of the teacher to the child's work often lack the objectivity and accuracy that written tests provide.

Record keeping is of utmost importance in classroom evaluation. Samples of children's work, test papers, the teacher's written observations of and impressions of pupil behavior, records of diagnostic procedures, and so on should be kept in folders on individual children. When these records are kept for a period of time, we can tell something about the child's educational progress. If the teacher relies on memory to retrieve this information at times when formal reports are due, it is not possible to prepare a very complete or well-documented report. What is then reported are impressions; and because inferences are sometimes made about the teacher's competence on the basis of pupil progress, it is natural that bias, however inadvertently, is brought into the report.

HOW ARE INFORMAL TECHNIQUES AND PROCEDURES USED TO EVALUATE SOCIAL STUDIES OUTCOMES?

The reader should now turn back to pages 4–6 and review the major goals of social studies education. The central question is, "How is the attainment of those goals by the pupils evaluated?" For purposes of study and analysis, we often examine teaching and evaluative procedures in terms of cognitive gain, attitude and value change, and achievement of skills. Although this separation is a convenient one, it is also an artificial one. In the practical sense these goals are intimately related, and this reality must be taken into account in evaluating pupil achievement of them. Just to cite one specific example: A child may score poorly on a test intended to measure cognitive gain. The test requires the child to read three paragraphs of prose and then arrange a series of events in the order in which they occurred. It happens that the child is a poor reader. One does not know if such an evaluative device is measuring the child's understanding of the substantive content or his or her reading skill. Perhaps the truth of the matter is that in this case it does not do either one. It is certain that no test will provide an assessment of a pupil's knowledge of concepts and content if he or she cannot read it with understanding. We should not place too much credence in test scores unless we also know what skills were needed to do the tasks required by the test and the attitude or mind-set of the child toward the activity.

If the reader will keep these precautions in mind, Chart 10–1 may be helpful in selecting evaluative procedures and techniques for various types of social studies outcomes.

CHART 10-1. *Techniques, devices and procedures commonly used by elementary school teachers to evaluate pupil progress in social studies.*

Outcome to be evaluated

Techniques, procedure, or device used	Cognitive gain
Group discussion	Things to note: How well do pupils use the appropriate vocabulary? Are essential concepts understood? Are important relationships understood? Are there important concepts needing further study? Is the factual base adequate for the ideas being discussed?
Observation	Do pupils Talk with understanding about the topics under study? Cite examples of out-of-school applications of ideas studied?
Checklists	Applied to behaviorally stated objectives that serve as criterion references of pupil achievement.
Conferences	Use individual pupil conferences to Discover evidence of confusion or misunderstanding of ideas. Clarify the kinds of assistance needed by the pupil. Discover the nature of needed remedial work.
Anecdotal records	Used to record specific observations of pupil behavior; items listed under Group Discussion and Observation will be appropriate.

Attitude and value change	Skill growth
Things to note: Extent to which pupils express like or dislike of topic. Presence or absence of comments suggesting racism, sexism, or prejudice. Extent of openness to new ideas. Evidence of responsible self-evaluation.	Things to note: Ability to express ideas in a group. Ability to use standards in evaluating work.
Do pupils Show respect for the ideas and feelings of others? Carry a fair share of the work load? Show evidence of responsible habits of work?	Do pupils Use relevant skills independently when they are needed? Have apparent deficiencies in skills? Avoid using certain important and needed skills?
Used to record observations of specific behaviors of pupils.	Checklists are developed to evaluate the use of a specific skill: giving an oral report, clarity of speaking, or use of references.
May be used to learn specific interests of individual pupils—likes, dislikes, preferred activities, books, topics, and so on.	Used to diagnose specific problems in the use of skills. Can be used to check the proficiency of skill use on an individual basis.
items listed under Group Discussion and	Observation will be appropriate.

SOCIAL STUDIES COMPETENCIES AND SKILLS

CHART 10-1. (continued)

Work samples	To note qualitative differences in pupil work products over time: a written report, booklet, map, or a classroom test.
Diaries and logs	Basically the same as Experience Summaries, Help pupils recall what has been learned.
Sociometric devices	Of no special use in evaluating cognitive gain.
Teacher-made tests	Used to evaluate understanding of concepts, generalizations, trends, and informational content through the use of such exercises as the following: Matching causes and effects. Arranging events in order or arranging steps in a sequence. Providing reasons or explanations for events. Selecting the best explanations from a list of alternatives. Determining the truth or falsity of statements. Providing examples of concepts. Supplying a generalization based on given facts. Being able to use key terms correctly. Providing ends to unfinished stories or situations based on facts. Placing events on a time line.

To note greater sensitivity to others in written work and artwork. To note increased concern for neatness of work; concern for punctuality in completing assigned work.	To note qualitative differences in proficiency in use of specific skills.
except that diaries and logs are kept on a Remind pupils of the gap between intentions and behavior.	continuing basis. Show incremental growth in skill use over time
Used to observe changes in the social structure of the group. Show how children have or have not won greater acceptance by the group. Show how leadership roles have changed over time. Show how the preferences of children for one another have changed over time.	Of no special use in evaluating skill growth.
Used to find out about likes, dislikes, interests, and preferences for activities through the use of such exercises as the following: From a list, select the things you liked best, liked least. Check what you like to do during your free time. Write ends to unfinished stories that deal with emotions, prejudice, and discrimination. Select words from a narrative that engender strong feelings.	Used to check the proficiency of skill use *or* to diagnose specific difficulties through the use of exercises such as the following: Placing geographic features on an outline map. Locating places on a map. Reading to find the main idea. Making an outline of material read; or finishing a partially completed outline. Using an index to find information. Skimming to find specific facts.

SOCIAL STUDIES COMPETENCIES AND SKILLS

The following are a few examples of teacher-made tests that could be used for evaluating social studies outcomes:

What's Going On Here?

Directions: Read each paragraph carefully, then write a sentence telling what the paragraph is describing.

Situation 1. It was the first Tuesday in November. On this day the fire station had the United States flag flying just outside the entrance. All day long people were going in and coming out of the fire station. A sign in the window said, "Polling Place."

What was going on at the fire station?

_____

Situation 2. A large number of people are in the room. At the front of the room, sitting behind a large desk up on a platform, is a man dressed in a black robe who seems to be in charge of things. As we watch, two men face each other in front of the man in the black robe. One man seems to be holding a Bible. He says to the other man, "Raise your right hand. Do you swear to tell the truth, the whole truth, and nothing but the truth, so help you God?"

What is going on in this room?

_____

Situation 3. A large crowd of people is in this huge room. There are signs and banners all over the place. There is much noise and confusion. People speak to the crowd, but many are not listening. The person who is now speaking has just said, "I yield five minutes to the delegate from the great state of Virginia."

What is going on here?

_____

Situation 4. People are scurrying around all over the place. Everyone seems to be in a hurry. Over the loud speaker, a voice is saying, "The East Concourse is now open."

Where is all this taking place?

_____

Figure 10-1.

EVALUATION PROCEDURES AND PROCESSES IN THE CLASSROOM

Do-It-Yourself Map

Directions:

1. On a clean sheet of paper, draw an outline map of an imaginary continent. You may make it any shape you wish, but you must include at least one peninsula and one bay.
2. Show a scale of miles in your legend for the map.
3. Draw east-west and north-south lines on your map.
4. Draw a mountain range running east and west across your continent but include at least one mountain pass. Place the symbol you use for your mountain range in your legend.
5. Show a city in the northern half of your continent and one in the southern half. Make each one a seaport.
6. Show a railway joining the two cities.
7. Show three rivers on your continent; show a lake and a swamp. Place all the symbols you use for cities, rivers, lakes, and swamps in the legend.
8. Place a third city somewhere on your map where you think a city should be. On the bottom of your map tell why you think a city should be where you have placed it.
9. Show boundary lines that divide your continent into three large countries and one small country.

Figure 10-2.

Matching Cause and Effect

Directions: Each of the events listed in the first column was the cause of an event listed in the second column. In the space provided at the left, place the letter of the result that matches each cause.

____1. Expanding factories needed many workers.

____2. Automobiles were mass produced at low cost.

____3. Trains and trolleys were built to take people to their jobs.

____4. Workers needed to live close to their jobs.

a. People with average income could buy their own cars.

b. Immigrant workers came in large numbers.

c. Workers lived in crowded and congested conditions.

d. People could have their homes farther from where they worked.

Figure 10-3.

SOCIAL STUDIES COMPETENCIES AND SKILLS

Knowing Their Meaning

Directions: The phrases in the right-hand column explain the words or terms listed in the left-hand column. In the space to the left of each phrase, place the letter of the word or term that matches the description.

a. Blimp
b. Drill
c. Mohair
d. Derrick
e. Raw Sugar
f. Helium
g. Gusher
h. Sulphur
i. Refinery
j. Flowing well

_____ 1. An oil well from which the oil shoots high into the air.

_____ 2. A building in which raw materials are changed into finished products.

_____ 3. The brown crystals that form when the juice of sugar cane is boiled and allowed to cool.

_____ 4. The framework that supports the machinery used to drill an oil well.

_____ 5. The tool used to bore holes into the earth.

_____ 6. An airship that floats in the air when filled with a light gas.

_____ 7. Cloth made from goat hair.

_____ 8. A very light gas.

_____ 9. A well from which a steady stream of oil flows without having to be pumped.

_____ 10. A yellow mineral.

Figure 10-4.

What Did You Like Best?

Directions: In the space to the left of each activity, write a letter "L" if you liked it and a "D" if you did not like it. Place a star (*) next to the two you liked best of all.

_____ 1. Making individual booklets on the unit.

_____ 2. Working in committees.

_____ 3. Dramatizing important events.

_____ 4. Writing summaries.

_____ 5. Doing map work.

_____ 6. Seeing films and filmstrips.

_____ 7. Reading different books.

_____ 8. Collecting pictures.

_____ 9. Taking the field trip.

_____ 10. Hearing the resource people.

_____ 11. Making a mural.

_____ 12. Preparing the exhibit.

_____ 13. Preparing the report.

_____ 14. Doing the simulation.

_____ 15. Working in the learning center.

Figure 10-5.

EVALUATION PROCEDURES AND PROCESSES IN THE CLASSROOM

CHART 10-2.

Checklist for Discussion (Middle Grades)	Always	Usually	Seldom	Rarely
1. States problems clearly				
2. Sticks to the point				
3. Shows respect for ideas of others				
4. Contributes regularly				
5. Raises questions on issues				
6. Helps in making decisions				
7. Uses evidence to back up points				
8. Helps in summarizing				

CHART 10-3.

Checklist for Discussion (Primary Grades)	Always	Sometimes	Not Often
1. Helps make plans			
2. Listens to what is said			
3. Takes turns			
4. Gives own ideas			
5. Considers what others have said			

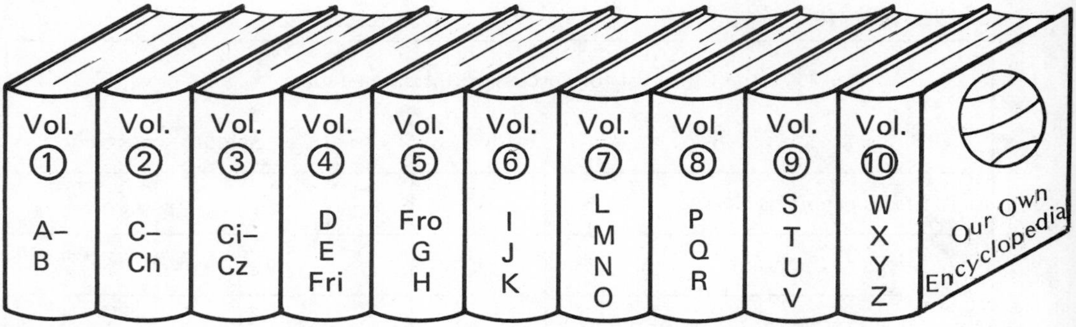

Using the Encyclopedia

Directions: Using the ten-volume *Our Own Encyclopedia* shown in this diagram, select the number of the volume in which you would find information about each of the items listed below. Write the number of the volume you select in the spaces on the left side of the sheet. Then list the volume number of *World Book* in which the same items are found in the spaces on the right side of the sheet.

Our Own   *World Book*

_____ 1. Earthquakes in Guatemala   1. _____

_____ 2. The French writer Crèvecoeur   2. _____

_____ 3. The history of rocketry   3. _____

_____ 4. The Peoples Republic of China   4. _____

_____ 5. Russia   5. _____

_____ 6. Apple growing in Washington state   6. _____

_____ 7. Jet aircraft   7. _____

_____ 8. Countries that are members of the   8. _____
                  United Nations

_____ 9. Unidentified flying objects   9. _____

_____ 10. The history of Czechoslovakia   10. _____

Figure 10-6.

245

EVALUATION PROCEDURES AND PROCESSES IN THE CLASSROOM

True or False?

Directions: The following list contains some statements that are true and some that are not true. Read each one and decide whether it is or is not true. If it is true, place a "T" in the space just to the left of the statement. If it is false, place an "F" in the space and *rewrite* the statement on the line below it to make it true.

_____ 1. Some of the dry land in Arizona and New Mexico is irrigated and produces fine crops.

_____

_____ 2. Colorado and Nevada were settled by people rushing east.

_____

_____ 3. The Mormons settled at Great Salt Lake in a region then owned by California.

_____

_____ 4. Gold was discovered in the Comstock Lode in the state of Nevada.

_____

_____ 5. The large area in the Rockies that is lower than the surrounding mountains is called the Continental Divide.

_____

_____ 6. The Indian house used by the Navajos is called a hogan.

_____

_____ 7. The Plains Indians lived in villages called pueblos.

_____

_____ 8. An early mission was established in what is now the state of Arizona by Father Kino.

_____

Figure 10-7.

SOCIAL STUDIES COMPETENCIES AND SKILLS

INTERN TASK 10-1

a. Turn to the teaching plan on pages 91–92. Notice that this plan does not provide for evaluation. Suggest evaluative procedures that might be added to the plan. Check your suggestions with your field associate teacher.
b. Make use of appropriate informal evaluative techniques and procedures in your teaching of social studies.

> **Field Associate Teacher Advisory**
>
> Make sure that the intern has experience in constructing and using some of the informal evaluative techniques and procedures discussed in the chapter. It is important for the intern to learn how to evaluate outcomes in the three major categories of social goals.
>
> Arrange to have the intern examine a standardized test appropriate for the grade and to read the test manual. Explain local policies in the use of standarized tests in social studies and explain the procedures involved in their administration. The intern should understand the teacher's responsibilities in the administration and scoring of these instruments.
>
> Involve the intern in reporting pupil progress to parents. The intern should assist in preparing report cards, if you use them, and should sit in on parent conferences. Also, involve the intern in completing cumulative record cards, if your district uses them.

WHAT STANDARDIZED TESTS ARE AVAILABLE FOR ELEMENTARY SCHOOL SOCIAL STUDIES?

Standardized tests are constructed by specialists who select test items on the basis of curriculum content that is common to a large number of schools throughout the nation. In the development of the instruments, the tests are tried out on a great number of pupils. This helps the test makers to eliminate weak items and to make the test technically correct. Items are arranged so that there is a gradual increase in the mean score from one year (grade) to the next. Because the test is given to thousands of pupils representing a national sample, the expected average scores and deviations can be established for each age or grade group. This process is known as establishing a *norm* and, therefore, these tests are called norm-referenced tests. This makes it possible to tell whether an individual pupil's score is at, above, or below the scores of other children of the same age and grade level. By grouping the scores for a class, school, or even a school district, comparisons can be made with the norming population.

Standardized tests are helpful in providing an objective yardstick to the achievement of pupils. They are not without their limitations, however, and in recent years they have come under increased criticism, particularly from members of certain ethnic minority groups. The most often cited objections to the use of standardized tests are these:

1. They are often misused by teachers who believe that all children must attain the average score and by teachers who teach specifically for the test content.
2. They rely on reading skill and, therefore, they often do not provide good measures of concept attainment and knowledge of informational content.
3. They may be used to label children as high or low achievers, thereby encouraging a self-fulfilling prophecy.
4. They may have the effect of limiting or "freezing" the curriculum to that of the content of the tests.
5. They are not able to accommodate adequately the local variations that are found in the social studies curriculums of American schools.
6. They not only test school achievement but life experiences and out-of-school learning of all types—that is, the tests have a sociocultural bias favoring children who come from middle and upper socioeconomic levels.
7. They focus on the measurement of easily identified objectives dealing with subject matter and information and often do not evaluate the broader goals of social studies education.

Many but not all of the limitations of standardized tests are less detrimental to sound instruction when the tests focus on essential skills rather than on subject matter. Somewhat the same skills should be taught in all schools, no matter what specific subject matter is included in the curriculum. Additionally, it is more difficult for teachers to abuse the use of skills tests by teaching directly for the test itself.

The following is a partial list of standardized tests that contain sections dealing with elements of social studies or whose contents are wholly social studies:

1. Stanford Achievement Test; Harcourt Brace Jovanovich, Inc.; New York.
2. Metropolitan Achievement Tests; Harcourt Brace Jovanovich, Inc.; New York.
3. SRA Achievement Series; Science Research Associates; Chicago.
4. Sequential Tests of Educational Progress: Social Studies, Level 4, Grades 4–6; Educational Testing Service; Princeton, N.J.
5. Iowa Every-Pupil Test of Basic Skills; Houghton Mifflin Company; Boston.

HOW IS PUPIL PROGRESS REPORTED TO PARENTS?

Each school district has its own procedures for reporting pupil progress to parents. These procedures vary from conventional report cards to individual parent conferences. Most districts use some combination of written and in-person reports to parents. *Evaluative comments to parents about their child's progress should always be documented by some type of data:* samples of the child's work, exact comments made by the pupil, a written record of observations that the teacher had made of the child's behavior, specific examples or instances of cooperation, helpfulness, consideration for others (or the reverse of these traits), test scores and/or test papers, and other documents and data that support what judgments the teacher is making of the child's work.

In general, parents should have at least three types of information about their child's progress in school:

1. How well the child is achieving in terms of his or her past record.

2. How well the child is achieving in terms of the achievement of his or her classmates.
3. How well the child is achieving in terms of children his or her own age.

To supply the parent with this information, the teacher will need to get data from several different sources. For example, standardized tests can be helpful in showing a child's achievement as it compares with that of others of his or her own age. How a child's achievement compares with that of his or her classmates depends on the type of class the child is in. A child achieving at an average rate might show up poorly in a class of gifted children. Social studies education concerns itself with a broad spectrum of goals and objectives; consequently, a broad range of evaluative devices and techniques must be used in assessing outcomes. Similarly, in reporting to parents, as much information and data as possible should be provided to give a clear picture of the status of the child in school.

SOCIAL STUDIES COMPETENCIES AND SKILLS

CHECKING YOUR PERFORMANCE

Intern Task Checklist

Task 10-1. a. Suggesting evaluative procedures for a teaching plan. P. 246. _____

b. Using informal evaluative devices in the classroom. P. 246. _____

Performance Checklist

In the field or in the clinic, the intern teacher has

1. Articulated a rationale in conversation or in writing for the use of _____
   evaluation as it relates to teaching.
2. Constructed and used a sample of informal evaluative techniques and _____
   procedures dealing with the three categories of social studies outcomes:
   cognitive gain, attitude and value change, and skill growth.
3. Assisted with the administration of a standardized test. _____

4. Participated in preparing pupil progress reports to parents and assisted _____
   the field associate teacher in making such reports.

> ### *Field Associate Teacher Advisory*
>
> Tasks and performances should be checked off or initialed and dated by the appropriate local official, or the intern teacher can use the checklists for his or her own record.

Chapter 11

Continuing professional growth in social studies

After completing her internship, securing a teaching position, and successfully teaching for two years, Mary Finch decided to begin work on her "fifth-year" requirements. She decided not to go back to Holy Names College where she did her undergraduate work. Not that there was anything wrong with Holy Names, but she wanted to get herself into a different environment. She discussed her plans with her former advisor at Holy Names, Sister Rose Anne, who suggested that she try a summer session at The University in another section of the United States, an institution reputed to have strong offerings in elementary education and social studies. Sister Rose Anne had completed a doctorate at The University and was able to help Mary establish contact with the institution. Mary had hoped to work toward a master's degree but needed to learn more about what was involved in making such a decision. She had taught long enough to know she needed to get back for more professional work, but beyond that her ideas were indefinite.

Mary found the summer session to be quite a different experience from her undergraduate work. As she remembered her classmates at Holy Names, they were all about her age, but her classmates during the summer session at The University tended to be older than she. Most of them had taught for many years. The variations in ability and motivation among her fellow students were very pronounced. Some seemed only interested in earning passing grades and credits; others were competitively seeking high grades; but most were concerned about learning something they could take back home with them and use in their classrooms. Summer session students at The University came from many different states and this in itself proved beneficial to Mary in helping her find out about educational practices in other parts of the country.

Mary Finch was surprised to learn of the extent of interest the instructors seemed to have in individual students at The University. This was something she had not expected at a large institution, which she had always believed to be impersonal and uncaring. At the time she completed her program planning for the summer, the professor who advised her said, "Miss Finch, this is a large institution, but you will be working with only a small part of it. I think you will find the people here friendly and helpful. We do not like to have students feel they are getting the run-around when they encounter problems. If you have any difficulties at all in your registration or in getting your program under way, come directly to this office and we will help you." Mary was encouraged by this assurance.

She found her classes more meaningful than she had as an undergraduate. Maturity and teaching experience accounted for some of this. She was pleased to be able to take classes from two professors who had written books she remembered using as an undergraduate. One was also an author of a textbook series used in her school.

During the summer her social studies professor made use of some of the publications of the National Council for the Social Studies. She knew this national professional association from her undergraduate days, but had never seriously thought of becoming a member. However, in her summer work she learned about and liked what the Council was doing in developing curriculum guidelines, concerning itself with academic freedom, promoting multiethnic education, and speaking out on students' rights and other social issues. She decided to become a member of the Council. Not only that, she and a couple of her colleagues decided to attend the annual meeting of the Council to be held that fall during Thanksgiving week in Atlanta, Georgia.

Mary found the convention to be an inspiring growth experience professionally. She pored over the many book exhibits and eagerly collected a couple shopping bags full of complimentary materials furnished by publishers. She attended several section meetings dealing with values, inquiry, and women's studies. A meeting she found especially interesting was one conducted by two elementary school teachers from Michigan who shared some of their work in implementing cultural pluralism in their curriculum. Another program that she found helpful was one dealing with values education presented by a group from the Harris County Department of Education from the Houston, Texas, area. For Mary Finch, however, the highlight of the convention was the banquet speech by Sam J. Ervin, former United States senator from North Carolina. She felt she was close to the heartbeat of the country as she listened to this great American expound in a simple yet thoughtful way on the freedoms guaranteed all citizens by the Constitution.

The summer session and convention experience made indelible marks on Mary Finch, fourth-grade teacher from Mill Town. She found her circle of professional contacts enlarging. Her "teacher talk" tended toward issues besides bread and butter matters. More frequently she found herself asking why she was doing something. She tried to do some professional reading each week. Her commitment to continued professional growth was already firmly established when in early January she received a letter from the Dean of the Graduate School at The University notifying her of her admission to the graduate program. The possibility of working toward a master's degree did not seem so far out of the question as it had just a year earlier.

Basic Competencies—Social Studies

The intern teacher

1. Understands the need for continuing education and knows where to turn for such education.
2. Knows the professional associations relevant to social studies and is familiar with their publications.
3. Develops a sense of professional identity.

INTERN ADVISORY

After completing this chapter, together with related work in the clinic and appropriate classroom experiences in the field, you should be able to do the following:

1. Articulate a rationale for the career-long education of teachers.

2. Identify where to secure information at the local level about requirements and opportunities for the postbaccalaureate education of teachers.
3. Identify local, state, and national professional associations concerned with social studies education and list a few of their major publications.
4. Claim some interest in your professional development as a teacher as evidenced by extensive reading in the social studies and related literature, by attending professional meetings, or by engaging in a social studies related activity or hobby.

WHY IS CONTINUING EDUCATION ESSENTIAL TO PROFESSIONAL GROWTH?

Teaching is one of a very few professions in which the certification-training program is combined with the requirements for a bachelor's degree. Because of the need for students to meet both the baccalaureate degree requirements and the certification requirements, colleges and schools of education tend to resemble arts and science colleges more than they resemble true professional schools such as those of law and medicine. The need to complete both certification and degree requirements in a four-year time period places constraints on both programs. This usually means that the professional training is limited in intensity and scope. Consequently, the graduate of a four-year teacher education program must be perceived as one who is prepared only for beginning teaching and is not in any sense a "finished product."

Most states recognize this limitation in the preparation of teachers and, therefore, require them to take additional college or university work to be completed within a specified amount of time. The usual requirement is an additional year of training before the teacher is eligible for a permanent certificate.[1] The practice of requiring the teacher to return for additional training before the certificate is renewed is firmly established not only in the United States but in most modern nations of the world.

But even if the teacher's initial training were wholly adequate, there would still be a need for continuing education simply to keep up with emerging developments in subject matter and methodology.

---

[1] These certificates go by a variety of titles: Permanent Certificate, Standard Certificate, and Life Certificate. In California the term *credential* is used in place of certificate.

There is a constant flow of new information and new teaching procedures into the mainstream of social studies education. Without having access to those new ideas and developing trends, the teaching soon becomes out of date. That is why in-service courses along with the programs and publications of professional associations are so important to the teacher—they put the practitioner in contact with the latest professional thinking in the field. Teaching experience in itself cannot do this for the teacher. It requires the input of ideas from some outside source if improvement is to occur. There is a big difference between having ten years of teaching experience and having one year repeated ten times, and the latter is likely to happen without the stimulation of new ideas.

It should be the teacher's responsibility to remain professionally alive and competent and to keep his or her teaching techniques up to date. But teachers have not had a good track record in this regard. The involvement of teachers in in-service courses, professional workshops, curriculum-development activities, or college and university summer sessions has usually been at the urging of supervisors, or because of state certification requirements, or because of the incentive of higher salary. Not many teachers continue their in-service education simply out of a sense of commitment to remain professionally competent.

As soon as the beginning teacher is situated in a district, he or she should inquire about the in-service education opportunities available locally. Larger districts often have an office for continuing education as a part of the central administrative services. In fact, information about such an operation will ordinarily be provided the teacher during the orientation period prior to or early in the school year. Some school districts provide generous offerings of in-service courses for teachers at little or no cost. Such courses usually do not carry college credit (although in some cases this can be arranged), but almost always can be counted as credits toward a higher position on the salary schedule. Such credits usually apply only to the district in which they are earned and cannot be transferred for salary purposes from one district to another. This, of course, would not be true of college or university credits, which could be applied anywhere.

The beginning teacher needs to have a clear understanding of the state requirements for college or university training beyond what is needed for initial certification. These requirements vary from state to state. The Student Advisory Office or the Student Teaching

Office in colleges of education will provide that information, or it can be obtained from any State Department of Education, Office of Teacher Certification. The information may also be available through school district personnel offices. It has been this writer's experience in working with hundreds of teachers through the years, that these requirements are often *not* well understood. In some cases they are not even understood by those who are supposed to be advising the teacher about the fifth-year requirements! As a result, the teacher may end up taking courses that are not needed or not having courses that should have been taken. The teacher should read the regulations himself or herself and not rely on information passed by word of mouth from one teacher to another. Better still, the teacher should request an evaluation from the State Certification Office or one of its agents of all work taken and get *in writing* a statement of what course work is needed in order to fulfill the fifth-year or permanent certificate requirements.

Teachers find it most convenient to attend colleges and universities during the summer. Summer sessions are often operated under somewhat different regulations than is the regular academic year. For example, some state institutions do not differentiate in the amount of fees paid by residents and nonresidents of the state during the summer session. This encourages teachers to do some summer work in a different section of the country, which is in itself a growth experience. Colleges and universities will categorize their summer session students in terms of how long the student is expected to be at the institution. If the student is to be on the campus for the summer session only, the admission procedure is much less complicated than if one is a degree-seeking student. In any case the deadlines for summer session application are ordinarily far in advance of the time classes begin. This may vary from a few weeks in the case of "summer session only" students to several months in the case of students seeking admission to graduate degree programs.

During a full summer session, usually nine to eleven weeks in length, a student can earn the same number of credits that are earned during one quarter of the academic year. In order to accommodate the summer clientele, colleges and universities often divide the summer session into two terms, thereby offering the students several choices in terms of the length of time and the amount of credit. Because the length and number of credits can vary from one student to another, the fee structure is also flexible.

As a service to teachers, colleges and universities in the local area may offer late afternoon, evening, or Saturday morning classes during the academic year. These may be regular classes that count as resident courses but are simply offered at times that are convenient to teachers. Credits so earned can be used in exactly the same way as credits earned at any other time of day. If, however, these courses are offered as extension classes, it is important to know that there are certain limits on how such credits can be used. The letter *X* appearing prior to or following the course number usually identifies it as an extension course, as, for example, Educ X465 or Educ 465X. The fact that the course is offered on the campus has nothing to do with its status as an extension course.

The teacher is usually advised against taking any courses during the academic year in the first year of service. After that the number of courses taken will depend on district policy on such matters, the demands of the courses taken, and the ambition of the teacher. Almost never is the teacher advised—or even allowed—to take more than one course a quarter if the teaching assignment is a full-time one.

Fifth-year certification requirements can often be combined with the requirements for a master's degree, both requiring about forty-five quarter credits of work.[2] Whether the teacher should combine these two requirements is a matter that must be resolved on an individual basis. There are advantages and disadvantages in doing it either way. Having the master's degree provides the holder with a generally recognized symbol of achievement. Many positions that are perceived as promotions require the applicant to have a master's degree. On the other hand, admission to master's degree programs is usually more rigorous than it is for fifth-year certification work only. The teacher in a master's degree program will usually have less freedom in selecting the courses that are taken. In other words, the master's degree program imposes certain course requirements that must be met, whereas the fifth-year programs ordinarily do not. It should be said, however, that in recent years many institutions have liberalized course requirements for the master's degree to the extent that there is little constraint on what the candidate can include in the program. The tendency is to tailor-make master's degree programs to fit the individual professional needs of teachers.

---

[2]Quarter credits can be converted to semester credits by reducing them by one-third—forty-five quarter credits are equivalent to thirty semester credits. Semester credits = two-thirds x quarter credits; quarter credits = 1½ x semester credits.

Fifth-year and master's degree course work should be a mix of academic courses and education courses. In social studies, teachers should reach into the social science disciplines for work in geography, sociology, economics, political science, history, and anthropology. Work in the arts and humanities is also valuable for the elementary school teacher in social studies. This substantive work is especially important for the teacher who may have had an undergraduate major in elementary education and, therefore, has not had in-depth work in the disciplines as an undergraduate student. There is a tendency for elementary school teachers to shy away from the academic offerings, and this results in lopsided preparation. Some academic departments provide special offerings of courses or workshops for teachers during the summer session to encourage more teachers to build their subject matter backgrounds.

In some cases school districts may allow travel experience, especially travel abroad, to count toward in-service education. Such arrangements must always be made with the district in advance of the travel and may require the teacher to do something beyond what an ordinary tourist would do on such a trip. In other words, the district may require that the teacher prepare a unit of study on the area covered, to collect instructional materials, to prepare a photograph collection or a filmstrip, or some such professional application of the travel experience.

Increasingly, public schools are providing teachers opportunities for professional leaves of absence, a practice well established at the college and university levels. Where such a policy exists, the leave may be available on a competitive basis after a specified period of service, usually six or seven years. The leave may be granted without pay or may provide partial salary for the leave period. In cases where a partial salary is paid, the teacher is obligated to return to the district following the leave for a period of one or two years. Naturally, leaves without pay are easier to obtain than are those with partial salary. For those who can afford it, a year spent in advanced study provides a fine opportunity for professional growth.

INTERN TASK 11–1

a. Find out what the requirements are for permanent or standard certification in the state in which you plan to teach.

b. Find out what procedures you are expected to follow in beginning your college or university work to fulfill fifth-year requirements in your state.

WHAT PROFESSIONAL ASSOCIATIONS ARE RELEVANT TO THE SOCIAL STUDIES FIELD?

The largest and most influential professional association relevant to social studies is the National Council for the Social Studies. Its headquarters office is at 2030-M Street, N.W., Suite 406, Washington, D.C. 20036. Membership in the Council is open to any person or institution interested in teaching the social studies. For the fifteen-dollar membership fee, each member receives a yearbook, a subscription to the journal *Social Education*, and the NCSS *Newsletter*.

The NCSS speaks to the professional needs of teachers and supervisors from the elementary school to college and university levels. It issues policy statements concerning curriculum guidelines, standards for the preparation of teachers, students' rights, academic freedom, and similar issues. Through its various publications, it keeps its membership informed about the trends and developments in the field. In recent years the NCSS has made an especial effort to accommodate the needs of the elementary school teacher.

There are state social studies councils that are affiliated with the NCSS in nearly all of the states. The state councils in turn have local council affiliates. These organizations address themselves to the professional concerns of social studies teachers at the local and state levels. Most of them meet once or twice during the academic year and provide their members with information through some type of publication. Sometimes the local and state councils cooperate with the National Council in sponsoring national or regional conferences on social studies.

The National Council for Geographic Education is another organization that is attractive to elementary school teachers who are interested in social studies. Its monthly publication, *The Journal of Geography*, often carries articles dealing with the teaching of geography at the elementary school level. Although this organization is primarily concerned with the teaching of geography, it does so, at least at the elementary school level, within a social studies framework. The National Council for Geographic Education also has state council affiliates.

The elementary school teacher is faced with a real problem when it comes to professional association membership. Most will become members of the National Education Association (NEA) or the American Federation of Teachers (AFT) and their corresponding local and state affiliates. Through the years these organizations have been concerned mainly with bread-and-butter issues: salaries, working conditions, contract negotiations, and so on. These organizations have been concerned with curriculum matters, too, especially in recent years, but it is fair to say that most teachers do not join them because of their work in the curriculum fields. Interested leaders in subject matter fields have developed organizations that deal mainly with curriculum matters relating to their disciplines: social studies, English, science, mathematics, art, music, reading, and physical education. The dilemma of the elementary teacher is to decide which of these several organizations to join.

It would improve the dissemination of professional information if every elementary school faculty had some teachers who were members of at least one of the professional organizations concerned with the subject areas that comprise the basic core fields of the elementary school curriculum: social studies, science, language arts, reading, and mathematics. This would ensure that those faculties had at least one or more members in direct contact with organizations that are concerned with the latest developments in content and method in those fields. This awareness and information could then be shared with colleagues, thereby making the entire faculty more alert professionally to curriculum developments in all fields. As matters now stand, if elementary school teachers belong to any of the special field organizations, they are likely to select reading and language arts. As a result, there is a void of knowledge about current developments in the other fields. More teachers need to become involved in the professional activities of organizations such as the local and state social studies councils and the NCSS.

INTERN TASK 11-2

a. Familiarize yourself with the journal *Social Education,* published by the NCSS. The periodical library on your campus undoubtedly subscribes to it.
b. Arrange with your field associate teacher to attend a meeting of the local or state council for the social studies.

HOW DOES A TEACHER DEVELOP A SENSE OF PROFESSIONAL IDENTITY?

Teachers begin to develop a sense of professional identity when they are concerned about the quality of professional practice and service beyond their own classrooms. As professionals, they are concerned that the schools are or are not addressing themselves to certain social issues. They are concerned that children may not be exposed to more than a single point of view. They are concerned about the rights guaranteed to all citizens, including those who are students.

Teachers who have an established professional identity desire to be centrally involved in the decision making that relates to their field of competence. *They* want to set standards of professional practice rather than have outsiders do it for them. *They* want to speak out on legislative issues affecting their field rather than have administrators or lay persons speak for them. *They* want to exert their influence in order that the boys and girls of this nation will be able to receive the best possible opportunity for an education befitting a free people.

But the question remains, "How does a teacher develop a sense of professional identity?" The answer to this question lies within each teacher. Professional identity comes to those who are concerned about keeping their teaching skills up to date. Such teachers are involved professionally with their colleagues. You see them at professional conferences. You see their names on curriculum committees and advisory committees in the local community. You find them involved when there is an assault on the professional integrity of one of their colleagues or when there is a violation of academic freedom. They are concerned and involved when textbook adoptions are underway. They find time to do some professional reading no matter how busy they are with other things. They find their way back to college and university campuses for additional training on a more or less regular basis. Although they are usually not motivated by selfish goals, they are, nonetheless, fully aware that *they* are the ones who have the most to gain and the most to lose when fundamental decisions are made about their particular field of expertise. And in the name of enlightened self-interest, they make it a point to see that the perspective of the professional teacher is well represented in such decision-making processes.

SOCIAL STUDIES COMPETENCIES AND SKILLS

CHECKING YOUR PERFORMANCE

Intern Task Checklist

Task 11–1. a. Finding out requirements for standard or permanent certif-   _____
icate in the local state. P. 258

        b. Finding out about procedures to initiate fifth-year college   _____
or university work. P. 259

Task 11–2. a. Becoming familiar with *Social Education.* P. 260   _____

        b. Attending a local or state social studies council meeting.   _____
P. 260

Performance Checklist

In the field or in the clinic, the intern teacher has

1. Stated in conversation or in writing a rationale for the career-long   _____
education of teachers.

2. Become familiar with sources of information at the local level that   _____
explain requirements and opportunities for the continuing education of
teachers.

3. Had some contact with local, state, and national organizations associated   _____
with social studies education; has read some of their publications; and
is generally familiar with their purposes and programs.

4. Shown some interest in pursuing social studies activities professionally   _____
and as a hobby. .

Field Associate Teacher Advisory

Tasks and performances should be checked off or initialed and
dated by the appropriate local official, or the intern teacher can
use the checklists for his or her own record.

INTERN ADVISORY

If you have studied the material presented in this text in a conscientious
way and if you are able to do the exercises suggested throughout the book at a

level that is acceptable to your field associate teacher, you should feel adequately prepared to begin teaching elementary school social studies on your own.

This is an appropriate time for your and your field associate teacher to make an over-all assessment of your performance as a teacher of social studies. This might be done by reviewing the list of Basic Competencies at the beginning of each chapter and the performance checklists at the ends of chapters. Perhaps there is still time in your internship to build increased competence in those areas that need improvement.

Certificate of completion

Name of Intern _____

College or University _____

Location of intern assignment _____

_____

Dates: From _____ To: _____
               Day   Month   Year   Day   Month   Year

Grade-Level Placement _____

Field Associate Teacher _____

School Principal _____

Clinic Instructor (social studies) _____

Field Coordinator (college supervisor) _____

_____

This is to certify that

_____

has successfully completed a teaching internship as described above and has
demonstrated competence in teaching social studies as evidenced by the completion of
the Intern Tasks included in this book.

_____

                          Field Associate Teacher

_____

               Clinic Instructor or College Supervisor

_____

   Date

Selected references

Banks, James A., ed. *Teaching Ethnic Studies: Concepts and Strategies,* forty-third yearbook. Washington, D.C.: National Council for the Social Studies, 1973.

Banks, James A. *Teaching Strategies for Ethnic Studies.* Boston: Allyn & Bacon, Inc., 1975.

Banks, James A. *Teaching Strategies for the Social Studies.* Reading, Mass.: Addison-Wesley Publishing Co., Inc., 1973.

Chapin, June R., and Richard E. Gross. *Teaching Social Studies Skills.* Boston: Little, Brown and Company, 1973.

Grambs, Jean Dresden. *Teaching About Women in the Social Studies: Concepts, Methods, and Materials,* Bulletin 48. Washington, D.C.: National Council for the Social Studies, 1976.

Hahn, Carole L., ed. "Eliminating Sexism from the Schools: Implementing Change," *Social Education,* 39 (March 1975), 113–147. (Seven authors contribute to this special issue on sexism.)

Hanna, Lavone A., Gladys L. Potter, and Robert W. Reynolds. *Dynamic Elementary Social Studies.* 3rd ed. New York: Holt, Rinehart & Winston, Inc., 1973.

Hunkins, Francis P. *Questioning Strategies and Techniques.* Boston: Allyn & Bacon, Inc., 1972.

Jarolimek, John. *Social Studies in Elementary Education.* 5th ed. New York: Macmillan Publishing Co., Inc., 1977.

Jarolimek, John, and Huber M. Walsh. *Readings for Social Studies in Elementary Education.* 3rd ed. New York: Macmillan Publishing Co., Inc., 1974.

Jarolimek, John, and Clifford D. Foster. *Teaching and Learning in the Elementary School.* New York: Macmillan Publishing Co., Inc., 1976.

267

Kaltsounis, Theodore, ed. "The Community: Laboratory for Social Learnings," *Social Education,* 40 (March 1976), 158–171. (Six authors contribute articles dealing with the use of the local community in teaching social studies.)

Keach, Everett T. "Simulation Games and the Elementary School," *Social Education,* 38 (March 1974), 284–285. (This article plus four others dealing with simulation games is included in the elementary education section of this issue. An annotated bibliography of published simulation games is included.)

King, Edith W. *The World: Context for Teaching in the Elementary School.* Dubuque, Iowa: William C. Brown Company, Publishers, 1971.

Manson, Gary, Gerald Marker, Anna Ochoa, and Jan Tucker. *Social Studies Curriculum Guidelines.* Washington, D.C.: National Council for the Social Studies, 1971.

Martorella, Peter H. *Concept Learning in the Social Studies.* New York: Intext Educational Publishers, 1971.

Michaelis, John U. *Social Studies for Children in a Democracy.* 6th ed. Englewood Cliffs, N.J.: Prentice-Hall, Inc., 1976.

Preston, Ralph C., and Wayne L. Herman, Jr. *Teaching Social Studies in the Elementary School.* 4th ed. New York: Holt, Rinehart & Winston, Inc., 1974.

Skeel, Dorothy J. *The Challenge of Teaching the Social Studies.* 2nd ed. Pacific Palisades, Calif.: Goodyear Publishing Company, Inc., 1974.

Index